color, class & country

EXPERIENCES OF GENDER

● ● ● ● ● ● ● ● ● ● ●

Edited by

GAY YOUNG &
BETTE J DICKERSON

ZED BOOKS
London & New Jersey

Acknowledgments

Our first thanks go to the Department of Sociology (Samih Farsoun, Chair) and the Women's Studies Program (Muriel Cantor, Director) of the College of Arts and Sciences of The American University for their support of the conference that was the source of this collection. A number of graduate students were also involved in a variety of capacities in the process of bringing the work to completion, and we thank them all: Oya Acikalin, Mona Danner, Ann Ewing, Lucía Fort, Philipia Hillman, Roberta Mildfelt, Johanna Rice, and Lisa Silverberg. Gay Young thanks Leila and Walid for waiting, Karim for constant encouragement, and all of them for what they continue to teach her about gender relations. Bette Dickerson thanks family and friends for unwavering support throughout this project – in particular, her mother, Rosa Anthony Dickerson, and all the other Anthony women whose lives helped shape her own construction of gender.

Color, Class and Country was first published by
Zed Books Ltd, 7 Cynthia Street, London N1 9JF, UK, and
165 First Avenue, Atlantic Highlands, New Jersey 07716, USA,
in 1994.

Copyright © Gay Young, Bette J. Dickerson
and individual contributors, 1994.

Cover designed by Andrew Corbett.
Typeset by Password Publishing & Design, Norwich.
Printed and bound in the United Kingdom
by Biddles Ltd, Guildford and King's Lynn.

All rights reserved.

A catalogue record for this book is
available from the British Library.

US CiP data is available from the Library of Congress.

ISBN 1 85649 179 X Hb
ISBN 1 85649 180 3 Pb

Contents

Introduction *Gay Young and Bette J.Dickerson* 1

Part I: Gendered Reproduction of Race-Ethnicity and Social Class *15*

1. "Becoming Somebody": Aspirations, Opportunities, and Womanhood
   Wendy Luttrell *17*

2. Chicanas in White Collar Occupations: Work and the Gendered Construction of Race-Ethnicity
   Denise A.Segura *36*

3. Urban Women's Work in Three Social Strata: The Informal Economy of Social Networks and Social Capital
   Larissa Lomnitz *53*

Part II: Gender and Challenges to the Construction of Social Class and Race-Ethnicity *71*

4. "I'm not your maid. I am the housekeeper": The Restructuring of Housework and Work Relationships in Domestic Service
   Mary Romero *73*

5. Fighting Sexual Harassment: A Collective Labour Obligation
   Stan Gray *84*

6. Ethnic Identity and Feminism: Views from Leaders of African American Women's Associations
   Bette J.Dickerson *97*

7. Race, Class, Gender and US State Welfare Policy: The Nexus of Inequality for African American Families
   Rose Brewer *115*

Part III: Reproduction of and Challenges to Gender Relations: Cases and Comparisons at the National Level — *129*

8. Gender Inequality around the World: Comparing Fifteen Nations in Five World Regions
   Lucia Fort, Mona Danner, and Gay Young — *131*

9. The State, Gender Policy, and Social Change: An Analysis from Turkey
   Nüket Kardam — *152*

10. Work Intensity and Time Use: What Do Women Do When There Aren't Enough Hours in a Day?
    Maria Sagrario Floro — *168*

11. Gender Stratification and Vulnerability in Uganda
    Christine Obbo — *182*

Part IV: Challenges to White Western Middle Class Gender Analysis and Agendas — *197*

12. "Lifting as We Climb": How Scholarship by and about Women of Color Has Shaped My Life as a White Feminist
    Kathryn B. Ward — *199*

13. The Place of the WID Discourse in Global Feminist Analysis: The Potential for a "Reverse Flow"
    Vidyamali Samarasinghe — *218*

14. Difference, Diversity, and Divisions in an Agenda for the Women's Movement
    Elizabeth Fox-Genovese — *232*

Index — *249*

Introduction

Gay Young and Bette J. Dickerson

In the fall of 1990, the Department of Sociology at The American University began its formal offering of Gender and Family as a field of concentration in the graduate program. In order to make this new part of the program more widely known, the department sponsored a conference on gender in April 1991. Through the scholars invited to participate and the topics they addressed, the intent was to convey the department's commitment to taking seriously the interconnection of gender, race, and class not only in the United States but internationally as well. That conference, entitled "Experiences of Gender: Color, Class, and Country," was the source of this collection. In the next three sections of this introduction, we clarify the concepts contained in the title: the nature of gender, the role of experience, and our understanding of the interlocking character of race-ethnicity, social class, and nationality in women's lives.

The meaning of gender

We recognize that gender is something fundamentally relational (Flax 1990; Hess and Ferree 1987) and that the relationship is always historically situated (Harding 1991). However, women and men do not experience themselves simply as *gendered* subjects, because the whole range of hierarchical social relations – race-ethnicity, social class, national location, and other systems of social demarcation – in which women and men participate operates to construct the experience of gender (Childers and hooks 1990; Harding 1991). Even when using gender as the primary lens of study, these other constructed hierarchies come into view, for gender is defined *with* not apart from race, class, and nationality (Minnich 1990; Spelman 1988).

The emerging analysis of the relation of gender to other forms of domination has expanded the category of gender and provided new direction in feminist thinking – too long restricted by the experience of white, middle-class, Western women (Childers and hooks 1990; Hirsch and Fox Keller 1990). Moreover, the insight that we neither experience nor can understand gender independently of other hierarchies implies that the entire matrix of domination is crucial to feminism (Spelman 1988).

Before we elaborate on this interconnection between gender and other forms of domination and the conjunction of feminism with other liberatory struggles, however, we address the issue of women's experience and its relationship to knowledge.

Experience and knowledge

We are committed to the idea that gender research, theory, and practice should start from women's lived experience (Harding 1991). Women share the experience of social relations organized to effect our exclusion; in particular, the sexual division of labor and the institutionalized subordination of women to (privileged) men represent key factors shaping women's experiences. But beginning from women's standpoint does not presuppose a common viewpoint among women – or one women's culture (Aptheker 1989; Smith 1987). Women's standpoint is grounded in concrete experience *and* does not negate the experience of any group of women (Sprague and Zimmerman 1993). As Sandra Harding (1991: 285) asserts, "to start thought from women's lives requires starting from multiple lives that are in many ways in conflict with one another and each of which has its own multiple and contradictory commitments." Indeed, women of color in the Third World and the US insist that the intersection of race, class, and nation demarcates women's position (Mohanty 1991) and that their particular perspective as outsiders within provides a unique standpoint (Collins 1991).

There are, then, two important concerns when garnering knowledge from experience: the problem of dominant experience and the issue of partiality. First, because women interpret experience through the operation of social relations of domination, women of dominant groups must be especially wary of the "authority of experience" – that their experience is what counts (Fuss 1989; Sprague and Zimmerman 1993). It is vital to have critical perspective on "spontaneous consciousness" and "obvious" beliefs – what one knows from experience – when they originate from a dominant social location (Harding 1991). Thus, women's standpoint is the place to begin inquiry – provided that one pays attention to how it is shaped by relations of domination.

Indeed, the lived experience of women marginalized by race-ethnicity (or social class or national location) is less suspect because the authority of their experience is constituted in struggle (hooks 1991). They are better able to see the line of fault (Dorothy Smith's [1987] term) between their experience and the dominant world-view, and they have a distinct angle of vision on the theories put forth, for example, by white feminists, Black male social thinkers, and the white male mainstream (Tuana 1993; Collins 1991). However, Nancy Tuana (1993) cautions that one's use of the notion of women being on the margin must take into account that a woman can be marginal in some ways – due to gender and social class – and at the center in others – because of race-ethnicity and national location. Moreover, there may be some locations that are altogether inaccessible to dominant group members (hooks 1989).

When considering the relation of experience to knowledge, the second concern is the issue of partiality. And when addressing partiality, two interrelated elements arise: one is recognizing that women's experience is embodied and linked to particular historical locations creating situated and partial knowledge (Sprague and Zimmerman 1993); and thus the second is giving up on both finding a common core of women's experience and establishing a single unitary explanation of women's oppression (Tuana 1993). This does *not* leave only knowledge that is completely and hopelessly fragmented, or mean that it is impossible to reduce the partiality and distortion of accounts of gender. The partial knowledge that has dominated thinking about gender relations has not simply been distorted but distorted in favor of the group that has had the ability to make its standpoint known (Minnich 1990). And that is being successfully challenged.

The standpoint injunction to start inquiry from *all* women's lives sustains the visibility of the multidimensionality of women's experience and compels the decentering of the dominant group in order to envision other groups' perspectives (Harding 1991; Aptheker 1989; Collins 1991). While it is reasonable to expect the cross-cutting and similarity of *some* of the experiences of some women with *some* of the experiences of others, there is no going back from the recognition that gender intersects with race-ethnicity, social class, national location, and other social demarcations to create particular experiences and generate situated perspectives (Sprague and Zimmerman 1993; Tuana 1993). Taking all of this seriously serves to reduce the partiality of knowledge about women and, instead of pronouncing a decisive statement, enlarges and adds complexity to knowledge based on the multiplicity of women's experience.

Finally, for experience to be a basis of feminist struggle the challenge of theorizing experience must be taken up. Teresa de Lauretis (1990: 260) asserts that one definition of feminist theory (of the female embodied social subject, the woman who lives at a particular historical juncture) is "theory of the relationship between experiences, social power, and resistance". Thus, critically analyzing personal experience – that is, understanding the material reality that undergirds experience – forms the foundation for theory (Childers and hooks 1990; hooks 1989; Mohanty 1992). Moreover, engaging in critical analysis of one's own experience is a way for even those with race, class, or national privilege to engender liberatory knowledge – if, through historical interpretation, they become aware of the grounds and the function of their privilege (Amott and Matthaei 1991; Harding 1991). Thus, the creation of liberatory knowledge requires full understanding of the interconnections among gender, race-ethnicity, social class, national location, and other social demarcations and divisions that situate women in the matrix of domination.

The intersection of color, class and country in women's lives

In our view, three conditions must be met in order for analysis of women's experience of gender to be fully liberatory. The first is to abandon "womanhood" as a universal category; the second is to move beyond the additive approach to gender "and" race-ethnicity, social class, national location, and other social demarcations; and the third is to analyze women's (often contradictory) positions in the matrix of domination formed by these social divisions.

The critique of theoretical universalism, one aspect of general trends in contemporary thought, has been accompanied by the breaking down of the feminist view of womanhood as a universal category. The recognition of the social and historical construction of gender cannot support a belief in the essential unity of womankind – as a totalizing whole – due to a common experience of oppression (Barrett 1992; Amott and Matthaei 1991; Haraway [1985]1990; Fuss 1989; Mohanty 1992). The notion of the "generic" woman allowed no space for race-ethnicity, social class, national location, or any other social demarcation and curtailed the analysis of the significance of women's heterogeneity (Spelman 1988; Haraway [1985]1990).

There is now wider acknowledgment that the phrase "women as women" really refers to women who are white and middle-class in Western industrialized countries. And like privileged men before them, these dominant few engaged in faulty generalizations that not only conflated their own situation with the situation of all women but also validated themselves as the norm, the ideal (Spelman 1988; Minnich 1990). One of the obvious ways this has been accomplished is through the language habit of referring to the dominant few (white, Western, middle-class) women as "women" with no "prefix": that without a qualifier is the universal, and the more qualifiers, as in "poor black women of the Third World," the further from the ideal (Childers and hooks 1990; Minnich 1990). Adrienne Rich points to the same problem with her phrase "white solipsism" – meaning whiteness is "realness" (cited in Childers and hooks 1990).

There is no seamless web of womanness and of being white, Western, and middle class, and many of the dominant few women now see the "noninnocence" of the universal category "woman" (Haraway [1985]1990). But the process of decentering white, Western, middle-class women – or pivoting the assumed center to include *all* women – while necessary (Aptheker 1989; Harding 1991; Mohanty 1991), has left some feminists wondering about the meaning of feminism. If all the complex differentiation of women is taken into account, is it no longer possible to articulate theory (Christian 1990)? Is nothing left but fractured discourse

(Hirsch and Fox Keller 1990)? Elizabeth Spelman (1988: 172) provides an answer that contains a challenge. Only from a position of privilege does ending the focus on (the dominant few) "women as women" signal the end of feminism; the issue is not one of quitting the analysis of gender but of moving forward mindful of "the full force of the idea that gender is a social construction."

A so-called additive analysis cannot meet this challenge. In an additive analysis, sexist oppression is something all women experience, but some women *also* experience oppression due to other forms of domination, for example racism. Such an approach fails to take into account the conditions under which women of color and white women experience sexism. Moreover, the additive approach not only means ignoring the race, class and national identities of white, middle-class women in the West but also masking the reality that such women take part in the perpetuation of racism, classism, and imperialism (King 1988; Spelman 1988; Ward 1990).

Moving beyond the additive approach to an integrated analysis requires a conceptual shift. Just as there is no generic woman (as Spelman [1988] has argued), there is no generic gender oppression (Amott and Matthaei 1991). Hierarchies of domination are constructed and experienced simultaneously, their dynamics permeating one another. And while they are socially constructed, they are not experienced the same way by all women. Attending to the interdetermining nature of sexism, racism, classism, and imperialism highlights the complexity and diversity of women's relationship to these structures of domination (Amott and Matthaei 1991; Collins 1991; Harding 1991; hooks 1989; Zinn et al. 1986).

The international dimension deserves particular note, for the world capitalist system makes inadequate the efforts to comprehend relations of gender, race, and class in one country alone. And, although world systems theory itself is critically lacking in this regard, we must move in the direction of analyzing these systems of domination on a world scale (Walby 1992; Ward 1993). Indeed, the "post-colonial subject" has seldom been understood as "an agent of labor migration" or as "a victim of globalizing managerial strategies" partly because the social structural model, in general, has thus far been inept at confronting the interlocking systems of domination (Barrett 1992: 213). Nonetheless, a key task ahead is to analyze women's conflicting positions in the structure of domination formed by the social divisions of gender, race-ethnicity, social class and national location.

Rather than a simple relation of oppressor to oppressed, these multiple systems of oppression intersect to locate women differently in the matrix of domination. Although each system needs the others to operate, these hierarchical systems do not generate identical experiences for all women, for they intersect to position women in particular historical junctures (Collins 1991; Mohanty 1991). For example, the oppression of Third World women is not attributable primarily to gender because racism and economic exploitation are prominent social arrangements oppressing Third World women. The position of women in society must be considered in conjunction with the position of the societies in which Third World women live. Indeed, women in the rich nations of the world participate in the oppression of women in poor countries (Johnson-Odim 1991).

Many women, in a variety of historical junctures of race, class, and nationality, have been readily able to identify their oppression within particular hierarchical systems. The fact that some women sustain other women's subordination has proven more difficult to bring into view. But as Patricia Hill Collins (1991: 229) points out, the "matrix of domination contains few pure victims or oppressors." For most women, location in the matrix of domination comes with both penalty and privilege, and determines the extent to which any woman will be victimized or will have the power to perpetrate oppression (Collins 1991; hooks 1989). It remains for feminists to analyze and articulate the simultaneity, for example, of being oppressed by gender and privileged by race or class or nationality (Childers and hooks 1990).

White, middle-class, Western women, in particular, need to engage in more complex analyses of their experience and fully comprehend the power they retain through other positions of privilege. While such women cannot change their race-ethnicity (or even their social class background or national location very readily), they can make deliberate decisions about where their loyalties lie (Russo 1990). It is not color, class, or country, then, that constructs the suitable ground for struggle against hierarchies of domination. Rather, it is the way feminist scholars think about race-ethnicity, social class, and nationality (as well as other social divisions) and the political links they choose to make among these struggles that ground the feminist movement as egalitarian and emancipatory (Mohanty 1991).

Overview of the volume

The key concern of the chapters that compose the collection is the interconnectedness of gender with other social divisions of race, class, and nation. Several contributors take up the theme both in terms of how gender operates in the reproduction of race-ethnicity and social class and how white working-class women and women of color are challenging the construction of social class and race-ethnicity. Other contributors focus on the reproduction of and challenges to gender relations in an explicitly international context. Finally, one group of contributors confronts white, Western, middle-class gender analysis and agendas. Contributors have adopted a variety of approaches. The empirical inquiries include case studies, group conversations, interviews, survey data and secondary statistics. Other studies are syntheses of earlier ethnographic work, bodies of literature, and critical reflections on social policy and personal practice. In no case do contributors treat the subjects of their analysis as interchangeable instances of some abstract universal, but rather as embodied women located in specific intersections of hierarchies of color, class, and country (Sprague and Zimmerman 1993).

The chapter by *Wendy Luttrell* introduces the section that analyzes the social reproduction of race-ethnicity and social class in women's lives. Through the voices of women from rural North Carolina and the city of Philadelphia she reveals the varying nature of the power relations operating in gender, race and class as social processes. A bottom-up approach to women's accounts of their youthful aspirations illuminates the simultaneity of these relations of domination as they link what society offers and what individuals choose to pursue. For example, Luttrell analyzes how both the meaning of "becoming somebody" and explanations for failed social mobility are shaded by women's race-ethnicity. Regarding mobility, black women saw their destinies as part of a collective journey and offered accounts of why they, as members of a group, had been rejected by the dominant white society. White women, accepting the ideology of mobility and believing in individual choice, felt compelled to explain why they personally had rejected the "move up." Moreover, white women's aspirations were set *outside* the white working-class world's opportunities for "women's work" in women's domain. Yet, black women's aspirations were *for* women's work other than serving white people and not set in opposition to cultural expectations of womanhood but in opposition to white society.

Indeed, a politicized understanding of women's work which is linked to the uplift of the racial-ethnic community exists among other groups of women of color, as *Denise Segura* asserts in her chapter on Chicanas and the gendered reproduction of race-ethnicity on the job. Chicanas recounted to her how conditions of work in white-collar jobs at a large university in California strengthen their social identities as women of Mexican heritage and their attachment to the ethnic community. This occurs in several ways. The confronting of discrimination embedded in the institution and the contesting of stereotypes that others bring to their interpersonal relations in the workplace reaffirm ingroup boundaries and reinforce the view that maintaining ethnic culture is important. In addition, Chicanas interpret their work as activity which strengthens the community – through "women's work" of helping/serving Chicano students as well as providing successful models to other community members. Finally, Segura analyzes how this market work also combines with traditional obligations for household work to intensify Chicanas' gendered responsibility for maintaining ethnic culture and community.

Concluding this section, *Larissa Lomnitz* reviews findings regarding gendered social networks in Latin America which are vital to economic activity *and* which operate to reproduce social class – in terms of assuring sheer survival among the poor, maintaining the perpetually threatened economic status of the middle class, and promoting the retention of economic privilege by the elite. These social networks translate into what Lomnitz calls "social capital" through the use of social resources for economic ends. In the Mexican upper class, "centralizing women" weave the social fabric in which the extended family network is embedded. And through this network – activated in the endless round of family rituals – passes the economic information which is vital for all business transactions. Middle-class Chilean women facilitate a system of reciprocal exchange of "favors" by creating an atmosphere of sociability. They fill their homes with relatives and friends who are well-placed in various bureaucracies and, by introducing them to one another, maintain a network of people willing and able to perform economically valuable services. Women in the lower class in Mexico meet their social security needs by building networks among immediate neighbors and kin. Typically, a central woman, who wields moral authority, organizes the domestic production unit and ensures that an adequate supply of goods and services flows through the network. Thus, women acting as gendered beings reproduce the material relations of social class.

In the next section, *Mary Romero* offers the first of the challenges to the construction of class and race – on the part of individual women. The contributions move next to challenges by women working in and with organizations and then finally to challenges at the level of the state.

In her study of Chicana domestic workers, Romero explores the circumstances in which paid reproductive labor occurs in order to illustrate the everyday rituals of class and racial domination that employers engage in, and the struggles on the part of employees to change working conditions. Rather than glossing over the structure of housework, as social psychological approaches tend to do, and treating it as an extension of the hierarchical relationship between the employer and domestic worker, she examines it as a site of class struggle. She asserts that the worker and employer define their interests in opposition and struggle for control. And only by gaining control can the employee restructure the work to eliminate demeaning and degrading practices. This active struggle by domestic workers to restructure housework and thereby improve their conditions of work centers around the elimination of personal services and creation of a situation where they are in charge of planning and organizing the work.

Struggle over the conditions of work is also the central theme of the chapter by *Stan Gray*, but rather than private households, the setting is a Canadian steel company. Gray recounts the novel challenge to the gendered construction of class relations made by Bonita Clark in her sexual harassment case. Clark claimed that the sexual harassment she was experiencing created "a poisoned work environment" and thereby transformed it from a problem of interpersonal relations to a health hazard – for which employers bear responsibility and against which unions can organize corrective actions. Framing sexual harassment as a collective labor issue instead of an individual woman's concern served to redefine a gender-specific experience of women into a more general class experience. To Gray, the significance of Clark framing her grievance – and the experience of powerlessness and struggle against the authority structure – in terms of typical working-class experience is the potential it holds for leading men in labor to see grievances of working women as their common interests. While he recognizes that sexual harassment is qualitatively different from other ways of exercising domination, as a union member he has also seen how the victimization of women has channelled class-based anger along irrational and destructive paths and deflected working men from the real source of problems. Defining and fighting sexual harassment as a health-and-safety issue is a means for class solidarity to overcome sexist attitudes of men in the workforce – and to forge stronger unions in the process.

In the next chapter, *Bette Dickerson* attests to the importance of inclusiveness and respect for diversity in building a stronger feminist movement. Her concern is to clarify the views of leaders of African American women's associations on ethnic identity and feminism. This process is critical, she believes, for mobilizing the capabilities of these women – and the voluntary organizations they lead – to address social problems stemming from the intersection of racism and sexism. An area about which (white) feminists are largely ignorant, voluntary organizations have provided opportunities for African American women to learn and apply skills needed for survival in the face of racist and sexist oppression. Using a methodology designed to reduce the distance between researcher and subjects, Dickerson involved the women leaders in group conversations on the concepts of leadership, ethnicity, feminism, and black feminism. Their understanding of leadership focuses on collective responsibility aimed at the empowerment of others. Their strong sense of ethnicity revolves around a feeling of collective identity and community which includes a common fate, shared interests, and valued heritage. Their role in the feminist movement has been quite problematic, but that has not weakened their resolve to end sexist oppression. Finally, their own feminism comprises dual concerns for black liberation and women's emancipation and thus calls for working *with* African American men to arrive at a new construction of gender relations.

The chapter by *Rose Brewer* takes up the challenge to the social construction of race, class, and gender at the level of state policy. These multiple inequalities form the foundation of African American women's poverty and that of families more generally. Brewer asserts that changed theoretical lenses – grounded in critical perspectives of political economy, not just culture – are necessary for studying Black family crisis. The situation of poor African American families is rooted in processes of economic transformation and restructuring, and the inequalities of race, class, and gender as they are implicated in state restructuring are at the core of the crisis engulfing many African American families. Brewer's task is to fill the gap in the analysis of state formation/change with respect to the complex interplay of race, class, and gender. Focusing on welfare state policy and African American family inequality, she analyzes issues of state legitimation and capital accumulation; then she outlines a policy agenda to respond to poor Black families which takes into account the simultaneity and relational nature of race, class, and gender hierarchies.

The next section, which includes both cross-national comparisons and country case studies of gender relations, begins with the study by *Lucia Fort, Mona Danner and Gay Young* which provides baseline indicators for assessing progress toward equitable treatment of women in fifteen of the nations that have signed the Convention for the Elimination of all Forms of Discrimination against Women (CEDAW). Measures of *gender inequality* were developed from official statistics collected in the 1980 census rounds (about the time CEDAW went into force) and compiled in the United Nations Women's Indicators and Statistics Database (WISTAT). Fort, Danner and Young define gender inequality as the departure from parity in the representation of women and men in five dimensions of social life: physical well-being, family formation, education, economic activity, and public power. They set the quantitative findings in the context of historical, cultural, political and economic forces which condition the gender system in individual countries. While they assume that a socially constructed status quo of female disadvantage exists in all countries, they also assert that international institutions can push changes that translate into policies which partially ameliorate women's disadvantage. And despite the problems aggregate data present, such numbers do count when analyzing and challenging the global inequality of women and men.

Nüket Kardam shares the concern over norms and rules regarding women which are formulated at the international level and the extent of compliance with these norms by national governments. Focusing on the Turkish response to the broad recommendation, coming out of the 1985 Nairobi conference at the end of the Decade for Women, to set up mechanisms to ensure that women "receive an equitable share of the benefits of development," she uncovers a struggle over the rules of gender discourse between the Turkish state and society. In 1990, a bill to set up a Directorate of Women's Status and Problems was introduced in parliament amidst the wide range of positions on women which existed in Turkish society – from socialist feminists to conservatives calling for (re)formation of the Turkish-Islamic family. According to Kardam, the bill became a lightning rod in the battle between secularism and religious conservatism that had been brewing for some time. She concludes that compliance with international norms is best gauged by the extent to which efforts arouse and alter domestic debate in a particular issue area. In this case, the bill fueled the discussion of appropriate gender roles as well as appropriate relations between the state and (women's) groups in society.

The converse of receiving an equitable share of the benefits of development is to shoulder an inequitable portion of the burdens of development. *Maria Floro* reviews a variety of settings in which structural adjustment policies adopted to direct the course of economic development have resulted in a longer and harder working day for women because of the gender-based pattern of labor reallocation. A significant lag exists between the labor restructuring of the economy and change in the gender division of labor within the household. When government policies limit the supply of basic goods and the provision of social services, demands on women's time increase. Floro asserts that one of the coping strategies women have developed for dealing with time pressure is to intensify their work, that is, to increase the incidence of overlapping activities and the simultaneous performance of two or more tasks. In developing countries, women often intensify their time use through homework or informal-sector employment which enables them to provide the income needed for subsistence and, at the same time, continue to perform essential childcare and household chores. Floro ends on a cautionary note, pointing to the losses in productivity, the decline in the quality of childcare, and the deterioration of woman's health brought on by women's work intensification – all of which affect the well-being of society as a whole.

Christine Obbo also focuses on the consequences of structural adjustment policies in her analysis of women and poverty in Uganda. She frames her probe into women's strategies to ward off encroaching poverty – which begins in the 1950s – with the system of kinship and gender relations in which women remain enmeshed. Women work for men, and their dependent position derives directly from the gender system. With structural adjustment women's marginalization in the labor market has become more extreme; young girls and women who sell newspapers and small quantities of such items as peanuts, candy, pencils and pens have emerged as the most visible group of hawkers in the streets. Moreover, Obbo points out that women's limited access to resources determines their access to health services. The main criterion for receiving health care is the ability to pay, and because men control cash while women produce food and manage the home, women may not be in a position to initiate medical care for themselves or their children because that requires as-suming financial responsibility. Truly, the women's development decade passed poor Ugandan women by. Obbo cites the Ministry of Women in Development as one more effort by elite women to speak to and for poor women – in the English language – thereby adding issues of class division to the gender system and "gender neutral" development policies which operate to the disadvantage of the majority of Uganda's poor women.

With the recounting of her personal journey to re-center her feminist analysis, *Kathryn Ward* begins the final section on challenges to white, Western, middle-class understandings of women's experiences of gender. She analyzes her earlier denial of how white, middle-class privilege mediated her position as a woman and her role in perpetuating domination by race and class. Like many feminists, she "understood" hierarchies of race and class because she was a woman and could refer to "analogies" with sexism. Moreover, her sociological training had not provided her with a vocabulary to probe the *intersection* of race, class, and gender. How she moved from this position to putting women of color at the center of analysis is the essence of her contribution. In part, it involved seeking specific training in curriculum integration, but it also meant coming to the realization that white women may need to be silent for a time and read, study, and listen to women of color. Ward also addresses how the scholarship by and about women of color helped her clarify the inter- national connections among gender, race, and class in terms of the treatment of women from currently developing countries and the situation of women of color and poor women in the United States. Breaking down the "intellectual ghettoization" of women in development (WID) research from scholarship on the intersection of race, class, and gender is also part of putting women of color at the center.

The positioning of WID research (a contested term to be sure) is the central concern of the chapter by *Vidyamali Samarasinghe*. She suggests reasons and strategies for moving Third World women's studies from the periphery to the center alongside Western feminist analysis. She argues that WID's (apparently) Third World-specific focus on poverty eradication and the purpose of WID strategies – incorporation of women into economic development projects – have inhibited a "reverse flow" to Western feminist analysis of knowledge from the Third World about the highly diverse realities of women. In her view, the strength of WID is in the rich accumulation of field-based empirical material on women generated over the past two decades. The lessons learned from this research can both expand the methodologies and tools available for probing gender subordination and enrich gender theory. She identifies areas of WID research where data emerging from particular methods of analysis have resulted in refinements of earlier ideas in order to illustrate the potential of a reverse flow in effecting a fuller feminist discourse. Ultimately, Samarasinghe is arguing for a corrective to the scholarly hegemony resulting from the one-way flow of feminist ideas from the West to the Third World, and to the paternalistic attitudes of Euro-American feminists in identifying the characteristics and setting priorities for these "other" women.

Finally, bringing the focus back to the US and the policy agenda of the US women's movement, *Elizabeth Fox-Genovese* criticizes the assumptions of universalism and essentialism which permitted privileged women to speak and act in the name of all women. In particular, the conflict of "equality versus difference" between women and men has tended to obscure diversity among women by assuming that all women are seeking/should seek equality with privileged white men, *or* that the differences between women and men are the differences which count, not those of race-ethnicity or social class. Fox-Genovese argues, on the one hand, that the existence of a women's movement depends upon agreement that at least some differences between all women and all men have sufficient significance to justify pursuing a policy agenda for women, *but,* on the other, that the vitality of the women's movement depends upon the recognition that women are divided by class and race, and that the crafting of policies which respond to these divisions among women is the real challenge for feminists today. In her view, to avoid the pitfalls of the dilemma of equality versus difference, feminists must recast women's issues as social issues, as opposed to individual or even sexual issues, and the agenda for the women's movement should emphasize health care, daycare, education, and benefits for part-time workers. Implementing and financing policies on this scale requires engaging and negotiating the divisions among women, and that is the most pressing item on the agenda of the women's movement.

As Elizabeth Spelman (1988: 187) asserted: "There are no short cuts through women's lives." The chapters that follow make that clear. But they also reveal how far feminist scholars have come in their efforts to confront the complexities – due to race, class, and nation – that constitute women's experiences of gender.

References

Amott, Teresa, and Julie Matthaei. 1991. *Race, Gender, and Work: A Multicultural Economic History of Women in the United States.* Boston: South End Press.

Aptheker, Bettina. 1989. *Tapestries of Life*: Women's Work, Women's Consciousness, and the Meaning of Daily Experience. Amherst: University of Massachusetts Press.

Barrett, Michèle. 1992. "Words and Things: Materialism and Method in Contemporary Feminist Analysis." In *Destabilizing Theory: Contemporary Feminist Debates,* edited by M. Barrett and A. Phillips, pp. 201–19. Stanford: Stanford University Press.

Barrett, Michèle, and Anne Phillips, eds. 1992. *Destabilizing Theory: Contemporary Feminist Debates.* Stanford: Stanford University Press.

Childers, Mary, and bell hooks. 1990. "A Conversation about Race and Class." In *Conflicts in Feminism,* edited by M. Hirsch and E. Fox Keller, pp. 60–81. New York and London: Routledge.

Christian, Barbara. 1990. "The Race for Theory." In *Women, Class, and the Feminist Imagination,* edited by K. Hansen and I. Philipson, pp. 568–79. Philadelphia: Temple University Press.

Collins, Patricia Hill. 1991. *Black Feminist Thought: Knowledge, Consciousness, and the Politics of Empowerment.* New York and London: Routledge.

de Lauretis, Teresa. 1990. "Upping the Anti (sic) in Feminist Theory." In *Conflicts in Feminism,* edited by M. Hirsch and E. Fox Keller, pp. 255–70. New York and London: Routledge.

Flax, Jane. 1990. *Thinking Fragments: Psychoanalysis, Feminism, and Postmodernism in the Contemporary West.* Berkeley: University of California Press.

Fuss, Diana. 1989. *Essentially Speaking.* New York and London: Routledge.

Haraway, Donna. (1985)1990. "A Manifesto for Cyborgs." In *Women, Class, and the Feminist Imagination,* edited by K. Hansen and I. Philipson, pp. 580–617. Philadelphia: Temple University Press.

Harding, Sandra. 1991. *Whose Science? Whose Knowledge?* Ithaca: Cornell University Press.

Hess, Beth B., and Myra Marx Ferree, eds. 1987. Analyzing Gender. Newbury Park: Sage.

Hirsch, Marianne, and Evelyn Fox Keller, eds. 1990. *Conflicts in Feminism.* New York and London: Routledge.

hooks, bell. 1989. *Talking Back: Thinking Feminist, Thinking Black.* Boston: South End Press.

hooks, bell. 1990. *Yearning: Race, Gender, and Cultural Politics.* Boston: South End Press.

Johnson-Odim, Cheryl. 1991. "Common Themes, Different Contexts: Third World Women and Feminism." In *Third World Women and the Politics of Feminism,* edited by C. T. Mohanty, A. Russo, and L.Torres, pp. 314–27 . Bloomington and Indianapolis: University of Indiana Press.

King, Deborah K. 1988. "Multiple Jeopardy, Multiple Consciousness: The Context of a Black Feminist Ideology." *Signs* 14: 42–72.

Minnich, Elizabeth K. 1990. *Transforming Knowledge.* Philadelphia: Temple University Press.

Mohanty, Chandra Talpade. 1991. "Introduction: Cartographies of Struggle." In *Third World Women and the Politics of Feminism,* edited by C. T. Mohanty, A. Russo, and L. Torres, pp. 1–47. Bloomington and Indianapolis: University of Indiana Press.

Mohanty, Chandra Talpade. 1992. "Feminist Encounters: Locating the Politics of Experience." In *Destabilizing Theory: Contemporary Feminist Debates,* edited by M. Barrett and A. Phillips, pp. 74–92 . Stanford: Stanford University Press.

Russo, Ann. 1991. "'We Cannot Live without Our Lives': White Women, Antiracism, and Feminism." In *Third World Women and the Politics of Feminism,* edited by C. T. Mohanty, A. Russo and L. Torres, pp. 297–13. Bloomington and Indianapolis: University of Indiana Press.

Smith, Dorothy E. 1987. *The Everyday World as Problematic.* Boston: Northeastern University Press.

Spelman, Elizabeth V. 1988. *Inessential Woman: Problems of Exclusion in Feminist Thought.* Boston: Beacon Press.

Sprague, Joey, and Mary K. Zimmerman. 1993. "Overcoming Dualisms: A Feminist Agenda for Sociological Methodology." In *Theory on Gender/Feminism on Theory,* edited by P. England, pp. 255–80. New York: Aldine de Gruyter.

Tuana, Nancy, 1993. "With Many Voices: Feminism and Theoretical Pluralism." in *Theory on Gender/Feminism on Theory,* edited by P. England, pp. 281–9. New York: Aldine de Gruyter.

Walby, Sylvia. 1992. "Post-Post-Modernism? Theorizing Social Complexity." In *Destabilising Theory: Contemporary Feminist Debates,* edited by M. Barrett and A. Phillips, pp. 31–52. Stanford: Stanford University Press.

Ward, Kathryn. 1990. "Introduction and Overview." In *Women Workers and Global Restructuring,* edited by K. Ward, pp. 1–22.Ithaca: ILR Press.

Ward, Kathryn. 1993. "Reconceptualizing World Systems Theory to Include Women." In *Theory on Gender/Feminism on Theory,* edited by P. England, pp. 43–68. New York: Aldine de Gruyter.

Zinn, Maxine Baca, Lynn Weber Cannon, Elizabeth Higginbotham, and Bonnie Thornton Dill. 1986. "The Costs of Exclusionary Practices in Women's Studies," *Signs* 11 (2): 290–303.

Part I

Gendered Reproduction of Race-Ethnicity and Social Class

Wendy Luttrell teaches in the Sociology and Cultural Anthropology Departments at Duke University.

Denise A. Segura is Assistant Professor in the Department of Sociology and Chicano Studies, University of California, Santa Barbara.

Larissa Lomnitz is Professor of Social Anthropology at the National University of Mexico. She is the author of several books, including *The Chilean Middle Class: The Struggle for Survival within Neo-Liberal Adjustment Policies.*

1. "Becoming Somebody": Aspirations, Opportunities, and Womanhood

Wendy Luttrell

> My parents they sit down and tell us, you going to be a school teacher. You know how they think. They told us what they wanted us to do, you know, so we wouldn't have to work as hard as them. But we knowed we weren't going to be. 'Cause we didn't have too many school teachers no way. The two schools we went to weren't but one school teacher.
>
> *So is that what you wanted to do – to be a school teacher?*
>
> I don't know, I guess a school teacher. That's the only thing we knowed. We didn't think about anything else.

> When I was in grade school they asked us what we wanted to be when we grew up. I wrote that I wanted to be a judge. The nuns got very upset with this and asked me if I had copied it from somewhere. I mean, what little kid from the neighborhood ever thought about being a judge?

Despite their distinct backgrounds and experiences, these two women share similar stories about childhood aspirations. Ola, born and raised in a southern rural community, recalls her parents' hopes that one of their eight children would become a schoolteacher, yet as a child she knew that such a possibility was a dream, not a reality. Throughout the rest of her interview Ola elaborates on and accounts for this gap between her dreams and her realities as a black woman growing up in the rural south. Joanne, born and raised in a northeastern, urban, industrialized neighborhood, describes how she first learned about the gap between her dreams and her destiny as a white, working-class woman. Having revealed her longings to be a judge, Joanne remembers the force with which she was challenged by school officials. For the remainder of her interview, Joanne explains how she came to take on her teachers' views as her own.

This chapter is about what two groups of women remember about their childhood aspirations and what we learn from their accounts about how gender, race and class shaped what they "knew" about their futures. Their stories are part of a comparative ethnographic study which analyzes the past and present schooling experiences of women learners in two adult basic-education programs to show the effect of social differences on women's knowledge and power. A number of compelling mobility studies document the statistical reality of the part played by social differences in people's life trajectories and chances. Yet, we know little about the narrative realities of these patterns or how social differences and inequalities come into being and are sustained. This chapter focuses on women's aspirational stories as windows into these narrative realities and suggests new ways to theorize issues of gender, race and class.

Admittedly, the process of social reproduction is complex. Of particular interest is how occupational aspirations link opportunity structures, or what society offers, and individuals, or what one wants or chooses at the cultural level. Several ethnographic studies have documented how aspirations serve at once to reproduce and challenge race, class or gender divisions and inequalities. For example, Ogbu (1974) argues that because African-Americans have faced (and continue to face) job ceilings and economic barriers, they have developed a set of folk theories about "making it" which do not always focus on academic pursuit. Moreover, African-Americans' aspirations, which reflect alternative strategies for making it outside of mainstream education and jobs, may serve to facilitate economic survival at the expense of upward mobility. Similarly, Willis (1977) argues that the white, working-class "lads" he observed based their aspirations on insights into the structure and organization of manual work for which they were destined. Through their counter-school culture, which opposed school styles and values such as official notions of time and the principles of achievement and meritocracy, the lads came both to accept and subvert the manual jobs and shop-floor culture which awaited them. Along similar lines, McRobbie (1978 and 1991) illuminates the ironies of working-class girls' opposition wherein they drew on traditionally defined feminine concerns to challenge school officials, values and styles that ultimately served to prepare them for subordinate roles as working-class wives and mothers. Holland and Eisenhart (1990) provide a detailed account of the downscaling of career aspirations among a group of black and white female college students, arguing that peer-group interactions which favored the culture of romance and attractiveness over school work and careers prepared the young woman to take on subordinate roles. In a similar study about the role of peer culture, Macleod (1987) documents the varied, yet leveled, aspirations of two groups of male teenagers in a low-income neighborhood. Each of these studies highlights pieces of the story, emphasizing race, class and gender as separate axes of social structure or as conflicting collective identities through which aspirations are constituted and practiced. This study highlights a different piece of the story by emphasizing the variability and simultaneity of gender, race and class in the formation of aspirations that link what society offers and what individuals choose.

My presentation of the interview material draws on cultural studies and narrative analysis to discern the meanings and conditions that shaped the aspirational stories told by the women (Carby 1982; Hall 1986; McRobbie 1978; Willis 1977; Chase 1991; Personal Narrative Group 1989; Mishler 1986). While there is much to recommend the use of this approach, I want to clarify its pitfalls. First is the problem of presenting the women's lives in a way that they may not recognize or agree with (Collins 1990; hooks 1990; McRobbie 1982; Oakley 1981; Smith 1987; Steedman 1987). Needless to say, the women I interviewed did not talk about their lives as "cultural texts," nor did they label their multiple and sometimes conflicting interpretations as oppositional or compliant "moments." With this in mind, I have tried to strike a balance between the women's version of the past and my own and to create a bridge between more abstract and everyday understandings of how the world works. Second is the problem of representation. I suggest that the women's stories be understood as both products and reflections of social divisions and imbalances of power which were negotiated between the women and me through the ethnographic enterprise (Clifford and Marcus 1986). Our mutual effort to talk across social differences and to recognize common concerns is itself part of the conditions which produced the stories as well as my interpretations (Mascia-Lees, Sharpe and Cohen 1989). Finally, there is a tendency to resolve rather than sustain ambiguities that arise in people's memories and interpretations of the past. I believe that studies are most successful when they preserve and highlight the multiplicity of views and voices that constitute the "circuits" of cultural production (Johnson 1986/87 :45–6).

The women in the study

I provide here a brief sketch of each group of women. My intention is to discuss the similarities and differences in how the women interpreted their lives and projected their futures, rather than to generalize about either group. The women will be referred to by locality as the Philadelphia and North Carolina women. In the past I have identified the women by race and class (Luttrell 1989). However, these labels can serve to fix the women's identities and make it difficult for the reader to focus on how gender, race and class are produced and negotiated, which is the subject of this chapter (Ginsberg and Tsing 1990).

All the Philadelphia women were white and had been raised in the same neighborhood, which, when the study began, was in flux and disarray because of industrial relocation and massive social-service cutbacks. They had all attended neighborhood schools during the late 1940s, 1950s and early 1960s; only 20 percent had finished high school. They had moved in and out of the workforce as clerical workers, factory hands, waitresses, hospital or teachers' aides; two women were displaced homemakers when the study began in 1980.

All the North Carolina women were black and had grown up in southern, rural communities where they had experience doing farm work; most had picked cotton or tended tobacco during their youth. They had attended segregated rural schools, but because of the demands of farm life, lack of transportation, and racial discrimination their school attendance had been sporadic. Only two of the black women had graduated from high school, one of whom had completed one year at a local black college. During the study all were employed at a university but shared similar work histories which included domestic work in white people's homes.

There were significant differences in the two groups of women. While equal numbers had gotten pregnant as teenagers, a higher proportion of the Philadelphia women had married as a result. More of the North Carolina than the Philadelphia women had been single heads of households, although during the course of the study this difference declined. The North Carolina women had lower incomes, earning no more than $8,000 a year; the Philadelphia women's income averaged $10,000. The women all shared one basic characteristic: they were mothers ranging in age between twenty-five and fifty with children still living at home.

There are many contrasting experiences to consider including race, region, ethnicity, religion, schooling, levels of economic deprivation, political participation, all of which give rise to the different voices and dialogues about childhood aspirations presented in this chapter. Interestingly, however, these voices converge around historically grounded and emotionally charged images of work and womanhood which offer us fresh insights into the process of social reproduction.

Aspirational stories

Central to the women's aspirational stories is what each group of women "knew" about their futures:

> The time I was coming along you could do housework, you could baby-sit, work jobs in the back of a kitchen, you know, or you could clean up outside.
>
> When I got grown up you couldn't find no job nowhere but tending to somebody's babies or cleaning somebody's house.
>
> If you were lucky you could end up like well, out there like where I'm working.

> In the neighborhood there were four choices: you could either be a secretary, nurse, mother, or nun (if you were Catholic).

> When I grew up the choices were clear – either a nurse, nun, secretary or mother. We didn't think about other things, we didn't know anything different.

Both groups of women shared the view that certain kinds of work awaited them and recalled that as children they had dreamed of escaping its most arduous demands. For example, Lilly, while explaining that she had wanted to be a nurse, remembered that "mostly I knew I didn't want to farm":

> But I really liked going to school, and I said a million times I wished that I could have stayed in school like other kids did cause I wanted to be a nurse, but that didn't work out. Mostly I knew I didn't want to farm because we got tired of farming. Whenever we farmed on half we always wind up with nothing. We farmed one year and ended up with one hundred dollars apiece, and I bought our first refrigerator and record player. But mostly we ended up with nothing. It was hard work – my sister and I we was just working with children, the man wouldn't hire nobody else. We had to go out in the field and prime tobacco; we had to get up on the barn and get on those tills and hang it. We had to set up at night, you know, so the tobacco could dry out in the barn. We had to do all that stuff and, well, we had a hard time then. I knew I didn't want to do that all the time.

Helen explained that her desire to become a secretary was a way to avoid factory work:

> I knew I wanted to be a secretary – which I am and I wish I weren't. I didn't know how crummy some secretarial jobs could be. But my sister was a secretary. I used to see her in the morning go to work, and she was all dressed up – she looked real nice. It was either that – and then I had another sister who worked in a factory. She always look like she was overtired, looked like a bum. I didn't want to do what that one did, I'd rather do what the other one did.

Lilly's and Helen's accounts are typical in that all the women's stories about aspirations were narrated "in the voice" and "in the image" of people they knew and valued (Holland 1988). What they "knew" about the future and how they learned not to "think about anything else" was inextricably linked and confounded with their feelings about and affiliations with those people who shared their destinies. Equally striking was how the women narrated their aspirations as part of an unfolding story about social differences and struggles within schools and workplaces. It was both within and against these two institutional settings that the women projected their futures and accounted for the gaps between childhood dreams and adult realities. But whereas the North Carolina women emphasized the organization of work, the Philadelphia women emphasized the organization of school in telling their aspirational stories. The contrasts in the telling of their stories enable us to explore the variable meaning and salience of gender, race and class in shaping aspirations.

North Carolina women's aspirations

The North Carolina women knew of limited options beyond life on the farm. If lucky they could "end up" doing domestic work in an institutional setting rather than in a private home, entitling them to benefits, such as vacation, sick leave and health insurance. Their view about the futility of education was as persistent as their knowledge about limited work options. In the telling of their aspirations, all but two of the North Carolina women told stories about people they knew who had gotten a "good education" only to find themselves working in laundries, banks, motels or schools as housekeepers:

> I know a lot of educated ones doing work no better than I'm doing now. Then a job is a job. It's nothin' against the job but when you got a little education I think you most likely will try to find somethin' better than cleanin'. My niece, she has herself a Masters, I was there at her graduation. But she's working at a laundry, she's been there some five years. She kept going to one interview after another, and she never would get a job. Maybe it was somethin' she said, but you would think that she could be workin' in a place better than a laundry with a Master's degree.

Beyond this recurring theme about the limited social mobility of blacks, what tied all the North Carolina women's aspirational stories together was a focus on work. Woven into every account were detailed descriptions of the racial organization of work, which included the difficulties blacks had finding anything but menial jobs, the working conditions of the jobs they could find and, most important, the social relations between blacks and whites that characterized the jobs they had held.

Lilly's story illustrates the typical sequence of how the North Carolina women narrated their childhood aspirations:

> I was wanting to be a nurse, but then we stopped school to help mama out and when she got straightened out then I didn't want to go back. I felt like all the kids that we went to school with had moved on. And then when we went back we went back with a younger group. I was ashamed to be so big so I started to work in my first job that I had in a restaurant. And the blacks had to be in the back, had to work in the back. Nobody could see you in the front unless they run short, unless the lunch hour would get busy and they couldn't keep up. Then they would pull somebody black from the back. I started as a dishwasher and helped the lady cook who was in the back. And then one day at lunch time when they couldn't keep up they would pull me out of the kitchen to make hotdogs. I still didn't get out on the floor to clean up, nothing like that. I had to stay behind the counter making hotdogs. All the white peoples was in the front and all the black was in the back. And you didn't see the blacks out until it was time for us to leave or if they needed some help. But I really liked going to school and I wished that I could have stayed in school cause I wanted to be a nurse.

Lilly's story begins with her dream of becoming a nurse, interrupted not only by family and work demands, but also by the shame she felt for having been left behind by others in school. Her story then shifts to a description of her first job working in a restaurant. Lilly describes the world of work in terms that were repeated throughout the North Carolina women's interviews. Her story highlights the marked divisions between blacks who were relegated to the "back" and whites who occupied positions in "front." Such divisions not only rendered the work of blacks invisible, but also devalued blacks in the eyes of the public. This racialized image of work, historically grounded in the Jim Crow laws of the segregated south, evoked charged memories that framed the North Carolina women's aspirational stories.

Gloria weaves the racial organization of domestic work into her story about childhood aspirations.

> I always wanted to be a seamstress. I used to make all my clothes. I would design them myself, and I even found me an old sewin' machine someone had thrown out. I cleaned it, greased it down and got it workin' like it was new. Then I was workin' at the time, since I was about ten years old for a white lady. I started with one of the daughters. You know, just go there and clean up her room and wash out her little laundry. I would go there three times a week. Then I started baby-sitting for her and went on through just like that. I enjoyed it cause I was always really wantin' my own money and I know if I didn't get out and earn it I wouldn't have none. I worked like that until I dropped out of school cause I was stayin' the lot.
>
> *What does it mean to stay the lot?*
>
> You stayed there all week and went back home on Friday night and then come back on Sunday. I got a baby during the time I was working there. There I was taking care of this young white girl's babies (she was not much older than me) while my mother took care of mine. I liked working for them, they treated me like one of the family. But it wasn't till I left and got my own place that I could take my sewing machine with me, you know so I could make clothes.

Gloria recalls that she enjoyed her job because she liked earning her own money. Yet, the racial and gendered structure of domestic work, in this case "staying the lot," required her to subsume her interests so as to meet the demands and interests of the white family of which she was "treated as part." This concept of being "treated like one of the family" (a phrase used by more than half of the North Carolina women to describe their domestic work experiences) is particularly telling in that it reveals as it disguises the race and gender relations which conspired to suppress black women's knowledge and worth, a point to which I will return.

But not all the women who worked for white families could claim that they had been "treated like one of the family." Ella's aspirational story begins with her effort to escape a life on the farm, then shifts to a description of the job that she secured up north, only to return home because she could not find adequate childcare for her baby. She concludes with her recollection that "some of the people were nice and some of them were not" who employed her as a domestic, the only job she could find:

> We would say if we did any kind of work it wasn't going to be nothing but baby-sitting, that's right, we would say that too. Haven't you heard me tell you how I worked for this lady? I worked for this lady and she fixed dinner for me. Her husband was in a wheelchair and she sat her dog and her husband up at the table and sat me off at a little table back (laughing). I'll tell you something, that hasn't been too long ago. I baby-sat for another lady. Some of the people were nice and some of them were not.

Told "in the voice of" and "in the image" of what other rural, black girls growing up in the segregated south "would say" about what they could anticipate for themselves, Ella speaks to the kinds of social relations that blacks learned to anticipate in the work they were forced to accept.

Louise told one of the most striking stories about the treatment of domestic employees as "dirt" and undeserving of human status (Rollins 1985). One day the white "lady" she worked for took out a can of Lysol to spray on Louise before she began her domestic chores:

> We was in the kitchen when she came at me with that can of spray. I wasn't going to let nobody spray me. I could feel my hand on the knife behind me on the counter. I might have killed that woman, I could feel the knife in my hand. But I got out of there before any damage could be done. Not all the white peoples I worked for were that bad, some of them was nice people, but then I could never forget. Black people were treated as dirt back long and then.

Charged memories of being invisible and worth less than whites (and lighter-skinned blacks) were persistent throughout the North Carolina women's descriptions of work as well as schools (Luttrell 1993). Their stories stress the profound effects of racial segregation and violence (as threats or as actual incidents) on what the women "knew" and how they learned not to think about anything else. Their anecdotes also speak to the risks attached to "knowing anything different, anything better than farming" (a familiar story told by black women authors).

Betty's desire to "be somebody" illustrates the risks as well as the social-psychological costs that at once fueled and constrained her aspirations to become a social worker:

> You can't imagine what people got beat out of in those days, how they had to answer to white people. It could make you ashamed to see them take it. But as my mother always say, that kindness don't hurt anybody. You can get more by being easy and

kind than you can by being harsh and ugly. She would say you can get right next to a person being nice, but you can't by being ugly. As ugly as that person talks to you, the nicer you be, that really does something to them. But I didn't see it like that. I wanted my mother to talk ugly to the teachers or to the man whose land we farmed. But see, she didn't do it. She took whatever it was and went on. And that's why I got mad with her. And I regret it. I reckon I'll regret it till I die. But I wanted to do it so – so much so that I wanted to talk for everyone, you know take up everybody's battle. I didn't want nobody thinking I was a coward. But I seen a lot of people being made to be cowards and some of them is cowards and some of them are just afraid they might say the wrong things. They're afraid they will say something that will hurt their own self or get someone else hurt. So that's why I wanted to be a social worker. I wanted to be somebody, that's why I always tried in school and was interested in learning.

Told as an unfolding drama about how best to understand and negotiate social differences and inequalities, Betty's account echoes the fears, shame, and rage that persisted throughout the North Carolina women's aspirational stories. Still, while their stories reveal what the North Carolina women "knew" about gender, race and class as barriers to social mobility, their explanations about their own "problem" or "downfall," which they attributed to individual traits of "stubbornness," "temper," and "lack of motivation," suggest yet another version of the past. Indeed, it would be a mistake to categorize the women's stories in dualistic terms, as simply oppositional or compliant. But in order to appreciate more fully what the North Carolina women blamed themselves for, it is useful to turn to the Philadelphia women's stories.

The Philadelphia women's aspirational stories

Whereas the North Carolina women's aspirational stories cohered around work themes, the Philadelphia women's stories cohered around school themes. All the Philadelphia women described their aspirations in the context of explaining school decisions and actions, particularly why they had not pursued a college education. Doris's account is typical of how the Philadelphia women narrated their aspirations:

> I always wanted to be a secretary. No let me backtrack. I guess I always preferred to go to college, but the idea that there was no money to go made it that you were going to be a secretary. You knew there just wasn't an option to pick something else. There was one thing definite; I wasn't going to work in the factory.

In telling their stories, all the Philadelphia women made a point of emphasizing that it was not that they did not *think* about going to college; the problem was that finances did not permit them to pursue this course:

> It wasn't that I never thought about college – it was just that nobody around me

ever went. We all knew that college was for kids whose parents had the money to send them. So we just didn't even discuss it.

I remember thinking about college in eleventh grade, but it wasn't feasible. You could sit around and think about it, but it just wasn't feasible.

Some women, like Peggy, provided insights into how schools "tracked" working-class students into working-class jobs (Bowles and Gintis 1976):

In high school I had signed up for commercial, but I got sent to kitchen practice.

What was kitchen practice?

Being a waitress, cook, chef. That was the worst course in school. There was really the low life in that course.

How did people get placed into kitchen practice?

I think they just went down and said, well this is a poor one and she's not going to do good; she probably doesn't have the mentality. Look at the income, look where she lives, she's not going to amount to anything so stick her in there. Once you got into ninth grade you ran into a lot of problems. It didn't matter how smart you were anymore, they didn't take that into consideration. It was where you lived and how much money you had backing you. There were academic courses where I went to high school, you know English and history and all. Only some of us were put into academic – I wasn't one of them.

Even though you were a really good student in junior high? [She had made the honor roll every semester.]

That's right. You know at the time I just didn't think anything of it. I accepted it. Then afterwards I thought about it, why did that happen? I could have been put into academic. If only I had pushed harder. I remember that I had wanted to become something professional, like a lawyer maybe. I did, I wanted to be somebody when I was younger.

Yet, despite these insights about how schools reproduce class inequalities, Peggy goes on to blame herself for "accepting it." Moreover, she disclaims her insights by explaining that she could not have envisioned herself in college because she "would not have been comfortable" with people she perceived as "different." College represented the unknown, an unfamiliar and potentially unfriendly territory that had not been explored by people the women knew or could identify with. Students who attended college were not only viewed as unfamiliar but as having unique characteristics which several of the Philadel-phia women referred to as "college material". As Pam explained:

Even though I was in the advanced track, the academic track, I really didn't think about being anything except a secretary. I wanted to stick to something I *knew* I could do.

And what was that?

I knew I could do all the things a secretary does – I had seen my older sister do it. She was great at it, and I knew I'd be good at it, too. I wasn't sure whether I was college material, I guess mostly because I didn't know anyone else who was.

The Philadelphia women's talk about college could be interpreted as a way to protect themselves from feeling like failures for not having achieved class mobility, what Sennett and Cobb refer to as one of the "hidden injuries of class" (1973). However, this interpretation misses the ways in which the Philadelphia women's stories highlight shared values about what "really matters" in life for working-class women. Anne makes this point as she tells about her childhood aspirations:

I wasn't interested in the academic track. I didn't know why I needed to study history and all. I was interested in learning what I needed for a job like typing, book-keeping, and the commercial courses. I couldn't wait to get out of school where I could be on my own, where I could be myself and do what I wanted to do. Some of it was to have my own money so I could buy what I wanted for myself, but we all, all the girls I hung with, all of us were in commercial and we knew what we wanted. We knew what we needed to do too, you know, about life, we knew about life even if we didn't know what they were teaching us about in school.

Anne's account draws on the images and voices of people she knew and valued to confirm and validate her school decision. She grounds her actions in the knowledge and judgments of "the girls I hung with " Sounding much like the low-income high school girls (white, black and Hispanic) in Michelle Fine's (1991) ethnographic study, the Philadelphia women recalled feeling trapped by dominant school values and traditions which did not apply to their own experiences or desires. To account for why they had dropped out of school, the Philadelphia women emphasized the role and value of "common sense" or "streetwise" as opposed to "schoolwise" knowledge in a successful future (Luttrell 1989 and 1993). Again, it would be a mistake to characterize the Philadelphia women's aspirational stories as either oppositional or compliant. Rather, their stories are complex cultural texts which at once reveal and disguise how gender, race and class differences and inequalities are reproduced.

Ironically, while accepting a view of school as a vehicle that could move them up the social ladder, the Philadelphia women persistently gave reasons for rejecting the ride. Their acceptance of the ideology of meritocracy served both to validate and undermine their working-class identities and interests. Joanne's story illustrates this paradox. Recall that Joanne began her aspirational account with her dream of becoming a judge, for which she had been reprimanded in school. She continues her account by describing her career in school, including her decision to drop out in response to family demands, and then shifts to a discussion of how she had traveled around Europe, and returned to work as a receptionist in a doctor's office and in a law firm. Joanne concludes her discussion of childhood aspirations in the following way:

> You know I think a lot of working-class people put professional people with educations on a pedestal. It is like with blacks – if all you see of blacks is that they are trash men, then you think they must all be like that. But I met a lot of professional people – people with more knowledge than me, and maybe more ambition, but they weren't really any better than me. They weren't really any different, even if they were somebody. You know, the thing is, with all the people I met I still married the boy on the corner. I just always felt most comfortable with him. Maybe I had a strong homing instinct, but that's just who I am.

On one level, Joanne's story reveals an acceptance of the deeply ingrained, yet implicit value of upward mobility within American culture, best captured by Lillian Rubin's observation that we judge people according to how well they "move up or down, not just through" the class structure (1976: 8–9). Joanne's description of "professional people with educations" being put on a "pedestal" and blacks being viewed as "trash men" exposes the inseparability and simultaneity of gender, race and class relations as the matrix of this value. Historically, it is upper-class, white women who are put on pedestals as cultural and symbolic figures of purity, moral superiority, virginity and domesticity. Having been relegated to manual, unskilled labor, blacks have been culturally and symbolically associated with "dirty" and undesirable work, thus justifying their lowest position in the class hierarchy. These gender- and race-based images promote and sustain the class differences and inequalities which Joanne is critiquing, and yet she borrows the same images and ideologies to make her point.

On another level, Joanne's description of marrying the "boy on the corner" could also be interpreted as a rejection of the value of upward mobility. Joanne contends that professional people are not better than she is and that she could have married one if she had chosen to. Instead, she chose to marry the boy she felt most "comfortable with," rejecting marriage as a vehicle of upward mobility. Joanne's decisions regarding both school and marriage illuminate the avenues of upward mobility she viewed were open to her. Ironically, however, the language and logic of her "homing instinct" masks the oppositional nature of her actions, actions which appear to her as "natural" rather than "social," as inherited rather than made. Reminiscent of the North Carolina women's concept of being "treated as part of the family," the Philadelphia women's concept of being "comfortable with" reveals as it disguises the class and gender relations which conspired to shape their aspirations.

Discussion

By juxtaposing how the North Carolina and Philadelphia women narrated their aspirational stories, we learn that both groups felt compelled to answer for their lack of social mobility, but with different emphases, implications and consequences. First, let us consider the thematic contrasts between the women's stories. Whereas the North Carolina women stressed the organization of work, the Philadelphia women stressed the organization of school to explain their failed mobility. I would argue that these distinct views are produced by institutional elements, such as the goals, structure and modes of control that are found within rural community vs. urban bureaucratic schools and within domestic vs. "pink collar" (that is, clerical and waitressing) work. For example, in contrast to the one-room rural schools attended by the North Carolina women, the comprehensive urban high school attended by the Philadelphia women was large, differentiated in its instruction, and bureaucratic; it was not analogous in structure and operation to either family or church as was the rural school. Moreover, the urban school, unlike the rural school, was isolated from other institutions and required its students to negotiate between class, race and gender practices found in schools and those found in families and workplaces (Hansot and Tyak 1988). Recall that domestic work and its gender, race and class practices were presented by the North Carolina women as part of a seamless web of contexts, each interwoven with and legitimating the other. However, the Philadelphia women viewed school as separate from and in conflict with both family and work life. Thus, one way to think about the women's stories is to pose them in institutional terms, to consider how different institutional structures, practices and rituals themselves shape aspirations.

Second, let us consider what these thematic contrasts suggest about the women's acceptance and rejection of dominant ideologies about upward mobility. For the Philadelphia women, the ideology of opportunity and mobility promoted in school made it appear that they had and could make individual "choices" about their futures. In contrast, the North Carolina women did not fully embrace this dominant ideology and thus could see their destinies as part of a collective journey. Put another way, whereas the Philadelphia women's versions account for why they, as individuals, had rejected upward mobility, the North Carolina women's version account for why they, as a group, had been rejected by white society. Both versions reject the official, authorized interpretation of their social situation.

Split images of womanhood: behind the official version of social mobility

An underlying coherence that tied all the women's stories together was an emphasis on women's work, particularly in terms of idealized but split images of womanhood. This more buried coherence illuminates the links between structural opportunities, gender, race and class-based ideologies of upward mobility, and what individuals choose or want. The Philadelphia women anticipated doing "women's work" as "secretaries, nurses, mothers, or nuns." These options (which they understood as both constraints and possibilities) charted a traditional, subservient and culturally sanctioned view of, and pathway through, womanhood. This path offered them the opportunity to achieve idealized images of femininity as clean, good, domestic, nurturing and selfless beings. Regardless of whether they anticipated doing "women's work" in the paid labor force (as secretaries or nurses) or in the home/church (as mothers or nuns), they learned to view their work and authority in dualistic and contradictory ways.

Ironically, the Philadelphia women's so-called opportunities worked for and against them. On the one hand, as "secretaries, nurses, mothers and nuns," they could look forward to establishing female bonds with each other through shared work, family, and religious rituals. Through the creation of a working-class female culture, they could expect to acquire and exercise their own distinct knowledge and authority, albeit in a separate sphere. Their common experience and camaraderie with girlfriends, sisters, or other female family members generated shared values and views of the work world and a confidence that they "knew what they were good at." As part of their work as women they could exercise their judgments, making choices based on these distinct values and views. Their stories about why they dropped out of school, chose the "commercial track," rejected college as an option, and married the "neighborhood" boy illustrate not only their working-class affiliation but also their claims to knowledge and authority as women.

Yet, these opportunities also *undermined* their claims to knowledge and authority as women. In anticipating their work as secretaries, nurses, mothers and nuns, the Philadelphia women learned to focus on what Dorothy Smith (1987: 81) calls the "concrete, the particular, the bodily" aspects of daily life which characterize "women's work." In the patriarchal division of labor, men (whether as bosses, doctors, husbands, or clergy) are freed from a concern about maintaining their daily existence which allows them to concentrate solely on the "abstracted conceptual mode of ruling." At the same time that "women's work" produces the conditions of men's ruling, it also produces the conditions of its own undermining, suppression and invisibility. As the Philadelphia women learned to concentrate on the "concrete, the particular, the bodily," they also learned to suppress their own knowledge in favor of patriarchal authority and knowledge. Such suppression was expressed by their aspirations. First, when aspiring beyond their "choices" as secretaries, nurses, mothers and nuns, the Philadelphia women projected themselves outside their working-class world (as "college material" or as "professionals"). Second, these aspirations were set outside what has traditionally been considered a "women's" sphere or domain (for example, Joanne's dream to be a judge and Peggy's dream to be a lawyer).

As domestics "working for white people," the North Carolina women anticipated a different path through womanhood. They were afforded fewer opportunities for achieving idealized images of womanhood but a greater chance to claim their own knowledge and authority as black women. First, race-based lines of authority in domestic jobs required that the black women answer not only to white men, but also to white women and children. And yet, these power relationships were mixed with the intimacies and inter- dependencies which come from doing domestic service work, the blurring of lines between who cares for whom, who depends on whom, and who knows about whom (Tucker 1988; Rollins 1985). In such a division of labor, white people need not attend to certain aspects of daily maintenance and thus are freed to attend to the conceptual modes of ruling. Consequently, the North Carolina women, who saw themselves destined for the "concrete" and "bodily" work of white society, learned to anticipate their invisibility in its workings and in dominant conceptions of power and knowledge.

Yet, at the same time, when it came to preserving their own families and communities, an act historically and currently viewed as outright resistance (hooks 1990; Davis 1971), the North Carolina women's attention to the "concrete, the particular, and the bodily" work of survival could not be ignored or minimized. In contrast to the Philadelphia women, they could expect to acquire knowledge and exercise their authority because of, rather than in spite of, their work as women. Indeed, the North Carolina women's aspirations illuminated their ability to resist the suppression of their own knowledge and authority as women. When dreaming of their destinies beyond "working for white people," they most often imagined themselves as teachers and social workers. While still viewed as "women's work," these jobs offered them an opportunity to contest dominant racist authority relations by advocating for black men, women and children. Thus, for the North Carolina women "being somebody" was projected in opposition to white society, but not in opposition to what is culturally expected from women. Segura (in Chapter 2 of this volume) finds a similar understanding of work among Chicanas in white-collar jobs.

Nonetheless, the North Carolina women were subject to what Pat Hill Collins calls "controlling images" of black womanhood, as "mammys" and "matriarchs", which divide black women against each other as "good" and "bad" women (1990: 67–90). These split images surfaced in several ways. First, more than half of the North Carolina women told stories about how skin color had shaped their aspirations, and all offered examples of how the color line had affected their school achievement (Luttrell 1993). Eloise's aspiration to be a majorette is one such example:

I wanted to be a majorette, you know those girls who represent the school. I wanted to be a majorette in the worst way. But at that particular time they wasn't takin' black girls in there. We, all of us were black, but I'm just saying they were not for the colored, you know. But that's what I wanted to be, a majorette, I wanted that in the worst way.

Second, split images of womanhood persisted throughout the North Carolina women's descriptions of work. The hard, dirty, and tiresome jobs they sought to avoid, their explanations of and emotions about who cared for their children while they were at work, their recurring references to why marriage had not occurred or worked out in their lives, and their persistent descriptions of typical interactions between themselves and the white "ladies" for whom they worked, were all told as counterpoints to idealized images of women as clean, domestic, married – that is, "good" – women. Third, whereas motherhood was mentioned as one of four "options" by the Philadelphia women, it was never once mentioned in that way by the North Carolina women. The Philadelphia women's discussions of motherhood, which revolved around their mistaken idealized images of marriage and domesticity, focused on how they had been misled about these aspirations and opportunities:

I started going with Bob. All the girls thought I was so lucky. I really wish I hadn't fallen in love that young. You know we all dreamed about white picket fences – a little house with flowers and staying home with the kids and all. You know, typical Father Knows Best family. We just had no idea that those things don't work out. Funny, my own family wasn't like that. My dad lost his job several times and my mom supported all of us, but that's how we thought it would be.

In contrast, the North Carolina women's discussion of motherhood was woven into their descriptions of work and interdependence on kin relations, predominantly other black women, wherein they reflected on their feelings about being "good" or "good enough" mothers. Geraldine explained that in order to support her children she had been forced to live apart from them:

I'll never forgive myself for that. Only one of my children I kept for any length of time. That one there (she points to the picture on her television). That is my biggest grief.

The North Carolina women who had been able to raise their children alone or in nuclear families did not view this outcome as either expected or ideal, but rather as the result of "luck" or chance. More important, it was an aspect of their womanhood for which they felt compelled to account. Indeed, historically grounded and emotionally charged split images of womanhood were woven throughout all the women's aspirational stories. These split images served both to tie and to divide the women from each other and from themselves as a group. Consider Helen's "choice" between the sister who worked in the factory and "looked like a bum" and the other sister who went to her secretarial job "all dressed up – she looked real nice," and Lilly's experience of being sprayed with Lysol, as variations on the same gendered theme about the process of social reproduction.

In light of these split images of womanhood, it is not surprising, then, that both groups of women mentioned nursing as a childhood aspiration. No doubt the history of nursing and the varied avenues through which poor and working-class women have been able to enter the profession (as hospital aides, LPNs, RNs, midwives, and so on) provide a clue to this common aspiration. Just as important, nursing is a role that builds on symbolic and idealized images of women as clean, white (as in their uniforms), nurturing, and subservient, while simultaneously promising professionalization and better pay than other types of women's work. Moreover, the gender-based divisions between what women as nurses are allowed to know and make judgments about, and what men as doctors are allowed to know and make judgments about, take precedence over race- and class-based differences between women. Indeed all of these factors may have converged in making nursing an aspiration within which women from varied class and race backgrounds could bridge available opportunity structures and ideologies about what a "good" or "ideal" woman should be.

Finally, these split images of womanhood undermined how both groups of women projected their futures. The women's shared images of good vs. bad, clean vs. dirty, black vs. white antagonists in the struggle for upward mobility served to mediate the effects of class- and race-based barriers; these false antagonists also served to mask the female subordination that all the women shared (Palmer 1983). Indeed, idealized but split images direct our attention away from what poses a threat to society: the collective agency of "bad" women, whether black or white, lower or upper class, married or single who refuse to accept patriarchal structures of family, work, or school.

Toward a bottom-up analysis of gender, race and class

What do the women's aspirational stories teach us about the narrative realities of social reproduction? In one sense we learn that the process of social reproduction looks quite different from the ground up than from the top down; that the tensions and fusions between what society offers (opportunity structures) and what individuals want (aspirations) are much more nuanced than current theories allow or account for. The women's version of social reproduction belies the notion that gender, race and class (whether as opportunity structures, ideologies, or collective identities) stage our sense of ourselves in direct or expected ways. Moreover, these stories about what it means to "be somebody" are better understood for their potentiality than for their resistance to or complicity with dominant social relations; indeed that is their drama.

In another sense, the women's contrasting tales about work, school and aspirations suggest new ways to theorize gender, race and class. A focus on gender, race and class as social products rather than social processes has dominated the field of sociology. These top-down approaches view gender, race and class in categorical terms, as separate features of experience or as variables which determine social mobility and status. Top-down theoretical accounts which use gender, race and class as abstract tools of analysis often lose sight of the fact that individuals experience these three relations simultaneously and in ways that are context-specific and vulnerable to change. The logic of these accounts stresses gender, race and class as divided and conflicting interests that are produced by the social structure and are seemingly impervious to all but complete social transformation, and thus do not leave enough room for what R. W. Connell calls "practical politics: choice, doubt, strategy, planning, effort and transformation" (1987: 61).

The women's aspirational stories offer a bottom-up approach to gender, race and class as interpretive devices rather than prescribed scripts for making choices, expressing doubts, and planning strategies about their futures. Their logic does not separate; it confounds structure and agency. The women's context-specific, historically grounded and emotionally charged stories illustrate that people move through a matrix of institutions in the course of a lifetime, each organized with different goals, structures and modes of control concerning gender, race and class. The variable meaning and salience of gender, race and class in different institutional settings encourages people to negotiate these relationships as shifting rather than fixed relationships of power. A bottom-up approach makes it easier to identify which gender, race and class practices and structures are harder to alter and which are more vulnerable to change, thus enabling us to develop a "practical politics." Finally, the further development of a bottom-up approach to gender, race and class depends not only on analyzing the experiences and views of diverse people, but also on people's experiences and views within diverse settings and circumstances.

References

Bowles, Samuel, and Herbert Gintis. 1976. *Schooling in Capitalist America.* New York: Basic Books.
Carby, Hazel. 1982. "Schooling in Babylon." In *The Empire Strikes Back,* edited by Centre for Contemporary Cultural Studies, pp.183–211. London: Hutchinson.
Chase, Susan. 1991. "Interpreting Women's Narratives: Towards an Alternative Methodology." Paper presented at the Southern Sociological Society Meetings, Atlanta, Georgia.
Clifford, James, and George Marcus. 1986. *Writing Culture: The Poetics and Politics of Ethnography.* Berkeley and Los Angeles: University of California Press.

Collins, Patricia Hill. 1990. *Black Feminist Thought: Knowledge, Consciousness and The Politics of Empowerment.* Boston: Unwin Hyman.
Connell, R. W. 1987. *Gender and Power.* Stanford: Stanford University Press.
Davis, A. 1971. "Reflections on the Black Woman's Role in the Community of Slaves." *The Black Scholar* 3: 3–15.
Fine, Michelle. 1991. *Framing Dropouts: Notes on the Politics of an Urban Public High School.* Albany: State University of New York Press.
Ginsberg, Faye, and Anna Tsing. 1990. *Uncertain Terms: Negotiating Gender in American Culture.* Boston: Beacon Press.
Hall, Stuart. 1986. "Gramsci's Relevance to the Analysis of Racism and Ethnicity." *Communication Inquiry* 10: 5–27.
Holland, Dorothy. 1988. "In the Voice of, In the Image Of: Socially Situated Presentations of Attractiveness." IPA *Papers in Pragmatics* 2 (1/2).
Holland, Dorothy, and Eisenhart, Margaret. 1990. *Educated in Romance: Women, Achievement and College Culture.* Chicago: University of Chicago Press.
hooks, bell. 1984. *From Margin To Center.* Boston: South End Press.
hooks, bell. 1990. *Yearning: Race, Gender and Cultural Politics.* Boston: South End Press.
Johnson, Richard. 1986/87. "What is Cultural Studies Anyway?" *Social Text: Theory, Culture and Ideology* 16: 38–80.
Luttrell, Wendy. 1989. "Working-Class Women's Ways of Knowing: Effects of Gender, Race, and Class." *Sociology of Education* 62 (January): 33–46.
Luttrell, Wendy. 1993. "The Teachers They All Had Their Pets: Concepts of Gender, Knowledge and Power." *Signs: Journal of Women in Culture and Society* 18 (3): 505–46.
MacLeod, Jay. 1987. *Ain't No Makin' It: Leveled Aspirations in a Low-Income Neighborhood.* Boulder, Colorado: Westview Press.
McRobbie, Angela. 1978. "Working Class Girls and the Culture of Femininity." In *Women Take Issue: Aspects of Women's Subordination,* edited by Women Studies Group CCCS, 96–108. London: Hutchinson.
McRobbie, Angela. 1982. "The Politics of Feminist Research: Between Talk, Text and Action." *Feminist Review* 12:46–57.
McRobbie, Angela. 1991. *Feminism and Youth Culture: from "Jackie" to "Just Seventeen."* Boston: Unwin Hyman.
Mascia-Lees, Frances, Patricia Sharpe, and Colleen B. Cohen. 1989. "The Postmodern Turn in Anthropology: Cautions from a Feminist Perspective." *Signs: Journal of Women in Culture and Society* 15(1):7–33.
Mishler, Elliot. 1986. *Research Interviewing: Context and Narrative.* Cambridge, Mass.: Harvard University Press.
Oakley, Ann. 1981. "Interviewing Women: A Contradiction in Terms." In *Doing Feminist Research,* edited by Helen Roberts, pp.30–61. London: Routledge and Kegan Paul.
Ogbu, John U. 1974. *The Next Generation: An Ethnography of Education in an Urban Neighborhood.* New York and London: Academic Press.
Ogbu, John U. 1988. "Class Stratification, Racial Stratification, and Schooling." In *Class, Race and Gender in American Education,* edited by Lois Weis, pp.163–82. Albany, New York: SUNY Press.
Palmer, Phyllis Marynick. 1983. "White Women/Black Women: The Dualism of Female Identity and Experience in the United States." *Feminist Studies* 9 (1): 151–70.
Personal Narrative Group. 1989. *Interpreting Women's Lives: Feminist Theory and Personal Narratives.* Bloomington: Indiana University Press.
Rollins, Judith. 1985. *Between Women: Domestics and Their Employers.* Philadelphia: Temple University Press.
Rubin, Lillian. 1976. *Worlds of Pain: Life in the Working-Class Family.* New York: Basic Books.
Sennett, Richard, and Jonathan Cobb. 1973. *The Hidden Injuries of Class.* New York: Vintage Books.
Smith, Dorothy. 1987. *The Everyday World As Problematic: A Feminist Sociology.* Boston: Northeastern University Press.
Steedman, Carolyn. 1987. *Landscape for a Good Woman.* New Brunswick, New Jersey: Rutgers University Press.
Tucker, Susan. 1988. *Telling Memories Among Southern Women: Domestic Workers and their Employers in the Segregated South.* New York: Schocken Books.
Willis, Paul E. 1977. *Learning to Labour: How Working-Class Kids Get Working-Class Jobs.* New York: Columbia University Press.

2. Chicanas in White Collar Occupations: Work and the Gendered Construction of Race-Ethnicity

Denise A. Segura

Chicana[1] employment is often depicted as "unique" – a solemn concurrence of categorical status-clashing. Simultaneously members of several oppressed groups – females, historically subordinated racial-ethnics, and the poor or working-class – Chicanas' distinct set of social locations intersect in ways which shape their life chances and perceptions of opportunity (Baca Zinn 1982; Segura 1986a and 1989; Zavella 1991).[2]

In the labor market, substantially fewer Chicanas work in higher-level jobs than non-Hispanic women (14.1 percent and 28 percent respectively; US Bureau of the Census 1991b). This profile demonstrates marked growth in white-collar jobs among Chicanas since 1980; however, the largest proportion of these women (38.9 percent) work in lower-level technical, sales, and administrative support (clerical) jobs (US Bureau of the Census 1991b). In spite of these developments, we know relatively little about the experiences of Chicanas in white-collar occupations and the ways in which their jobs reproduce gender and/or race-ethnicity within the labor market and the ethnic community.

This chapter explores some of the dilemmas white-collar work poses to 152 Chicanas employed at a major public university in California. I argue that many Chicana workers, even in relatively secure white-collar jobs, view themselves as uniquely placed/positioned through their combined gender, race-ethnicity and class backgrounds. They work in jobs which reaffirm prevailing occupational hierarchies (by race-ethnicity, class, and gender) as well as reinforce and strengthen gendered constructions of ethnicity. Their experiences suggest gender informs the way women and men perceive the values, roles, and responsibilities of their ethnic group and the most appropriate ways to enact them.

---

* Research for this project has been supported by funding from the Academic Senates of the University of California, Davis and UC Santa Barbara as well as the UC Consortium on Mexico and the United States (UC Mexus).

The cues Chicanas receive vary according to the social setting. With respect to employment, Chicanas speak of a set of constraints which are structural (embedded in the organization), interpersonal (employee–employer; worker–worker), and cultural (affirming Mexican traditions). Chicanas' views that their experiences are distinct (from white workers and Chicano men) reaffirm the ideological boundaries of their ethnic community. And what Chicanas like about their jobs often intersects with what is esteemed in the Chicana/o community. Structural features of work and interaction with colleagues concurrently reinforce ongoing labor-market stratification, which, in turn, can strengthen Chicanas' attachment to their ethnic community's ideologies regarding work and opportunity for Mexican women in the United States.

This chapter explores these possibilities. First, I present an overview of Chicanas and employment. This is followed by an analysis of new survey and qualitative data gathered from Chicana white-collar workers. I conclude by offering my views on the implications of the intersection of employment and family for the reproduction of a gendered construction of ethnicity among Chicanas in this study.

Chicanas and employment: some relevant issues

Research on the intersection of gender and race-ethnicity in employment often analyzes unequal labor-market outcomes between men and women (for example, occupational sex segregation) or between Anglo workers and racial-ethnic minorities, both of which reproduce hierarchies at work and reinforce social inequality. Relatively little of this literature focuses on Chicanas despite the fact that they belong to the second largest racial-ethnic group in the US with soaring labor-force participation rates in recent years (Almquist 1984; Cattan 1988; Tienda and Guhleman 1985). This shortcoming in the literature notwithstanding, we can glean several key insights on labor-market dynamics which are relevant to Chicanas and which indicate they encounter "unique barriers", such as unequal access to good jobs, gender/race-ethnic inequality embedded in the organization of work, and on-the-job interaction difficulties with co-workers/supervisors related to differences in culture or class background (Zavella 1987; Pesquera 1985; Romero, Chapter 4 in this volume; Segura 1989), as well as a uniquely framed "second shift" (Hochschild 1989).

Like most women, Chicanas tend to work with other women primarily in service-oriented jobs. However, Chicanas are overrepresented in low-paying or seasonal jobs with limited opportunities for advancement and which typically employ other women and men of color (for example, operatives, farmworkers).[3] Chicanas, like other women of Color, tend to be over represented in the secondary labor market of unstable, seasonal jobs or in jobs with limited promotional opportunities. When Chicanas work in large organizations with recognizable job ladders, they tend to be supervised by white women or men (Malveaux and Wallace 1987; Segura 1986b and 1989). In these jobs, Chicanas tend to be unequally distributed in the lower echelons of an organization.

These observable features of labor-market dynamics have several important consequences for Chicanas. They reinforce existing work hierarchies, maintain social inequality, create conditions which exacerbate divisions among workers, and, in the case of Chicanas, contribute to a gendered construction of their ethnicity. That is, workplace conditions often provide Chicanas with opportunities to enact behavior, pursue relationships, or interpret their work in ways which reinforce their social identities as women of Mexican descent.

Ethnicity is marked by a set of norms, customs, and behaviors different from the dominant or majority ethnic group, as well as "a shared feeling of peoplehood" (Gordon 1964; Keefe and Padilla 1987). Baca Zinn notes that "it has been assumed that one's ethnic identity is more important than one's gender identity" (1980:23). She points out, however, that discussions of gender and ethnicity have been limited in scope and typically situated within the context of the family. Within the ethnic community, Chicano ethnicity is affirmed in the family when Spanish is taught, cultural values instilled, ethnic pride emphasized, and interaction with other Chicanos esteemed.

Within the labor market, Chicano/Mexican ethnicity is reinforced by discrimination (both objective and perceived) and social exclusion from the dominant group (Barrera 1979; Nelson and Tienda 1985). In addition, there are other, less obvious ways in which a gendered sense of Chicano/Mexican ethnicity may be reinforced. That is, organizations may structure jobs in ways which reaffirm Chicanas' sense of themselves as women from a unique racial-ethnic group. Or Chicanas may themselves act in ways which either consciously or unconsciously serve the Chicano community. As one example of the first possibility, Chicanas who work in jobs structured to "serve" a racial-ethnic clientele (for example, minority students) may encounter a reward system which affirms their ethnic identification while they do their job. In the second case, Chicanas who work in jobs which are not overtly structured to accomplish race-ethnicity may nonetheless reaffirm their ethnic identity. They can commit themselves to staying in white-collar jobs even if they experience social isolation or discomfort; they have a sense of themselves as role models. That is, their "success" indirectly enlarges the options of other Chicanas.

Chicanas' labor in low-paying female-dominated jobs not only can reinforce their ethnic identity; it also upholds patriarchy (male domination/female subordination). Women employed in jobs where they earn salaries inadequate to support their families remain economically dependent on men to live above the poverty level (Hartmann 1976; Kuhn and Wolpen 1978; Smith 1987). In addition, these jobs often offer women occasions to strengthen their gendered conceptions of themselves (Fenstermaker, West and Zimmerman 1991). Since many female-dominated jobs involve "helping others," or "serving men", women in these jobs often reinforce social conceptualizations of femininity. Their gendered sense of self can be reinforced even further when they have children and families to care for. (Fenstermaker 1985:204) argues that when women engage in housework and childcare, one social product is "a reaffirmation of one's *gendered* relation to the work and to the world. In short, the 'shoulds' of gender ideals are fused with the 'musts' of efficient household production."

For Chicanas, there may be another dimension to this process with important cultural implications. Like other women, Chicanas often encounter a "second shift" (Hochschild 1989) – bearing primary responsibility for household work in tandem with market work. Unlike other women, however, this dual set of responsibilities may be perceived by Chicanas as part of a distinct cultural heritage – a necessary unity of household and economic work which has sustained their ethnic community historically and is part of what renders them distinct from the majority white population (Segura, forthcoming). Inasmuch as the value of Chicano/Mexican culture is constantly being undermined by outside social pressures, the need or motivations to continue traditional patterns may be more problematic for Chicanas. That is, for Chicanas to challenge Chicano male privilege renders them susceptible to the charge they are acting "like white women" – an act of betrayal to *la cultura*, a possible harbinger of its end, and something to be avoided among many women who give priority to maintaining traditional Chicano/Mexican culture (Nieto-Gomez 1974; Orozco 1986; Segura and Pesquera, forthcoming).

This possibility appreciates that a Chicana's decision to change traditional patterns comprises more than effecting personal empowerment; it also involves the politically charged issue of culture maintenance. In this sense, Chicanas' performance of housework or childcare may be part of the social reinforcement of their gender identity and racial-ethnic culture as well. Such strain adds another dimension to our understanding of the tenacity of triple oppression in the lives of Chicana/Latina women, as the following analysis demonstrates.

An empirical study

In Fall 1989/Winter 1990, in collaboration with Dr Beatriz Pesquera of UC Davis, I distributed a questionnaire on "women and work issues" to all Hispanic-identified women employed at a large public university in California. The survey asked women a battery of closed-ended questions concerning work, the intersection of family and work, gender ideology, feminism, ethnicity and political ideology. A total of 152 women, 47.5 percent of the total, completed the survey. In addition, my co-investigator and I interviewed thirty-five women randomly selected from the survey respondents.[4] This chapter undertakes analysis of the survey and interview data on selected work issues to demonstrate how the intersection of gender and race-ethnicity, as women participate in a stratified workforce and in the family, reproduces a gendered sense of race-ethnicity among Chicana workers.

Most of the informants are of Mexican descent (75 percent) with the rest either of Latin American or Spanish origin. All but fifteen women were born in the United States. Sixty percent of the respondents are bilingual in Spanish and English. All but three women received high school diplomas; one hundred and eighteen have education beyond high school; forty-three have a B.A. or above. Their educational levels are much higher than the California norm for Chicanas (11th grade). Ninety-four women (61.8 percent) are presently married/partnered: of those, 45.8 percent are married to Mexican/Chicano men, 10.6 percent are married to "other Hispanic" men, and 40.4 percent have non-Hispanic husbands. Three women declined to state their husbands' ethnicity. The respondents' ages range from 20 to 60 years old, with an average age of 36.5 years. One hundred and eleven women have children. The mean number of children is 2.1.

Objective job characteristics

Chicanas' employment profiles reveal the intersection of gender and race-ethnicity both in the organization of the workplace, the dilemmas they encounter at work, and their family responsibilities. By and large, the Chicana workers in this large, public organization are employed in female-dominated jobs where most of their co-workers are female (59.2 percent) and/or Anglo (80 percent). Of the 152 respondents, 41.4 percent work in jobs I classified as "lower-level clerical"; 28.9 percent are "upper-level clerical workers"; 5.9 percent are "technical aides and service workers", while 19.7 percent are "professional/ managerial workers".[5] Six women declined to provide information on their occupations.

The informants' incomes are greater than those of many women workers; the mean is $23,288[6] annually. This income profile allows me to explore the intersection of gender and race-ethnicity among Chicanas in jobs which are relatively good (that is, secure) as well as in professional jobs. The selective nature of the occupations, however, makes it important to note that the form and contours the intersection of gender and race-ethnicity takes among this group of women probably differs from that of Chicanas in different jobs with lower incomes. Nonetheless, the analysis offers one interpretation of ways in which gender and race-ethnicity influence Chicanas' lives.

Subjective job characteristics

Exploring the job characteristics which Chicanas value and dislike offers one way to gain insight into labor-market mechanisms which maintain gender and racial-ethnic work hierarchies. Many white-collar jobs (especially clerical) provide limited advancement opportunities. Despite this shortcoming, women tend to seek and keep these jobs. Women's attachment to female-dominated, service-oriented jobs reinforces labor-market boundaries (Segura 1989). Much of their job attachment can be explained by economic need. However, research also indicates that women's job commitment may be enhanced by the presence of valued subjective job features (for example, quality personal interaction; providing services to their community) (Neil and Snizek 1987; Agassi 1979).[7]

In the present study, 70.4 percent of the Chicana workers reported they were satisfied with their current jobs. Only 21.7 percent indicated they were not satisfied with their jobs. The job characteristics Chicanas value may also reinforce a gendered sense of their race-ethnicity. That is, insofar as a Chicana connects her job to a larger group (the Chicano community), she may be affirming her gendered relation to the world and reinforcing her racial-ethnic sense of self. At the same time, a Chicana's experiences in these jobs can either maintain or expand her sense of what is possible for herself and for other Chicanas.

When I asked women to identify three features of their jobs they liked the best, 60.3 percent indicated "having control of my own work;" 56.3 percent chose "the pay;" 39.7 percent replied "it makes me feel good;" 38.4 percent selected "doing different things at work;" 30.5 percent listed "my co-workers;" and 25.8 percent indicated "ability for me to make meaningful changes." I should note that about one-sixth of the women indicated they enjoyed more than three work features, while seven women replied they didn't like anything about their jobs.

There were a few interesting variations by occupational groups. A much higher proportion of lower-level clerical workers and service/technical workers listed "co-workers" as important to their job satisfaction (42.9 percent and 44.4 percent, respectively) than did either Upper Clerical (18.2 percent) or Professional workers (17.2 percent). On the other hand, Professional and Upper Clerical workers were much more likely to indicate that the job "makes me feel good" (55.2 percent and 43.2 percent, respectively). Few women indicated they valued their jobs because of the "prestige" or "chances for promotions." Professional workers were the least likely to mention promotions as a key feature of their jobs (3.4 percent).

My discussions with women about their jobs and what they liked (or disliked) about work revealed two major patterns. First, women discussed job features and job satisfaction in terms which affirmed social conceptualizations of femininity. Second, their accounts revealed a sense of affinity or connectedness with their racial-ethnic group. For example, one Upper Clerical worker described what she valued about her job as:

> I need to do that [work] because for your self-esteem [it's important] to feel that you're doing something and you're helping other people accomplish themselves. In that sense it's good for my health and also for my kids. I think if they see that you're involved with something, it helps them reach beyond their own world to see that there is an outside world there. And, that there's things that they can pursue that they enjoy.

A Professional Worker said:

> It is very satisfying when you're working with a Chicano student or with a black student who really wants to become a veterinarian. To see them being admitted to a Vet school is really very satisfying and to see them graduate is just incredible. I just graduated my second class, and every year they'll say, "Thanks!" And, God – the parents will say, "We never thought we'd have a doctor in the family!" So, that's really neat to feel that way, but I'm still limited in that I'm not doing enough.

Both women worked in jobs where their clientele included numerous male and female racial-ethnic minority students as well as white women. Throughout her interview, the first woman quoted discussed a range of problems she had experienced in her specific workplace (racial discrimination in promotion). Nonetheless, she valued her job because it enhanced her self-esteem. Like other women in service-oriented jobs in the University she derived satisfaction from "helping" other people. Moreover, she saw herself as a "role model" helping to extend the boundaries of what is possible for her community. The second woman articulated similar feelings. In addition, she expressed a sentiment common among the professional workers – that of "not doing enough" for their communities.

Many of the respondents valued jobs which allowed them high levels of autonomy, that is, to feel "in control" of their work. Women tended to like jobs where their supervisors practiced minimal intervention; where women were "left alone" to "get the job done." Feeling in control of their jobs was important to the informants because it facilitated their abilities to help others (a value associated with traditional femininity). In the view of many, job control indirectly expanded the job range of Mexican descended women (a value associated with helping the ethnic community). Women's preference to feel in "control" of what they do at work implicitly expresses a politicized sense of themselves as racial-ethnic women. That is, having "control" expands the job range of Chicanas. Women remark how their jobs "are different" from those of other relatives and friends who work in jobs (largely in racial-ethnic labor markets) where this control does not exist. (See Romero,

Chapter 4 in this volume, for analysis of the importance of control of the labor process among Chicana domestic workers.) Others note that their jobs allow them to "help others" and "help Chicanos." Critical here is that the gendered act associated with women – that of "helping others" – is often linked by Chicanas to the betterment of the racial-ethnic community.

Discrimination on the job and the consequences for Chicanas' gendered construction of race-ethnicity

By and large, Chicanas' experiences at work included either direct or indirect encounters with discrimination and harassment based on gender and/or race-ethnicity.[8] In this study, 44.1 percent of the informants reported discrimination in securing a job or a promotion based on their gender and/or race-ethnicity. The vast majority of these women felt this discrimination was based on their combined gender/race-ethnicity as opposed to gender only.

One Upper Clerical worker described how she had been denied a promotion in the recent past:

> one time I wanted a job at [unit x][9] and a white woman got it because she'd already been in the position. I should have gotten the job. But they didn't even interview me because they knew I was completely qualified for the position. And so I thought, well I could take it further, but if you take it further that means [unit x] would never hire me because I was a troublemaker.

Her words point to several problem areas referred to (in varying degrees) by other Chicana workers. The sense that white women have an advantage in securing better-paying jobs or promotions compared to Chicanas was widely shared. In large organizations, Chicanas are underrepresented in supervisory positions. This may reflect overt discrimination or prior race-or-sex ascription in the organization of work. Baron and Newman's (1990) research on the California state civil service in 1985 indicates that white women and non-white women and men are victims of ascription; that is, that jobs done primarily by women, white or non-white, and by non-white men are devalued vis-à-vis equivalent work performed by white men. They document that white women and non-white women and men earn substantially lower pay in similar occupations in state civil services which are predominantly female and/or minority.

Women indicated that the credentials and work histories of women of color are also subjectively devalued by supervisors and co-workers. One Upper Clerical worker asserted:

> I think you have to demonstrate that you can do a job – I mean I've seen it! In interviews with a white candidate. They see it written on the paper and they say, "Isn't this great!" But, when you bring a Latina woman in, it's almost like

they're drilled. "Tell us." "Give us examples." "How long did you do it?" Some say to prove yourself, and that's what I feel. You always have to prove yourself that you are just as good even when it's all there. It's all written. You almost have to fight harder to demonstrate that you can do a job just as well!

One consequence of their subjective devaluation in the workplace may be job downgrading, as the same Upper Clerical worker related:

> This position that I have now, before me was a Word Processing Supervisor. None of them [prior job occupants] had the work load that I have now. In fact, they just surveyed my job, and it's increased 130 percent. Yet, I'm a Senior Word Processor. I've had to fight tooth and nail to be classified back [up]. Even then, it's been procrastinated. They know it has to be done, but why is it taking so long? It's just obvious. It just makes you think – those were all white women prior to me. What's the difference?

Baron and Newman's (1990) research suggests that recent efforts to improve pay for majority women and minority women and men including upgrading female-dominated jobs (for example, comparable worth) is not helping all groups equally. They demonstrate that Hispanic and other non-white females encounter greater penalties (for example, lower pay) when they work in new job titles (created since 1978) where other women of color work than do white women employed in female-dominated jobs generally. They suggest that "perhaps efforts to upgrade the standing of jobs done by blacks and white women have occurred partly at the expense of these other minority groups which have been less outspoken on pay equity" (1990: 167). This possibility may be relevant to the current study. Chicanas' perceptions that their efforts to gain access to better-paying jobs are not being supported, and that the organization appears more adept at upgrading jobs held by white women, could be other illustrations of the effects of ascription found by Baron and Newman's study.

Several women also discussed "subtle discrimination;" that is, comments which depreciate their culture and/or features of their combined gender/race-ethnicity. As one Upper Clerical worker reported:

> It's subtle discrimination. I haven't gotten a job because of, or I don't know if I have gotten a job because of, my color. You know, subtle stuff – that subtle baloney that people pass you over because they think that women of color aren't as brilliant as they [Anglos] are. That sort of thing. Actually, they can be condescending to me.

A Professional worker said:

> I'm usually asked because of my accent – they say you have a funny accent.

> And, I always say, "I'm Mexican." And people are really surprised. They say, "You don't look Mexican." And so I ask, "How many Mexican people do you know?" And they say, "Oh, just you."

The words of these informants attest to the potent role of gender and race-ethnicity in social interaction at work. Moreover, they present how Chicanas perceive non-Chicano workers as possessing certain beliefs regarding Chicanos (dark-skinned, Spanish-speaking, unsophisticated accents, less competent). Chicanas feel they are bound by these views and expectations. When these socially constructed assumptions are brought to the workplace, Chicanas and other workers experience a sense of where gender and racial-ethnic boundaries lie. When these limits are contested in daily interaction on the job, the boundaries of what is possible for Chicanas (to themselves and to the non-Chicano worker) may expand. Concurrently engaging in such struggles reinforces Chicanas' sense of difference from non-Chicano co-workers and connects them to similar expectations experienced by other Chicanas. This serves to reaffirm existing in-group boundaries of the Chicano community.

The Chicana respondents argued that differences in skin color, accents, language skills, and cultural mannerisms shaped their occupational chances. Interestingly, many of the women who indicated they had not personally experienced job discrimination (although they were careful to note their belief in its importance) argued this was due to their fair or light complexions. As a Professional worker put it:

> Maybe I haven't felt as much discrimination because I'm not . . . I'm kind of fair complected. So, a lot of people don't know, or don't even assume that I'm Mexican. They're real surprised when I say, "Yeah, I'm Mexican."

Discrimination at work plays an important role in reinforcing gender and/or racial-ethnic boundaries in the organization. Many women also offered analyses of the consequences of gender and race-ethnicity for Chicana inequality in employment. Some argued that discrimination is the primary reason Chicanas are overrepresented in lower-level positions in the organiza-tion. And while others cite individual inadequacies (especially education), they acknowledge the importance of social networks in the organization and differential treatment by supervisors. Research on ethnicity indicates that individual and institution-level discrimination help maintain a "sense of peoplehood" among the group. Chicanas interpret their personal experiences of discrimination as part of the shared experiences of the larger racial-ethnic community. While most of the Chicanas in this study assert that maintaining their culture is important to them, discrimination within the institution serves to hold them accountable to this resolution. In this way, the organization reinforces Chicanas' gendered construction of their ethnicity.

One-third of the survey respondents belong to a Hispanic Workers Advocacy group at their worksite. Women feel this group promotes a positive image of Chicanos/Latinos and believe it will help erode the power wielded by negative cultural stereotypes currently embedded in the institution. These women demonstrate a politicized sense of their ethnicity.

Employed Chicanas' family obligations and the gendered construction of race-ethnicity

Historical research on Chicanas highlights women's responsibility to transmit Chicano-Mexican cultural values as well as care for the family unit (Garcia 1980; Griswold del Castillo 1984). Chicano families tend to be mother-centered, with women responsible for the majority of household/child-rearing decisions and tasks, and they also embody a patriarchal ideology (Baca Zinn 1975, 1979). Coltrane notes that "the routine care of home and children... provides opportunities for women to express and reaffirm their gendered relation to men and to the world" (1989: 473). Moreover, among Chicanos, the image of "la madre" as self-sacrificing and pure as the Virgen de Guadalupe (the Catholic patroness of Mexico whose portrait graces many Mexican immigrant and Chicano houses and churches in the Southwest) is a powerful standard against which Chicanas often compare themselves (Melville 1980; Mirande and Enriquez 1979; Alarcon 1987; Fox 1983). The family is a site for Chicanas to affirm a gendered way of teaching and practicing Chicano culture but, especially among the 111 Chicana respondents with children, family care-taking also constrains chances for mobility in the world of work.

Chicanas in this study struggle to meet the expectations of their families, their communities, and their employers. Often women try to carve out two separate worlds where, in reality, there is but one world and one woman trying to meet the demands that continually compete for her time. As one Professional worker said:

> For the most part, my job doesn't interfere too much with home. When I leave work, I leave my work. I switch stations to do whatever I need to do for the family. But, there are times when, yes, work does tend to tire you out and you *do* carry it home with you in terms of less energy and not having the energy to deal with the family. That's really hard, especially when both of you come in very tired and you sort of want the other one to do something because you're too tired to deal with it. Then it's hard. The poor kids, they don't understand. They just know that they're hungry and "how come you guys won't feed us?"

This woman speaks to the dilemma of reconciling what Hochschild refers to as the "competing urgencies" of family and work.[10] Interestingly, women in this study downplayed the spillover between work and family. In the survey and in their interviews, women consistently reported that their jobs "almost never" (27 percent) or only "occasionally" (47.7 percent) interfered with their abilities to manage their family responsibilities. Yet, their discussions of the intersection of family and work reveal they are experiencing considerable tension and stress in this relationship

Ironically, ideological changes which have expanded the domain of women's competencies may impede women's articulation of the stress experienced in meeting family and work responsibilities. As one Professional worker argued:

> I think as women, maybe the progress has been kind of negative in some aspects. You know, we go out and say that we can do this – we can work, we can raise a family, and all that. And yet at the same time, I feel like maybe we've hurt ourselves because we can't do it all. I don't believe there is super woman.

An additional constraint felt by many of the Chicana workers is their responsibility to maintain Chicano/Mexican cultural traditions and forms. Chicanas often do not engage in overt struggle for egalitarianism in the household division of labor. An overwhelming majority of our survey respondents reported "little" (39.4 percent) or "no" (40.4 percent) difference of opinion on the household division of labor between married women and their spouses. Yet, when asked about the *actual* division of labor, women reported doing most of the housework and wished their partners/spouses would do more. Among Chicanos, women's household work is often legitimized as part of a distinct cultural heritage which is under assault by outside social pressures (Baca Zinn 1975 and 1982; Segura, forthcoming). This pressure contributes to the resilience of Chicano family structure and social dynamics within the family and larger community which are difficult to challenge. When Chicanas contest traditional patterns they can become enmeshed in the competing demands for personal empowerment and their gendered responsibility for maintenance of the culture.

Thus, some women cast the household division of labor in cultural terms. That is, Mexican/Latina women take on much of the caretaking work in the household as one expression of Chicano culture, described this way by an Upper Clerical worker:

> I'm just happy who I am and where I come from. Our women, Latino women, do things just a little bit differently because of who we are and where we came from. There are certain things that we do for our husbands that I know that other women, white women, have problems doing, for instance – and I've seen it because my brother-in-law was married to a white woman. You're eating and you go to the stove to maybe serve yourself a little more. It's just normal, I think. You're brought up with that real nurturing, with "Honey, do you want some more?" And her comment was, "Well, he can get up by himself." Just

the real independence on their side, and I think we're brought up a little more nurturing to our male counterparts. Maybe there's more machismo there too – whatever. It's the way you're brought up.

Traditional gender roles and gender ideologies are particularly resistant to change when they are framed within what Caufield (1974) terms a "culture of resistance." Consistently, Chicanas refuse to engage in sustained struggle with husbands/partners over the division of household labor even when they admit they often feel, as one Chicana Professional worker said, "too stressed and torn between career and family responsibilities to feel good about the accomplishments!" Rather, Chicanas conform to their community's culturally gendered expectations, reaffirming both their womanhood and their culture. This relationship is strengthened in those cases where women work in jobs which give priority to services to other women and/or Chicanos on the campus. As the same Professional worker said:

> Chicanas feel that working – we see ourselves as social change agents. We see it as being done in a partnership basis with our families. We get hurt by things that people in our culture do, but we don't turn against them. Maybe that hurts in the end, but I think we want to keep a forged relationship and a partnership. As painfully as it may be. And that's where I want to be. Yes.

Summary and conclusion

This study has explored the multiple meanings of Chicana white-collar workers' distinct set of social locations, in particular the intersection of gender and race-ethnicity. Located in a stratified labor market divided by gender and race-ethnicity, Chicanas weave their way through obstacle-laden paths. The effects of prior gender-and-race/ethnic ascription in the organization are keenly felt and often challenged. But the need to contest gender and/or racial-ethnic discrimination advances another effect: a gendered construction of race-ethnicity already set in motion by women's experiences in her family and ethnic community.

Chicanas' participation in many white-collar jobs coupled with the perform- ing of traditional family responsibilities reinforce a gendered construction of culture and ethnicity in the Chicano community. Women enjoy their jobs, but their work is not so much "liberating" as intensifying their accomplishment of gender both in the tasks they do at work as well as the female-associated tasks they continue to do at home. Moreover, their attachment to "la familia" is linked ideologically to the survival of the culture, which renders their accomplishment of gender an overt act of ethnic or cultural politics.

The Chicana workers in this study also tend to assist male faculty members under the supervision of white women or males (in academic departments) or to work with Chicano students – a dynamic which reinforces gender/race-ethnic hierarchies at work. Through their words, Chicanas revealed a clear sense of the boundaries of their gendered racial-ethnic social locations. Concurrently, they exposed tensions between traditional conceptualizations of gender/race-ethnicity and their individual quests for job control and mobility. While this discourse is largely contained in the notion of "helping" others, Chicanas may increasingly find that meeting their goals requires sustained contestations of the social boundaries which surround them.

Notes

1. The terms "Chicana" and "Chicano" refer respectively to a woman and to a man of Mexican descent residing in the United States without distinguishing immigrant status. "Chicano" also refers generically to the category of persons (male and female) who claim Mexican heritage (e.g. the "Chicano" community). These labels offer an alternative to the more common ethnic identifiers, "Mexican" and "Mexican American". Other terms associated with people of Mexican descent include "Hispanic" and "Latino". Both of these terms typically include Spaniards and a variety of ethnic groups who were colonised at one time by Spain. Readers interested in the history and significance of different labels used by the population of Mexican origin are referred to Candace Nelson and Marta Tienda (1985) and John A.Garcia (1981).

2. I use "racial-ethnic" as defined by Maxine Baca Zinn (1990): Racial Ethnic groups are *groups labelled as races in the context of certain historical, social, and material conditions. Blacks, Latinos, and Asian Americans are racial groups that are formed, defined, and given meaning by a variety of social forces in the wider society, most notably distinctive forms of labor exploitation. Each group is also bound together by ethnicity, that is, common ancestry and emergent cultural characteristics that are often used for coping with racial oppression. The concept racial-ethnic underscores the social construction of race and ethnicity for people of color in the United States. (80 n.1)*

3. The US Bureau of the Census estimates that, in 1991, 14.9 percent of Chicanas worked as operators, farbicators, and laborers, compared to 32.1 percent Chicano men, 19.1 percent non-Hispanic men, and 7.6 percent non-Hispanic women (US Bureau of the Census 1991b: 12).

4. At present, Dr Pesquera and I are planning to interview an additional fifteen women. We do not expect to find significant differences from the interview data explored here. Our intention is to expand and enrich our existing qualitative database for future work on gender ideology and ethnic identity among Chicana workers.

5. The response rate, 47.5 percent, is an overall average and does not provide information on possible under/overrepresentation of Chicana workers from various occupations. This shortcoming is inevitable given that the personnel list we obtained from the organization did not provide us with information on women by occupation (which would have allowed us to estimate the degree of representativeness of the final respondents). The occupational categories were derived in consultation with the personnel manual of the research site and two personnel analysts. In general, Lower Clerical occupations (levels 1–3 in this organization) are non-supervisory. Upper Clerical occupations (levels 4–6) are often supervisory. Professional occupations include managers of academic and staff units as well as a variety of specialized jobs that are mainly administrative (e.g. Counselor, Personnel Analyst) or scientific (Staff Research Associate). Service and Technicians tended to be lower paid workers in laboratories (Laboratory Helper) or custodians. Since we received a relatively high number of responses from white-collar workers and few from non-white-collar workers, it is likely the latter are underrepresented, although without better organizational data we cannot provide an estimate of this. Because of the low

response rate from non-white-collar workers, I do not discuss their jobs or perceptions of opportunity.

6. National median incomes in 1989 for white female full-time workers was $19,873 and for Hispanic females was $16,006 (US Bureau of the Census 1991a). The average for the group obscures the income range of the respondents. Fourteen women earned less than $15,000; 33 earned between $15,000 and $19,999; 57 earned between $25,000 and $29,999; 13 earned between $30,000 and $34,999; 11 earned more than $35,000.

7. It is important to note that the role gender plays in workers' evaluations of their jobs is a source of debate. When occupation and organizational level are controlled, Brief and Aldag (1975) find no significant gender difference in what workers value about their jobs. Other researchers (e.g. Neil and Snizek 1987; Agassi 1979) find that women are more likely to emphasize job competence and good personal relations on the job. Others argue that women value social aspects of their job more and place less emphasis on career-related values (Crewley, Levithin and Quinn 1973).

8. In this study, about one third of the respondents reported experiencing sexual harassment (n =50). Of these women, 60 percent reported doing something about it. Typically, this meant, "telling the person to stop," "talking with friends and family," or "complaining to the appropriate personnel officer." Eleven women did nothing and another nine women acted as if nothing had happened.

The women interviewed for this study believe that sexual harassment is one of the most underreported problems in organizations. They indicate that women often do not know the definition of sexual harassment; at other times they are reluctant to pursue a complaint out of fear of recrimination or being cast as the instigator by co-workers and/or supervisors rather than the victim. This information points to the need for additional work in this area.

9. The specific occupations and units mentioned by this informant and others have been changed to protect their anonymity.

10. This phrase was coined by Arlie Hochschild and quoted in Rubin (1983).

References

Agassi, Judith B. 1979. *Women on the Job: The Attitudes of Women to their Work*. Lexington: Lexington Books.
Alarcon, Norma. 1987. "Traddutora, Traditora: A Paradigmatic Figure of Chicana Feminism." In *Changing Our Power: An Introduction to Women's Studies*, edited by Jo Whitehorse Cochran, Donna Langston, and Carolyn Woodward, pp. 95–203. Dubuque, Iowa: Kendall-Hunt.
Almquist, Elizabeth M. 1984. "Race and Ethnicity in the Lives of Minority Women." In *Women: A Feminist Perspective*, edited by Jo Freeman, pp. 423 – 53. Palo Alto, CA., Mayfield.
Baca Zinn, Maxine. 1975. "Chicanas: Power and Control in the Domestic Sphere." *De Colores, Journal of Emerging Raza Philosophies* 2: 19–31.
Baca Zinn, Maxine. 1979. "Chicano Family Research: Conceptual Distortions and Alternative Directions." *Journal of Ethnic Studies* 7: 59–71.
Baca Zinn, Maxine. 1980. "Gender and Ethnic Identity among Chicanos" Frontiers 5: 18– 23
Baca Zinn, Maxine. 1982. "Mexican-American Women in the Social Sciences." *Signs: Journal of Women in Culture and Society* 8: 259–72.
Baca Zinn, Maxine. 1990. "Family, Feminism, and Race in America." *Gender and Society* 4: 68–82.
Baron, James N., and Andrew E. Newman. 1990. "For What It's Worth: Organizations, Occupations, and the Value of Work." *American Sociological Review* 55(2): 155–75.
Barrera, Mario. 1979. *Race and Class in the Southwest: A Theory of Racial Inequality*. Notre Dame: University of Notre Dame Press.
Brief, A.P., and R.J. Aldag. 1975. "Male–Female Differences in Occupational Attitudes Within Minority Groups." *Journal of Vocational Behavior* 6: 305–14.
Cattan, Peter. 1988. "The Growing Presence of Hispanics in the U.S. Work Force." *Monthly Labor Review* 8: 9–14.
Caulfield, Mina Davis. 1974. "Imperialism, the Family, and Cultures of Resistance." *Socialist Revolution* 2: 67–85.

Coltrane, Scott. 1989. "Household Labor and the Routine Production of Gender." *Social Problems* 36: 473–91.
Crewley, Joan F. Teresa E. Levitan, and Robert Quinn. 1973. "Facts and Fiction About the American Working Woman." Ann Arbor: Survey Research Center, University of Michigan.
Fenstermaker Berk, Sarah. 1985. *The Gender Factory: The Apportionment of Work in American Households*. New York: Plenum.
Fenstermaker Sarah, Candace West, and Don H. Zimmerman. 1991. "Gender Inequality: New Conceptual Terrain." In *Gender, Family, and Economy: The Triple Overlap*, edited by R. Lesser-Blumberg, pp. 289–305. Newbury Park: Sage.
Fox, Linda C. 1983. "Obedience and Rebellion: Re-Vision of Chicana Myths of Motherhood." *Women's Studies Quarterly* 11: 20–22.
Garcia, John A. 1981. "Yo Soy Mexicano . . . : Self-Identity Among the Mexican Origin Population." *Social Science Quarterly* 62: 88–98.
Garcia, Mario T. 1980. "The Chicana in American History: The Mexican Women of El Paso, 1880–1920 – A Case Study." *Pacific Historical Review* 49: 315–37.
Gordon, Milton M. 1964. *Assimilation in American Life: The Role of Race, Religion, and National Origin*. New York: Oxford University Press.
Griswold del Castillo Richard. 1984. *La Familia: Chicano Families in the Urban Southwest, 1848 to the Present*. Notre Dame: University of Notre Dame Press.
Hartmann, Heidi. 1976. "Capitalism, Patriarchy and Job Segregation by Sex." In *Women and the Work Place*, edited by M. Blaxall and B. Reagan, pp. 137–69. Chicago: University of Chicago Press.
Hochschild, Arlie R., with Anne Machung. 1989. *The Second Shift, Working Parents and the Revolution at Home*. New York: Viking.
Keefe, Susan E., and Amado M. Padilla. 1987. *Chicano Ethnicity*. Albuquerque: University of New Mexico Press.
Kuhn, Annette, and AnnMarie Wolpe. 1978. *Feminism and Materialism: Women and Modes of Production*. Boston: Routledge and Kegan Paul.
Malveaux, Julianne, and Phyllis Wallace. 1987. "Minority Women in the Workplace." In *Women and Work: Industrial Relations Research Association Research Volume*, edited by K.S. Koziara, M. Moskow and L. Dewey Tanne, pp. 265–98. Washington, D.C.: Bureau of National Affairs.
Melville, Margarita B. 1980. "Introduction" and "Matrescence." In *Twice a Minority: Mexican-American Women*, pp. 1–16. St. Louis: C.V. Mosby.
Mirande, Alfredo, and Evangelina Enriquez. 1979. *La Chicana*. Chicago: University of Chicago Press.
Neil, Cecily C., and William E. Snizek. 1987. "Work Values, Job Characteristics, and Gender." *Sociological Perspectives* 30: 245–65.
Nelson, Candace, and Marta Tienda. 1985. "The Structuring of Hispanic Ethnicity: Historical and Contemporary Perspectives." *Ethnic and Racial Studies* 8: 49–74.
Nieto-Gomez, Anna. 1974. "Chicana Feminism." *Encuentro Femenil* 1: 3–5.
Orozco, Cynthia. 1986. "Sexism in Chicano Studies and the Community." In *Chicana Voices: Intersections of Class, Race, and Gender, Conference Proceedings*, National Association for Chicano Studies, edited by T. Cordova, N. Cantu, G. Cardenas, J. Garcia, and C. Sierra, pp. 11–18. Austin: University of Texas, Center for Mexican American Studies.
Pesquera, Beatriz M. 1985. "Work and Family: A Comparative Analysis of Professional, Clerical and Blue-Collar Chicana Workers." Ph.D. dissertation. University of California, Berkeley.
Rubin, Lillian B. 1983. *Intimate Strangers: Men and Women Together*. New York: Harper and Row.
Segura, Denise A. 1986a. "Chicana and Mexican Immigrant Women in the Labor Market: A Study of Occupational Mobility and Stratification." Ph.D dissertation. University of California, Berkeley.
Segura, Denise A. 1986b. "Chicanas and Triple Oppression in the Labor Force." In *Chicana Voices: Intersections of Class, Race, and Gender, Conference Proceedings*, National Association for Chicano Studies, edited by T. Cordova, N. Cantu, G. Cardenas, J. Garcia, and C. Sierra, pp. 47–65. Austin: University of Texas, Center for Mexican American Studies.
Segura, Denise A. 1989. "Chicana and Mexican Immigrant Women at Work: The Impact of Class, Race, and Gender on Occupational Mobility." *Gender and Society* 3: 37–52.
Segura, Denise A. Forthcoming. "Ambivalence or Continuity?: Motherhood and Employment among Chicanas and Mexican Immigrant Women." *AZTLAN, International Journal of Chicano Studies*.

Segura, Denise A., and Beatriz M. Pesquera. Forthcoming. "Chicana Feminisms: Their Political Context and Contemporary Expressions." In *Women, A Feminist Perspective*, Fifth Edition, edited by Jo Freeman. Mountain View, California. Mayfield.

Smith, Dorothy E. 1987. "Women's Inequality and the Family." In *Families and Work*, edited by N. Gerstel and H. E. Gross, pp. 23–54.Philadelphia: Temple University Press.

Tienda, Marta and P. Guhleman. 1985. "The Occupational Position of Employed Hispanic Women." In *Hispanics in the U.S. Economy*, edited by G.J. Borjas and M. Tienda, pp. 243–73. New York: Academic Press.

US Bureau of the Census. 1991a. "Money Income of Households, Families, and Persons in the United States: 1988 and 1989." *Current Population Reports*, Series P-60, No. 172. Washington D.C.: US Government Printing Office.

US Bureau of the Census. 1991b. "The Hispanic Population in the United States: March 1991." *Current Population Report*, Series P-20, No. 455. Washington D.C.: US Government Printing Office.

Zavella, Patricia. 1987. *Women's Work and Chicano Families: Cannery Workers of the Santa Clara Valley*. Ithaca: Cornell University Press.

Zavella, Patricia. 1991. "Reflections on Diversity Among Chicanas." Frontiers 2: 73–85.

3. Urban Women's Work in Three Social Strata: The Informal Economy of Social Networks and Social Capital

Larissa Lomnitz

This chapter analyzes the role of women in creating and maintaining social networks which translate into "social capital" – as some have named it lately (Coleman 1990; Lomnitz 1988). Such networks are found among all social classes in Latin America, and their economic importance ranges from status maintenance among the privileged to physical survival among the poor. Here I will present three case studies from the urban upper, middle, and poor strata in two Latin American countries: Mexico and Chile. In each of the cases studied, there is an exchange pattern which supplements the formal economy; patterns of exchange are gendered in specific ways as women play particular roles in these social networks. The activities of these Latin American women, which reproduce social class in a material sense, share similarities but also depart from the social reproduction in which US women of color and white working-class women take part (Luttrell, Chapter 1 in this volume; Segura, Chapter 2 in this volume).

A social network is a field of social relationships among individuals as defined by some underlying variable (Barnes 1954; Mitchell 1969; Wolfe 1970). This variable may refer to any specific aspect of the relationship (for example, kinship, drug traffic, and activism in women's movements.) My own interest is the study of social networks as defined by an exchange of goods, services and economically relevant information among members. The use of social resources for economic ends creates what I call "social capital" (Lomnitz 1988).

In spite of considerable variations as to structure, function and other characteristic features, the networks on which I focus have certain important principles in common. For example, the status of the exchange relation between any two partners is defined by means of a psycho-social variable called *confianza* or trust. This *confianza* is a shared perception of the effective social closeness which promotes, induces or maintains the desired exchange. The presence of *confianza* often depends on the active participation of women, who frequently specialize in centralizing, maintaining and consolidating the networks in various ways.

The informal economy

For decades, the term "informal economy" referred to the urban poor or "informal sector" of Latin American cities. In a previous study, I defined it as the sector of the working class characterized by its chronic state of economic insecurity, both in terms of income and permanence of work. Accordingly, the informal sector was composed of urban workers who were not articulated into the formal, modern sector of the economy and thus lacked job stability and the benefits of modern labor legislation and welfare supports (Lomnitz 1977).

Other definitions from the 1970s included that proposed by the ILO, which saw the informal economy as related to the persistence in a formal, urban market economy of certain traditional practices which characteristically involve a "tendency toward affiliations, utilization of local resources, family business, small-scale operations ... in non-regulated competitive markets" (ILO 1974: 9). Thus, the ILO regarded the organization of production as the main defining characteristic of the sector. The unit of production (family enterprise or self-employed individuals) became the center of analysis, as did the ways in which informally produced goods and services articulated with the formal sector (Souza and Tokman 1975; Tokman 1986). Roberts, on the other hand, characterized the informal economy as "the persistence of the importance of family, traditional rural activities, and rural ways in the cities" (1974: 1).

As the analysis has advanced, the term "informal economy" has moved away from what was called the "informal sector." Castells and Portes say it is no longer a euphemism for poverty, but a term denoting a "process of income-generation characterized by one central feature: it is unregulated by institutions of society, in a legal and social environment in which similar activities are regulated" (1989: 12). De Soto (1987) also uses the same definition: the informal economy is one that, aiming at achieving goals which by themselves are legal, uses illegal or deregulated forms to reach those ends.

For Castells and Portes, the informal economy is manifest in "production relationships through the articulation of formal and informal activities" (1989: 12). In other words, "informality" is linked with formality, as in fact there is an interdependence between the two sorts of "economies." The large literature on developing, centrally planned, and advanced capitalist economies shows this to be the case (see Mars and Altman 1983; Portes et al. 1989).

Indeed, as modern states develop, they create ever more regulations on economic activity, which lead people to find informal ways to by-pass them. I claim that those activities are done through the use of social networks where a substratum of trust has been built among members, which allow unregulated or sometimes illegal exchanges to take place (Lomnitz 1988). In the three examples that follow, I show how women help to create networks which are vital to economic activity in urban Latin America.

An upper-class network

Entrepreneurial groups based on kinship affiliation are common in Mexico. The present example concerns the history (since 1850) of a family stock comprising over 400 individuals. At present, the family includes five main branches: two upper-class entrepreneurial branches and three middle-class ones, including members who practice liberal professions, who have white-collar employment in private enterprise, or who are shopkeepers or owners of small and medium industries (Lomnitz and Perez-Lizaur 1987).

The Latin American entrepreneur depends to a considerable extent on social resources for economic ends (Long 1979; Aubey 1979; Lipset 1967). As Greenfield and Strickton (1979) have pointed out, social relations that engender confidence and trust are critical resources in the entrepreneurial venture. These ideas were confirmed in our study of the Gomez family. We found that social relations among Mexican entrepreneurs have acquired an economic relevance which is generally unrecognized in the literature on the structure of business communities of the developed world.

Three major aspects of the economic utilization of social resources may be singled out in Latin America generally and Mexico specifically: action groups, social networks for the circulation of information, and social networks for facilitating access to economic resources.

(1) *Action groups* refers to the pattern of diversification typical of Latin American industrial development (largely because a state of insecurity prevails). Initially, an entrepreneur may attend to his business personally in all aspects, but with growth and diversification, people of *confianza* are placed in positions of trust. Usually they are brothers-in-law, sons, or nephews of the entrepreneur, who, in effect, become brokers between family enterprises and the national system. The entire kinship network of each entrepreneur represents a pool of managerial personnel as well as eventually constituting a network of peripherally related enterprises. Although privately owned by members of the family, the result is akin to a corporation: all these owners and related clients become a corporate group centered around a "patron" entrepreneur.

(2) Access to *information* depends upon networks. Economically valuable information is circulated constantly within the kinship network and allied networks beyond family boundaries. And information is a prime resource in Latin American economies. Because the markets are thin and public information is scarce and unreliable, networks represent the main source of business intelligence. Occasions for information exchange are provided by innumerable ritual family gatherings at which relatives are expected to be present. At family parties, business conversation is quite active, even among the women. Such a gathering rarely occurs without a new business deal being made. For this reason alone, family affairs are not to be missed.

(3) Access to *economic resources* also comes through social networks. An entrepreneur is typically an innovator. Usually the innovations introduced by the entrepreneur consist in identifying and using new technologies, developing new products, or opening up new markets. In this case from Mexico, the most remarkable innovative aspect was the development and use of social networks for tapping economic resources. For example, contacts with the Church hierarchy during the last decades of the nineteenth century allowed the first entrepreneur to get access to capital; his son became attached to the post-revolutionary regime from which licenses and financial support were secured; later on, contacts with the Spanish banking community allowed another member of the family to get access to capital as well.

Women and the economic use of social resources

In our study of this elite Mexican family, we found a series of "centralizing" women throughout the generations who maintained the family spirit and emotional links among its members. These women were also great information transmitters, being in charge of circulating gossip which contained "the latest" on everybody. For example, Leopoldo, the first entrepreneur, had very strong emotional ties with his widowed mother and one of his sisters. Both women were very active in centralizing information about all family members, keeping track of important events such as births, weddings and the like, and in organizing family reunions in their homes. Moreover, they were often approached by relatives who were in need of economic aid and/or jobs.

Social stratification begins in the second generation and becomes clearly established by the third. The two wealthy lineages have become the "patrons" of members of the non-wealthy branches, many of whom work as employees (even if for only a short period of time) or with help have established themselves as independent businessmen in fields of production related to the patron entrepreneur's main lines of production.

At this stage, three central women figures emerge. The first is an illegitimate daughter of Leopoldo's half brother, once "adopted" by Leopoldo's sister, who works as a switchboard operator in one of the family enterprises. She is a spinster, and she regularly visits the members of the lower-middle-class branch who live in her neighborhood. Through her constant contact with them, she finds out about illness, job problems, or other needs and uses the telephone to tell one of her middle-class aunts about all these matters. This information goes to a second woman, who is the sister of one of the family's tycoons, and is married to a cousin from another middle-class branch. She centralizes information about that branch also and intercedes, when necessary, with her brother for his help both in money and in getting jobs for members. The third example of a centralizing woman is the daughter of Leopoldo, who married a *Porfirian* aristocrat architect and whose descendants became important entrepreneurs in the construction industry. She carried on a very active social life among the wealthy members of the family and did extensive entertaining and visiting. She kept in daily touch by telephone, as well, with everyone of the grandfamily and with the other centralizing women. Thus, the centralizing women connect the various branches of the family.

By 1988 (the fifth generation), there were over three hundred living descendants of the Gomez stock, plus a larger number of affiliated kin. Several women have taken upon themselves the task of centralizing the information and coordinating the needs and problems of the various branches of the family. They keep the clannish spirit of the family alive through sociability. This includes family reunions among socioeconomic equals, as well as acts of inter-branch solidarity, such as helping to place poorer or unemployed relatives in the family business or organizing joint participation in ritual occasions and family events. As these women grow older their influence increases through their children and because of their experience in family affairs.

Business affairs are normally transacted between economic equals, among whom exchange of information is particularly important. And contacts among men are largely limited to business affairs, except when they gather socially in the company of their wives. The men of the poorer and the wealthy branches meet only at such ritual occasions – or as boss and employee at work. They depend on their wives, mothers, and sisters for information on personal events. And this is the basis for the *confianza* on which the creation of action groups depends.

The entire stock functions as a network or set of interlinking networks (branches) in which solidarity is based on economic motive. The wealthy members of the network depend on their peers for business support (information and introduction to individuals from whom needed resources can be secured). Even if they are competitors, they present a solid front, which is convenient when dealing with banks or the government. The poorer members depend on their rich relatives for jobs or for help in starting new enterprises; in return, they offer a degree of dependability and loyalty which their employers have come to expect from family members.

Within this context, the role of women is one of maintaining the family united and transmitting an ideology of belonging and solidarity. Through centralizing and then diffusing vital information of a personal nature, they maintain the social fabric in which the network structure is embedded. In the endless round of family rituals organized by women, economic information is circulated among those family members who attend. Thus, women are indispensable intermediaries in the process of the utilization of social relations for economic purposes in the urban upper class in Mexico.

Middle-class networks in Chile

The middle class in Chile is a social category which can be characterized better by what its members are not than by what they are. They do not own the "means of production", but they differ from the lower classes by their rejection of manual labor. The social survival of this group has come to depend to a great extent on its access to, and intimate knowledge of, the bureaucracy. Social resources are used for economic ends. In the studies done in Chile in 1970 and then in 1988 (Lomnitz 1971; Lomnitz and Melnick 1991), I found an informal system of reciprocal exchange of economically valuable services within a network of relatives and friends. These networks provide the channels for a system of reciprocity which consists of a continuous exchange of favours; an ideology of friendship and social closeness motivates the exchange.

In 1970, the favours tended to be "bureaucratic" in nature and usually consisted of preferential treatment in dealing with red tape and/or priority access to one of the services offered by the state, often setting aside the rights and priorities of third parties. This system consists of a tacit dyadic contract, or a chain of such contracts, between persons linked by mutual friends who acted as intermediaries. The initial favour was usually granted without any specific idea of how it would be returned: the required reciprocity was held in reserve for future use, should the need arise. This social institution, which was called *compadrazgo*, or *relaciones*, operates effectively among socially equal women and men: people who have gone to the same schools, who have undergone similar political experiences, who occupy similar positions in the economy, who move in the same social circles, are typically members of that exchange system. The services rendered are called *favores* and are motivated and justified by means of an ideology of friendship.

The most typical "favour" obtained through social relations is getting a job (normally in the public sector). This entails a mental review of all personal relationships until hitting upon a friend with some link to the personnel department of the specific agency where employment is sought. In the same way, when candidates for some vacancy are required, a list of friends is gone over until the appropriate person is found. Other typical favours include the expediting of certificates, licenses, permits, passports and other of the numerous documents the acquisition of which normally requires a considerable waste of time in bothersome red-tape procedures.

Most of these services entail economic advantages for the individuals who receive them, because they open up a higher level of material life. A typical feature of salaried middle-class people in Chile is the absence of savings and the recurrence of economic difficulties in a situation of chronic inflation. These middle-class people live in economic insecurity, yet their outward standard of living is patterned after the life style of the middle classes of more prosperous societies.

Money may be scarce, but a well-placed friend in a loan association or bank can facilitate a loan by providing information or by guiding his or her friend's application to the top of the pile. Another friend might be helpful in getting one's children admitted to a public, but prestigious, school where the children can meet other children who will become members of *their* networks for life. Friends may give advice on job openings, scholarships, medical services in public hospitals, tax problems, political patronage, customs facilities, public housing, and so on. The opportunities to be helpful to one's friends are endless. The ideal of the middle class is always to have the "right friend at the right place and at the right time" (Lomnitz 1971: 96).

Since the key to having friends is being sociable, an attitude of sociability is encouraged from early childhood on. In each family, there are overlapping networks around the wife, the husband and both. In each of these networks there are relatives and friends of both sexes. The degree of friendship is continually reassessed and, consciously or not, rated on a scale of *confianza*, which in this case may mean an approachability and readiness to exchange favors. Close friends are people who see each other regularly, who socialize frequently at each other's homes, and who may drop in unannounced. They are treated as relatives and may actually be entrusted with more intimate information than many relatives. A readiness to request and perform services among such friends is considered a duty, for, as the Chilean saying goes: "What else are friends for?"

The Fernandez family is a typical of the Chilean middle class. He works as a white-collar employee; she teaches at the University. Both have many friends and relatives. One day, Alicia, a close friend of Mrs Fernandez, called with a request: she would like to get her son admitted to a certain public high school which had an excellent reputation and therefore an immense waiting list. Alicia knew that Mrs Fernandez was a close friend of the head of the high school; the two had known each other since their own school days and saw each other professionally as well as socially. It turned out that the director "owed" Mrs Fernandez a favor; thus there was no problem in calling him up and getting Alicia's son admitted to the school. This kind of favor is rated very highly: there are not many people in a position to perform it, and schooling is the basis of a person's social network for life. Circumventing the rules of admission can only be done rarely, and Mrs Fernandez could not do it for anyone else for a long time. Thus, Mrs Fernandez was not only performing a valuable service to Alicia, she was also closing a door to her own nephews and nieces who might conceivably need the same service in the future. This incident reinforced the degree of *confianza* between the two friends.

Some time later, Mrs Fernandez's son happened to need a private telephone. The waiting list for new connections was such that there was no hope at all of getting it for several years. Mrs Fernandez immediately remembered that Alicia's husband had a close friend who worked at the telephone company. She contacted Alicia and succeeded in obtaining the prompt installation of a phone for her son.

This case exemplifies the point that the Chilean middle class contains a structure of open, flexible networks of reciprocity featuring a continuous exchange of services among social equals. These services are economically valuable, although in themselves they are not available for money. Typically, such favors are bestowed within the culture of sociability, without any overt expectations of reciprocity, and they are absolutely incompatible with money transactions of any kind.

In general, women interact with men on an equal footing and with the same easy spirit of camaraderie. In addition, women have a special role in maintaining active reciprocity networks because of the central importance of hospitality revolving around the home, not only for family rituals and gatherings (as is the case in Mexico), but also, and very specially, as the place where friends meet all the time. Women who are able to create an informal atmosphere of welcome or who surround themselves with highly placed friends and like to introduce them to one another are particularly valued. A social invitation may represent a favor in the context of reciprocal exchange. Thus, hospitality received is felt as an obligation to be returned in various ways. In many of those networks it is women who centralize the information and who organize the necessary social contacts needed for expanding the network to embrace an ever-widening circle of friends for all occasions.

It should be pointed out, however, that the specific role of women in Chilean middle-class networks is not as distinctly gendered as in the Mexican urban networks I have studied. This is partly because of the primary importance the grandfamily has in Mexico within which a woman keeps her "proper place" at home. In Chile, by contrast, the counterpart of the grandfamily is the *grupo de amigos* – the individual's and the family's friends. Moreover, there exists a higher degree of equality and independence between women and men in Chile. Middle- (and upper-) class women may not only count on the economic means to engage in exchanges but also take credibility from the historical tradition and the cultural feature of strong womanhood in Chilean life.

In the study cited, women participated on equal terms with men in social networks, and their friendship was valued for their reciprocal performance exactly as in the case of men. I found no social taboos concerning the requesting and granting of favors between men and women: the ideology of friendship appears to make no gender distinctions. Hence, the social resources of husband and wife tend to be equivalent in scope and kind, and may be utilized separately or jointly as the case requires.

Changes in the economic use of social resources

The example previously offered and the system described were typical of what I found in my 1970 field work. Almost twenty years later, I did a study of a group of school teachers in order to examine the effects on the middle class of the new economic model introduced by the military government. Among the many changes introduced within the profession were the abolition of job tenure and demolition of the professional organizations which represented the *gremio* (those who belong to the profession). During this time there was also a ban on all political parties in the country; parties had represented a means of access to the state apparatus or an avenue for defense of the interests of particular groups of people, particularly the civilian middle class.

Public administration came under the control of another sector of the middle class – the armed forces – which was involved in other social networks, traditionally separate from those of civilians. As a result of job insecurity and the deterioration of living conditions (public health services, education and housing were privatized), teachers needed to use their social networks more than ever, although for physical survival rather than for class maintenance as in the earlier period. The open structure of friendship networks was replaced by closed family ones, with only a small circle of "intimate" friends left with whom to exchange favours. And those changed in nature, resembling more what the poor exchange: food, lodging and loans of money, rather than bureaucratic favors.

For example, an informant confessed to receiving boxes of food regularly from his mother, who lives in another town. And a female teacher who plans to send her child to a private school for better education admits that "I will spend at least $10,000 pesos a month, but then he can go and have lunch with my mother. My mother will help us out once again." However, a prime way to get a job in the late 1980s was still through personal social networks. Several of the younger informants reported having gotten their first jobs through their mothers or relatives, who were themselves teachers.

The informants also talked about the help they received in relation to the care of their children. This help also usually came from the mother of one member of the couple or in some cases from a sister or a sister-in-law. Such a service becomes an economically important one when both husband and wife need to work to maintain a minimum standard of living. Where money is specifically concerned, most of the demands are now channeled through the family: "My mother is like an open credit line. That is, any difficulty I have, she can lend me money, and as long as I can pay her back, I accept her help. She has offered me money when I have no prospect of repaying her as well, but I try not to accept it if I possibly can."

Housing is another important area of need among the present-day Chilean middle class. Rents often cost as much as an employee's salary, and the lack of public investment for middle-class apartments makes it impossible for a young teacher to buy even the smallest property. As a result, all the informants we interviewed mentioned that, at some period or another in their lives, they had to return to their parents' homes and live with them for a while.

All of these examples show that under conditions of economic insecurity, where not only the position of the middle class is endangered but also its survival, the networks and the services exchanged through them resemble more the situation found among the poor than what was common among the same class during the previous regime. In the current case, the family is the center of the exchange network, and within it the mother is the main agent of assistance.

Informal sector networks in Mexico

In order to be able to survive during recurrent periods of unemployment, members of the popular classes (previously called *marginados*) in Latin American cities make full and varied use of their social resources (Lomnitz 1977). This stratum is typically composed of migrants and descendants of migrants from the landless peasantry who have congregated in large cities. They occupy an economic position characterized by chronic insecurity of income because of their tenuous relation to the urban industrial economy. The informal sector in which they operate is generally not protected by social security or other formal programs; participants' activities are unregulated or illegal due to legislation that controls health, housing, and labor norms, among other things.

In *Networks and Marginality* (1977), I showed the way members of this stratum generate their own security mechanisms by means of reciprocity networks, mainly among neighbors and kin. Among the social resources utilized are intra-family cooperation (for example, to complement the men's wages, wives make tortillas for sale, children shine shoes or beg, old people raise animals or carry water) as well as inter-family cooperation. The latter occurs through networks typically consisting of four or five nuclear families who dwell in adjoining quarters or under the same roof. Non-kin neighbors may be incorporated into such informal networks by means of an intense exchange of goods and services, which usually leads to fictive parenthood (*compadrazgo*). In addition to physical and social proximity, one key variable governing membership of networks is *confianza*, the psycho-social measure of trustworthiness and willingness to engage in reciprocal exchange.

Confianza is born first of all out of sociability; it is generally among the kin in extended grandfamilies where this trust appears as part of a cultural norm. However, it is developed when partners jointly suffer similar fates of economic deprivation. Women make daily requests for cooperation among neighbors – for baby-sitting or the borrowing of small amounts of food or money. Hence, women in the shantytown I studied were the basic agents in the formation of the network structure. I found all networks organized around a female figure, such as a mother, older sister, or a neighbor with a forceful personality, who cared for others and who set the tone for mutual assistance. In the absence of such a female moral leader, the network tended to disintegrate. The networks were composed of nuclear families, not individuals; however, the active participation of men was often overshadowed by the role of women in the daily reciprocity of goods and services which knit the network together.

Women and the household economy

The household within this stratum represents not only a unit of consumption, but also a unit of production and internal cooperation ensuring security and survival. Census data, which take into account only the income generated by the head(s) of the family, yield only part of the total economic activities which take place within that domestic unit. Women help their husbands in their small family enterprises as unpaid family laborers, have their own food-preparation enterprises, do washing for middle-class people, pick up scrap metal or paper to resell, and raise animals such as pigs or bird stock. Children shine shoes, carry water, wash cars, sell chewing gum at street lights, and collect food. They also help care for animals raised by households, deliver *tortillas* made for sale by their mothers, and take care of their brothers and sisters when their mothers go out to work. Old people carry water, sit long hours in front of tables selling peanuts or candies, and help women take care of children.

What we find is an informal economy of subsistence which adds to the declared economic activity of the household. To a great extent, it is the responsibility of a centralizing woman to maintain this social group running harmoniously as an economic one. Three examples illustrate the point

The Figueroa household

This extended household of seventeen members lives in an 800-square-foot plot and shares expenses and cooking arrangements. The male head of the household is a peasant migrant. He and his wife had sixteen children – thirteen of whom are alive. Seven children sleep in the room next to the parents'; a son and daughter are married and live in adjacent rooms with their spouses and children. There is a grandfather living in a shac. The four other sons and daughters live in another part of the city.

Mr Figueroa has obtained an informal concession to pick up the garbage of an apartment building. Officially a municipal truck should provide that service. However, it is not uncommon that truck drivers sell those privileges to scavengers, while themselves receiving their formal municipal salaries. At midnight, Mr Figueroa leaves with two of his sons (aged 11 and 13) to pick up garbage and bring it home. Since this is an illegal activity, it has to be done at night. The following morning the whole family participates in the sorting-out process, separating paper, cloth, glass and metal objects from the food. The first three are sold, while the food is used to feed animals raised by the household.

Mrs Figueroa takes care of the animals; she sends her children out every day to ask for leftover food from middle- or upper-class houses and to pick up green leaves left over in vegetable markets in order to feed the animals. The family raises pigs (there are usually around ten), chickens and turkeys, one cow and, on the rooftop, rabbits. The cow has to be taken out daily to graze. This is done by Mrs Figueroa and her older children. She also milks the cow, keeping most of the milk to feed her children, while selling what remains to neighbors. The grazing is done in the rainy season in unbuilt lots; otherwise, the cow is fed with the vegetable leftovers which the children bring. Mr Figueroa also sells manure as fertilizer for private gardens. Several times a week, private, unregulated buyers come through the shantytown to buy pigs, turkeys or chickens. The rabbits are usually consumed by the family, and their skins are sold.

We see in this example that women not only raise a family, but participate very actively in the family "enterprise" which has been built around the husband's main economic activity. Without the active participation of children and the role of the mother as organizer, the enterprise would have been impossible.

The Gonzalez household

This four-generation extended family living together on a single plot includes six nuclear families, five of which share expenses. The sixth one shares the plot and use of the privy but keeps its own economy separate. The five families sharing expenses have a single kitchen. Everybody shares in the rent payment, and as new nuclear families are formed, small rooms have been built to accommodate them. At the time of the study, twenty-five persons lived in the plot, distributed in seven rooms, plus kitchens and privy.

The female head of the household was a widowed great-grandmother, aged 68. She had one daughter and three sons, two of them dead at the time of the study. All the sons, when married, settled on the plot, and their descendants (fourteen of them) live there, as does the daughter, who is a single mother, with her own child. One of the daughters-in-law is from the neighborhood and maintains active exchange relations with her former family network, as does one of *her* daughters who lives nearby with her husband's family.

The men, who work in different occupations, bring a large proportion of their income to the elderly powerful grandmother who centralizes the organization of this domestic unit. Preparation of food is in her charge, together with one of her daughters-in-law; other available women and girls assist. They make breakfast and dinner for all those who participate in the expense-sharing arrangements. All earning members contribute to food expenses; there are no fixed quotas, and anyone who is laid off may stop contributing. They, and their dependents, continue eating from the communal kitchen. Each nuclear family also has additional foodstuffs bought with their own money, and generally these are not shared.

Several women go out to work as maids for middle-class households. Their children are taken care of by the women who stay home. In general, the upbringing of the household children is a communal affair, including the daily bath, done by two or three women who carry water and firewood and are in charge of heating the water in buckets and scrubbing the children before they go to school.

The economy of this extended family is financed as follows. The main income of the household is earned by the men, and men change occupations as the need arises. At the time of the study, one of them was a trucker's helper, another a bricklayer, the third a truck driver. One of the grandsons sells newspapers. They all give most of their earnings to the grandmother, who distributes it according to the needs of keeping the household running. Two or three women work as daytime maids and bring their salaries home; they and some children collect stale bread and tortillas for the pigs which are raised on the plot as a joint project of the household group. If, at a particular moment, the family is raising no animals, the stale tortillas and bread collected are sold to other animal-raising families. Two of the women make tortillas for sale in the neighborhood. Children are in charge of their distribution. Women also go out regularly to collect *nopales* (prickly pear cactus leaves) both for sale and for family consumption. In those outings, they collect firewood as well as metal cans and scraps of paper to sell.

This household operates as a socioeconomic unit. Family solidarity allows its members to survive. And its holding together depends to a great extent on the cooperation of the women who compose the group. The importance of the grandmother's centralizing role cannot be overestimated. Without a moral authority, the group would fall apart; thus, that role is an economic one.

The Contreras network
This neighborhood-concentrated network consists of an extended family and two unrelated families. It includes five nuclear families in all, living in adjoining rooms with separate entrances. The unifying element of the network is kinship: two brothers and one sister, with their spouses and descendants, plus the two other nuclear families. Each family lives in its own residential unit and maintains its own economy.

The men of the household are a single labor unit under the leadership of one of the brothers, who was the first to migrate to the city. The sister works as a daytime maid, and in the evenings she makes dresses which are bought by the neighbors. Her 17-year-old daughter also works as a maid, and older boys go to junior high school and work with their father in their free time. Another woman settles everyday in a construction site and, with the help of a child, prepares *quesadillas* for workers to purchase for lunch.

Each nuclear family pays rent, prepares its own food, and educates its own children. All share the same outdoor facilities, including the kitchen, outhouse, storage places, and laundry vats. There is a continual exchange of assistance: money loans, loans of tools and artifacts, services such as the care of children and the sick, assistance in building new housing facilities, job assistance, migration assistance, ritual expenses, and so on. In addition, each household member has his or her own network of relatives or friends who live in other parts of town or in the countryside. Those networks are called on when needed by each person (or family) to find jobs, move to a different part of town in case of eviction, get emergency loans, and so forth.

The use of social resources for economic ends among the poor

The previous cases are examples of the importance of social networks for the survival of the urban poor. In Mexico, the basis of an individual's social network is the family, particularly the extended grandfamily. In the case of the urban poor, the household becomes an economic unit of consumption and production which allows that stratum of society to survive. Networks often coincide with households, but they normally include other individuals, families and households, within the shantytown. Because of needs and emergencies which arise daily, the intensity of exchange will depend not only on social distance but also on physical propinquity, as poor people do not own cars or telephones but still require a constant flow of exchanges. In these circumstances, it is very important to create networks within the same neighborhood. Reciprocal exchange prevails within these networks; reciprocity is a sort of exchange which takes place between equals, through time, and as part of a long-term social relation.

Women play a major role in creating and maintaining the social networks that form the underpinning of the exchange system. Not only are they crucial to the maintenance of family unity, but they also continually meet female neighbors and create new ties. Because trust is necessary for exchanges to happen, the role of women is essential in creating a foundation of *confianza* and solidarity among participants, and thus maintaining an adequate flow of goods and services circulating within the network. On the other hand, men get together with other men from many different places at work, creating external networks which are reinforced by common drinking bouts and football playing. Those bonds, however, do not include the female members of the family; they represent a network of individual males, rather than one that contributes to the family's survival.

The goods and services exchanged within the reciprocity networks may be classified as follows: (i) information, including instructions for migration, tips on residential opportunities and jobs, general or specific orientations to urban living; (ii) job assistance, in both finding one and training newcomers or young members of the family in skills to be sold in the labor market; (iii) loans of all sorts; (iv) accommodation of migrants from the countryside, including feeding and providing for the primary needs of families during the initial period of urban adaptation, assistance to friends and relatives in need, and a host of minor, but not unimportant, services such as shopping and taking care of children; (v) moral support, as networks are mechanisms that generate solidarity, and this solidarity is extended to all events in the life cycle.

In the shantytown, networks can be classified according to the intensity of exchange among their members. They range from networks with high intensity of exchange, where physical, social and economic distances are minimal and trust is maximal – as in the cases of the intra-household networks previously described – to networks where the intensity of exchange is minimal, consisting of families which are neighbors but not related by kinship or fictive kinship. In intermediary situations, networks are composed by relatives as well as non-related neighbors. Finally, each individual also possesses social resources spread out within the city (work mates, in-law relatives, friends) and in the rural areas where the migrants originated. These wide-ranging networks (similar to those of the middle class, above) could eventually be mobilized for services needed on special occasions: to move to another part of town if a shantytown is erased, to get special loans, or to return to the village if one's luck had not been good in the city.

Conclusions

I have presented ethnographic material from three different urban strata in Latin America to show the manner in which women participate in various types of informal economies. In each stratum, the persistence, or rather the adaptation to urban conditions, of certain features commonly associated with traditional economies has definite survival value and forms a pattern of socioeconomic responses revealed in women's activities.

In each case, a system of informal exchange emerges to complement the informal economy. These informal systems are embedded in long-term social relations (primarily kinship, but also fictive kinship, neighborliness, personal friendship, and "school-tie" solidarity). The characteristic feature of such systems is a tendency towards the formation of networks which can be converted into economic assets: security, status, power. For the poor in the popular classes the problem is one of sheer physical survival; among the middle class it is the maintenance of a perpetually threatened economic status; while among the very wealthy it is the retention of their economic privilege.

Women play a major role in creating and maintaining the social networks that form the underpinnings of the exchange systems. Apparently men have not developed the social skills necessary to create *confianza* to the same extent that women have. In the Mexican shantytown, for example, women are continually meeting and conversing with their female neighbors, while men are normally at large within the city; reciprocal exchange among neighbors is vital for the satisfaction of daily needs and coping with everyday emergencies. Networks are dependent on morally powerful female figures, who specialize in the organization of solidarity, by creating an emotional and ideological climate conducive to mutual help, as well as coordinating economic activities between networks.

Similarly, among the Mexican upper-class family "clans," it is women's business to keep information on relatives moving across economic barriers, while men are usually cast in rigid roles which prevent them from socializing across the class hierarchy within the family. Yet it is precisely the conversion of social resources into economic advantages which lends power and stability to such family-based networks. A similar role was played by Chilean middle-class women who created an atmosphere at home for the development of friendship and kinship networks in order to negotiate the bureaucracy; then, with changes brought by the military regime, mothers became central to middle-class survival much like the powerful female figures in the shantytown.

In all three cases, women specialize in communication, that is, the circulation of information among members of the network. The importance of communication for network continuity may be gathered from the fact that shantytown networks are dependent on next-door-neighborliness, while the middle classes and the upper class both depend on the telephone for contact. As a result, middle-class and upper-class networks are spread all over town, while shantytown networks are restricted to walking distance. In every case, however, the importance of women in the informal aspects of the economy hinges on the specific role assigned to them in the rites of sociability, in the forms of economic exchange, and in the cultural rules which determine trust. Insecurity is not a monopoly of the poor in the shantytowns; it is an intrinsic fact of Latin American life. Hence, maintaining active social networks has become a crucial aspect for economic survival in all social strata. Women have a central role in building the social networks upon which social capital accrues.

References

Aubey, R. 1979. "Capital Mobilization and Patterns of Business Ownership and Control in Latin America: The Case of Mexico." In *Entrepreneurs in Cultural Context,* edited by S. Greenfield, A. Strickton and R. Aubey, pp.225–42. Albuquerque: University of New Mexico Press.

Barnes, J.A. 1954. "Class Committee in a Norwegian Island Parish." *Human Relations* 7: 39–58.
Castells, M., and A. Portes. 1989. "World Underneath: The Origins, Dynamics, and Effects of the Informal Economy." In *The Informal Economy,* edited by A. Portes, M. Castells, and L. Benton, pp.11–37. Baltimore: John Hopkins University Press.
Coleman, J. 1990. *Foundations of Social Theory.* Cambridge, Mass.: The Belknap Press of Harvard University.
De Soto, H. 1987. *El Otro Sendero.* Buenos Aires: Sudamericana.
Greenfield, S., and A. Strickton. 1979. "Entrepreneurship and Social Change: Toward a Populational, Decision-making Approach." In *Entrepreneurs in Cultural Context,* edited by S. Greenfield, A. Strickton and R. Aubey, pp. 329–50. Albuquerque: University of New Mexico Press.
Grossman, G. 1977. "The 'Second Economy' of the USSR." *Problems of Communism* 26: 25–40.
Grossman, G. 1989. "Informal Personal Incomes and Outlays in the Soviet Urban Population." In *The Informal Economy,* edited by A. Portes, M. Castells, and L. Benton, pp. 150–72. Baltimore: Johns Hopkins University Press.
International Labor Organization (ILO). 1974. "La politica del Empleo en America Latina: Lecciones de la Experiencia de PREALC." Santiago.
Lipset, S. M. 1967. *Elites in Latin America.* New York: Oxford.
Lomnitz, L. 1971. "Reciprocity of Favours in the Chilean Middle Class." In *Studies in Economic Anthropology,* edited by G.Dalton, pp. 93–106. Washington, D.C.: American Anthropological Association.
Lomnitz L. 1977. *Networks and Marginality.* San Francisco Academic Press.
Lomnitz, L. 1988. "Informal Metworks in Formal Systems." American Anthropologist 90: 42–55.
Lomnitz L., and X. Perez-Lizaur. 1987. *An Elite Family in Mexico.* Princeton: Princeton University Press.
Lomnitz L., and A. Melnick. 1991. *The Chilean Middle Class.* Boulder: Lynn Reiner.
Long, N. 1979. "Multiple Enterprise in the Central Highlands of Peru." In *Entrepreneurs in Cultural Context,* edited by S. Greenfield, A. Strickton and R. Aubey, pp.123–58. Albuquerque: University of New Mexico Press.
Mars, G., and J. Altman. 1983. "The Cultural Basis of Soviet Georgia's Second Economy." *Soviet Studies* 32(2): 218–34.
Mitchell, J. C. 1969. *Social Networks in Urban Situations.* Manchester: Manchester University Press.
Roberts, B. 1974. "The Provincial Urban System and the Process of Dependency." Mimeo.
Portes, A., M. Castells, and L. Benton. 1989. *The Informal Economy. Baltimore: Johns Hopkins University Press.*
Souza, P. and V. Tokman. 1975. *El Sector Informal Urbano.* Santiago: CLACSO.
Tokman, V. 1986. "The Informal Sector: Fifteen Years later." Paper presented at Conference on Comparative Study of the Informal Sector. Harper's Ferry, West Virginia, 2–6 October.
Wolfe, A. 1970. "On Structural Comparisons of Network Situations and Social Networks in Cities." *Canadian Review of Sociology and Anthropology,* 7(4): 226–44.

Part II

Gender and Challenges to the Construction of Social Class and Race-Ethnicity

Mary Romero is Associate Professor in the Sociology Department at the University of Oregon. She is the author of *Maid in the USA*.

Stan Gray is a former trade unionist and Director of the Ontario Workers' Health Center. He currently works for Greenpeace.

Bette J. Dickerson is Assistant Professor, Department of Sociology, the American University, Washington DC. She is the editor of *African American Single Mothers: Perspectives on Their Lives and Families*.

Rose Brewer is Associate Professor, Afro-American and African Studies, University of Minnesota. Her most recent book is *Bridges of Power: Women's Multicultural Alliances*.

4. "I'm not your maid. I am the housekeeper": The Restructuring of Housework and Work Relationships in Domestic Service

Mary Romero

While domestic service has drastically declined in importance to other sex-segregated occupations which dominate women's work in the labor force, the occupation has persisted through slavery, feudalism and capitalism. A strong sentiment exists that the occupation is vanishing and being replaced with the commercialization of most services outside the home. However, when I interviewed Chicana household workers, they presented a different view about paid reproductive labor. The women did not complain about the difficulty of finding a job as a private household worker but rather the difficulty in finding employment outside the dead-end, low-status, and low-paying market of household labor and childcare. They described changes in the reproductive labor process but did not forecast a demise of the occupation.

The predictions made by social scientists have been primarily based on the notions that (i) technology has eliminated much of the work, and (ii) egalitarian and humanitarian ideals are incompatible with the personal service extracted from domestic service. Lewis Coser (1973) argued that the emergence of modern technology in our industrialized and developed economy has replaced household workers and has shifted much of the family's reproductive labor into the market place. Coser, David Chaplin (1978), Vilhelm Aubert (1970) and others claimed that the traditional mistress–maid hierarchical relationship was inconsistent with a democratic society. Furthermore, the employment of household workers was no longer a necessary status symbol in middle-class life. Aaron Levenstein (1962) pointed to the decreasing numbers of domestic workers as evidence that the character of US citizens had changed and workers were unwilling to engage in servitude. Consequently, domestic service was identified as a "bridging occupation" providing intergenerational social mobility among European immigrants and rural women.

---

* This paper appears in part in *Maid in the U.S.A.* (New York: Routledge, Chapman and Hall 1992). The research was funded by a grant from the Business and Professional Women's Foundation and the University of California President's Fellowship. (Broom and Smith 1963).

The "changing character" thesis was apparent in Harold Wool's (Wool and Phillips 1976) suggestion that there exists a causal relationship between the deplorable working conditions and the composition of a predominately immigrant and minority workforce. Most recently, Susan Tucker (1988) attributed the low wages in the occupation to the definitions of femininity that both African American employees and white women employers shared.

Previous theoretical constructions used to describe paid household labor have been challenged by research based on participant observation and extensive interviews with women of color employed as domestics. Unlike depictions of domestic service as a "bridging occupation", Evelyn Nakano Glenn (1986) found that women of color experienced an "occupational ghetto." Linda Martin and Kerry Segrave (1985) rejected Wool's argument that the low status of the occupation was related to the workers and pointed out that the occupation has traditionally been low-status and that groups left the service when other opportunities became available. Rather than using the concepts of "changing character," researchers have turned their attention to investigating the race relations embedded in the employer-employee relationship which reflect social inequalities in society.

The major area of concentration in the studies on women of color employed as domestics is the interpersonal relationships between employee and employer, particularly the methods used by women employers to maintain superiority and control while creating an informal and companionable relationship. Judith Rollins (1985), Wendy Luttrell (Chapter 1 in this volume), Glenn (1986), and Tucker (1988) explored the dialectic of intimacy and domination between employees and employers. Rollins identified the degradation rituals of deference and maternalism and showed how they functioned to confirm the domestic's inferiority and the employer's superiority. In general, Judith Rollins, Bonnie Thornton Dill, Shellee Colen, Susan Tucker, and others have analyzed domestics' actions within a social-psychological framework. Struggle is primarily understood as a fight for dignity and respect. For instance, Rollins investigated African American women's ability to cope and found that they did not identify with the oppressor because their moral system provided an "understanding of the meaning of class and race in this country, and their value system, which measures an individual's worth less by material success than by 'the kind of person you are,' by the quality of one's interpersonal relationships and by one's standing in the community" (1985: 213). Dill (1988), Colen (1989), and Luttrell (Chapter 1 in this volume) also considered membership of the African American community as an essential factor in protecting household workers from the stigma of domestic service and an important means to retain self-esteem.

Within the social-psychological framework, women-of-color domestic workers are perceived as powerless to change working conditions and their actions are analyzed as acts of resistance and coping mechanisms. Rollins

(1985: 227) described domestics as having few choices and consequently having to "pretend to be unintelligent, subservient, and content with their positions" or "they know the position could be lost." Dill (1988: 50) identified a wide variety of strategies used by African American women "to achieve some kind of parity within the confines of a relationship of domination." Presented as "stories of resistance," the strategies involved incidents of confrontation, chicanery, or cajolery with the employer. Likewise, Tucker (1988: 106) found that "one way black domestics dealt with such feelings of powerlessness was by tricking whites (employers) – by manipulating the situations in which they were perceived as childlike, lazy, or inferior."

Limiting the analysis of domestics' struggles to a framework of interpersonal relationships of domination directs our attention to workers' individual characteristics rather than to structural opportunities. Dill's examination of "stories of resistance" highlights the domestics' personal management skills. Similarly, Colen (1989: 187) explains everyday struggles on the basis of individual attributes: "the women in this study are strong, determined, secure and confident". In her book on domestic service in South Africa, Jacklyn Cock (1980: 103) referred to strategies of silence and mockery of employers as "muted rituals of rebellion." She asserted: "The domestic worker's main mode of adaption is the adoption of a mask of deference as a protective disguise" (103).

However, there is much to be gained by shifting the analysis away from interpersonal relationships and idealistic "dialectics" of intimacy and domination and on to an examination of the labor process itself. Domestic work is not a vanishing historical artifact; however, it has undergone significant changes. Race relations remain at the center of the occupation, which has traditionally been and currently remains dominated by non-white women. However, the context of the interaction between the white woman employer and the woman-of-color employee has not been fully examined. Exploring race relations alongside the conditions under which paid reproductive labor occurs illustrates the everyday rituals of class, gender and racial domination and the struggle to change working conditions. Social-psychological approaches tend to gloss over the structure of housework and treat it as an extension of the hierarchical relationship between women from different class and racial backgrounds. However, the relationship is best conceptualized as an employee–employer relationship and an instance of class struggle. The Chicanas I interviewed described their struggles to restructure housework and strategies for changing relationships with their employers. Like so many other employee–employer relationships under capitalism, control over the work process is not cooperative. Worker and employer define their interests in opposition and struggle for control. Only by gaining a measure of control can employees restructure the work to eliminate demeaning and degrading practices. Based on my research on Chicana household workers, the following discussion explores efforts made by workers to change domestic service.

Restructuring paid household labor

The shift from live-in to day work

The most significant change in domestic service has been the establishment of day work. While live-in situations continue today, particularly among immigrant women, the most common working conditions involve day work. In his characterization of the "hourly 'cleaning lady,'" replacing "the uniformed maid who was part of the household," David Katzman (1981: 378) captured the importance of the shift in changing social relationships. Glenn (1986: 143) attributed the establishment of non-residential jobs to the bringing of domestic work closer to industrialized wage work: "Work and non-work life are clearly separated, and the basis for employment is more clearly contractual – that is, the worker sells a given amount of labor time for an agreed-upon wage." Shifting from live-in to day work continues to be part of the struggle for improving working conditions. As noted in her study on black domestics in New York City and the surrounding suburban area, Soraya Coley (1981: 255) included moving out of the employer's home in a list of techniques "used to enhance or safeguard their personal dignity or to protect their physical and emotional well-being." Women unable to find day work continued to live in but rented a room elsewhere in order "to act independently and resist the potential ill-treatment of the employer" (260). Day work placed limits on the number of hours and increased the opportunities for autonomy.

Day work gradually effected a change in domestic service from a situation where employees had one employer to one where they have several employers at one time. Glenn (1986: 162) describes the advantages of the arrangement: "Domestics working for several families were less dependent on one employer. Work hours could be adjusted to fit in with the workers' other interests and responsibilities." Now workers were in a bargaining position and were able to quit employers and seek new ones. Similar situations were reported by Chicana household workers I interviewed. They increased the number of employers to two or three in one day (Romero 1992). Having several employers at one time allowed workers to replace one employer with another without affecting the entire work week. Some of the women increased their wages annually by requesting raises or quitting one employer and raising the rate for new employers.

Control over the labor process

As day work becomes the norm in many communities, the struggle for autonomy and independence becomes a struggle over the control of the labor process. Household workers attempt to negotiate a work structure that gives them control over the planning and organization of the housework, as well as the work pace and the method. Glenn (1986) noted the apparent conflict between employers and employees by pointing to the various ways that each tries to control the work process. Employers want the work done in a specific way; they monitor employees closely to ensure that the worker would not "loaf or cut corners" (1986: 161). Conflict that arises over the amount and pace of the work highlights the ongoing struggle over control. While employers strive to expand the work day and the workload, employees try to cut back the number of hours and the amount of work.

A significant strategy for gaining control is to define the limits of the work. Like Japanese American women in Glenn's study, Chicanas negotiated work arrangements by tasks rather than time and referred to this arrangement as "charging by the house" or charging a "flat rate." This type of arrangement eliminated employers' attempts to add more tasks and force the domestic to increase the pace of the work. Charging a "flat rate" was a critical strategy for eliminating emotional labor and placing boundaries on the job description. Negotiations concentrated on identifying a routine set of housework tasks and eliminating personal services such as baby-sitting, laundry, or ironing. Establishing a verbal job description also functioned to define the workers' social relationships to employers and their families.

Workers resisted employers' and their families' attempts to structure housework around rituals of deference, particularly those that involved emotional labor attached to personal services. One strategy used to avoid the personalization of the employee–employer relationship was to eliminate ways that household labor included personal service. A statement made by Mrs Fernandez, a 35-year-old household worker, illustrates the conscious effort made to draw distinctions between different types of paid household labor:

> They [the employer's children] started to introduce me to their friends as their maid. "This is our maid Angela." I would say "I'm not your maid. I've come to clean your house, and a maid is someone who takes care of you and lives here or comes in everyday, and I come once a week, and it is to take care of what you have messed up. I'm not your maid. I'm your housekeeper."

None of the women I interviewed referred to herself as a maid. Personal services or any act of serving was the crucial distinction. Mrs Montoya's statement clarifies the appropriate expectations for employers and employees:

> I figure I'm not there to be their personal maid. I'm there to do their housecleaning – their upkeep of the house. Most of the women I work for are professionals and so they feel it's not my job to run around behind them. Just to keep their house maintenance clean and that's all they ask.

Structuring household labor around rituals of deference was equated with maids' work, as Mrs Rojas's comment reveals:

> One or two [employers] that I work for now have children that are snotty, you know they thought that I was their maid, or they would treat me like a maid, you know, instead of a cleaning lady.

The most definite way to structure work as a meaningful and non-degrading activity was to remove employer supervision. The women wanted to enter the employer's home, decide where to begin, arrange the appliances and cleaning products, and pace themselves accordingly. Chicanas presented themselves as expert household workers and let employers know that they had extensive knowledge and experience. Mrs Fernandez's description of meeting a new employer illustrates the attention given to signs of supervision, monitoring and unreasonable expectations.

> You can tell if they're [employers] going to trust you or not. If they're not overlooking – see, you know, over you all the time. If they start looking or saying "I don't want this moved or I don't want this done or be careful with this" – well, you know, you can be so careful but there's accidents happen. So if they start being picky I won't stay.

Mrs Lopez evaluates employers' willingness to turn over the work process during their first encounter:

> I have had ladies that have said "I know you know what to do so I'll leave it to you" or they pull out their cleaning stuff and tell you "this is for this and this is for that" and I say "I know I've done this before." [And they say] "Oh, O.K. I'll let you do it."

For many Chicanas, minimizing contact with employers was the key factor in improving working conditions. Consequently, they preferred employers who worked outside the home, and they avoided working for employers who were full-time homemakers.

After establishing a verbal agreement about the specific tasks to be completed and wages, the women took responsibility for all decisions involved in getting the job done, including the work pace, establishing the cleaning routine, and in many cases the selection of work materials. Being in charge of the housework included scheduling a rotation of monthly or bi-monthly tasks, such as cleaning the refrigerator and stove.

Several of the women recalled employers who were insistent on supervising. In these cases, the worker frequently created situations to convince the employer that she should either relinquish control or do the work herself. Tactics included doing only the tasks requested and nothing else, not bothering to inform the employer that the worker used the last vacuum bag or used up the cleaning materials, and refusing to offer the employer assistance in fixing a simple mechanical problem on an appliance.

Informal networks provided a resource for restructuring housework and the relationships between employees and employers. Like workers in Coley's (1981) study, most of the younger Chicanas I interviewed began doing paid housework by working with a friend or relative for several days or weeks until she decided to work alone. Mrs Rodriguez and Mrs Garcia illustrate how this informal apprenticeship program served to "train" and socialize new recruits into domestic service:

> She [her sister] would go look it over and see if I missed anything. Or like in the bathroom, you have to polish all the chrome, and I didn't know that; so I cleaned it, and it was clean, but she's the one that gave me all these tips on polishing up the chrome and stuff.
>
> When I was working with my sister, I told her she shouldn't be cleaning by the hour because it's not worth it to be cleaning by the hour. You are there too many hours and you don't make much money that way.

The apprenticeship not only offered useful training about different cleaning techniques, new products and appliances, but also functioned to teach new household workers how to structure the work to increase autonomy and independence, and successful negotiation strategies for improving working conditions and wages. The apprenticeship served to socialize new workers to expect a higher wage scale, shorter work days, and certain working conditions. Recruiting new workers through informal networks served to maintain a set of standards in the occupation.

Both employees and employers actively help friends and neighbors find each other. Working through the informal network exposes both potential employees and employers to existing working conditions and helps to maintain standards. In describing how employees and employers find each other in the underground labor market, Chicanas revealed the way in which employers are tied to the network. Mrs Chacon's statement points to the way new employers are socialized to appropriate expectations through the network.

> I right away tell them what I do and what I expect to get paid, and they already know because of their friends – because they have already discussed my work.

Moreover, hiring through the workers' informal network gives workers the opportunity to expand their individual struggle to include collective efforts to improve working conditions, higher wages, paid vacations, and social security.

Discussion

Domestic service is not a vestigial remnant of feudalism, but is an occupation which has been modified and shaped by capitalist social relations. Coser's and others' depictions of the occupation as a fleeting memory of bygone years were based on the faulty assumptions that modernization would eliminate the drudgery of household labor for women in the United States and that modern society no longer relied upon status symbols. However, technology has not resulted in the elimination of reproductive labor. While studies may dispute the actual decrease of hours spent by women on housework and cooking, there is clear evidence that standards of cleanliness and childcare have easily stepped in to counter any savings. In addition, more and more women, many of whom are mothers, are joining the ranks of the employed. However, like previous generations of women, they are still delegated the responsibility for homemaking and childcare. While some reproductive labor has become commercialized and services can be purchased in the market, the cost and quality of pre-prepared food, childcare and other services remain a problem for many families. Consequently, women who can afford to hire household workers and childcare workers will do so. Unfortunately, many women and men seeking household help take advantage of the limited employment options for poor and immigrant women of color. Paying low wages and denying social security and work benefits, these employers maintain poor working conditions in domestic service.

Since women of color face the worst working conditions in domestic service and offer employers the greatest opportunity for exploitation, race relations remains central to the social relationships between employees and employers in the occupation. The extensive research addressing the dialectics of intimacy and domination, and the functions of rituals of deference and maternalism, clearly refutes Coser's argument that the servant is no longer an important status symbol. As Rollins points out, the interpersonal rituals are used to reinforce inequality and to confirm the domestic of color's inferiority and the white employer's superiority. The emotional labor extracted from women of color as household workers indicates employers' families' attempts "to absorb the total personality" and to tie the worker "to the household in a totalistic manner" (Coser 1973: 31). The emotional labor involves nurturing, caring and enhancing the employer's status. As Rollins, Dill, Glenn and others have pointed out, employers do hire domestics for emotional labor. Emotional labor is a commodity. However, employers rarely pay for the emotional work extracted from the employee. The additional labor is not acknowledged and thus becomes shadow work (Illich 1980). Conflict and tension arise over the exchange value of the labor, particularly in the case of unpaid labor extracted through the manipulation of "gifts" or under the disguise of "family" and friendship obligations. So although certain aspects of the servant role marking the position as a status symbol for employers may have disappeared, such as the use of uniforms, back entrances, separate eating and drinking utensils (see Luttrell, Chapter 1, p.26 in this volume), women of color employed in white households experience social relationships and work assignments shaped by the racial, class and gender hierarchical system of domination.

Yet, at the same time, women of color employed as household workers do not react entirely as powerless victims. Analysis of twenty-five work histories of Chicanas uncovered a wide range of efforts made to improve working conditions and increase their wages. The women's description of interaction with employers and their families include findings similar to those reported by Rollins, Dill, Glenn, Colen, Luttrell and others; however, they also describe a wider range of relationships coexisting in the occupation. The women I interviewed have not resigned themselves to "muted rituals of rebellion" but are actively struggling to improve their working conditions by changing the structure of housework. While they express awareness and concern over the employee-employer relationship, their main concern is focused on eliminating personal services from the list of household tasks and creating a situation whereby they are in charge of planning and organizing the work. The detailed description the women provided about the establishment of verbal contracts and the struggle to maintain certain working conditions expands Glenn's analysis of the struggle over the work process and draws our attention to the direction of changes in the occupation.

I would argue that many of the situations coded by Rollins, Dill and others as "coping strategies" are not necessarily limited to workers' struggles to maintain dignity and self-worth, but rather are deliberate ventures aimed at restructuring paid household labor. In her study of union and non-union members of the National Committee of Household Employment (NCHE), Coley analyzed structural factors in relation to strategies used by workers. Union members expressed an occupational identity and felt they had "achieved control over their work", whereas non-union members perceived the work "as merely a means to an end" and expressed a powerless resignation (1981:276). Coley analyzed various tactics which were similar to the "management skills" described by Dill, including direct confrontation, trickery and quitting. Trickery and confrontation were cited as particularly useful in resisting employers' attempts to increase the workload and in helping to maintain the boundaries of tasks. Employees expressed a preference for craftiness and trickery because those tactics minimize risk and economic hardship; however, confrontation was the most frequently cited form of resistance, and "confrontation was often the more expedient mode of establishing a clear understanding between the employee and employer on one's expectations" (1981: 277).

When household workers are in a seller's market and are in a bargaining position, they can select employers who allow workers to structure the housework and who do not include emotional labor. Chicanas facing limited job opportunities approached domestic service as an alternative to other low-paying and low-status jobs because they were able to be selective and sought employers who were themselves employed outside the home. Similar strategies are cited in other studies. For instance, Dill and Tucker found that domestics attempted to control wages and benefits by carefully selecting wealthy employers. Dill referred to the strategy as "building a career," explaining that domestics find wealthy employers who can provide high wages and benefits, which increases the domestic's social position and feelings of self-worth. Coley noted a similar technique among unionized members who created upward mobility for themselves by assessing the occupational structure and selecting the job description that conferred more money and status. The use of informal networks to find new employers is another strategy aimed at upgrading standards and increasing wages.

Domestic service is an occupation which is undergoing transition as it extends beyond the underground economy to the commercial house-cleaning agencies. Just as a few generations ago when women struggled to replace live-in with day work, private household workers continue to struggle to improve conditions. The narratives of women of color indicate that the struggle has turned to restructuring the work. Maintaining dignity and self-worth is largely a struggle fought out in the workers' attempts to eliminate emotional labor which affirms and enhances the status of employers. Determining their work pace, cleaning methods, and the planning and organization of the work are all strategies household workers have devised to gain control over the labor process.

References

Aubert, Vilhelm. 1970. "The Housemaid – An occupational Role in Crisis." In *Society and the Legal Order,* edited by Richard Schwartz and Jerome H. Skolnick, pp.559–68. New York: Basic Books.

Broom, Leonard, and S.H.Smith. 1963. "Bridging occupations." *British Journal of Sociology* 14: 321–34.

Chaplin, David. 1978. "Domestic Service and Industrialization," *Comparative Studies in Sociology* 1: 97–127.

Clark-Lewis, Elizabeth. 1985. "This Day Had A'End: The Transition from Live-In to Day Work." Working Papers No.2. Memphis, Tenn.: Center for Research on Women, Memphis State University.

Cock, Jacklyn. 1980. *Maids and Madams. A Study in the Politics of Exploitation.* Johannesburg: Raven Press.

Colen, Shellee. 1989. "Just a Little Respect." In *Muchachas No More: Household Workers in Latin America and the Caribbean,* edited by Elsa M. Chaney and Mary Garcia Castro, pp.46–70. Philadelphia: Temple University Press.

Coley, Soraya Moore. 1981. "And Still I Rise: An Exploratory Study of Contemporary Black Private Household Workers." Ph.D. dissertation, Bryn Mawr College.

Coser, Lewis. 1973. "Servants: The Obsolescence of an Occupational Role." *Social Forces* 52: 31–40.

Dill, Bonnie Thornton. 1988. " 'Making Your Job Good Yourself': Domestic Service and the Construction of Personal Dignity." In *Women and the Politics of Empowerment,* edited by Ann Bookman and Sandra Morgen, pp.33–52. Philadelphia: Temple University Press.

Glenn, Evelyn Nakano. 1986. *Issei, Nisei, War Bride, Three Generations of Japanese American*

Women in Domestic Service. Philadelphia: Temple University Press.

Illich, Ivan. 1980. *Shadow Work.* Cape Town: University of Cape Town.

Katzman, David. 1981. *Seven Days a Week: Women and Domestic Service in Industrializing America.* New York: Oxford University Press.

Levenstein, Aaron. 1962. *Why People Work: Changing Incentives in a Troubled World.* NY: Gowell-Collier Press.

Martin, Linda, and Kerry Segrave. 1985. *The Servant Problem: Domestic Workers in North America.* Jefferson, North Carolina: McFarland.

Rollins, Judith. 1985. *Between Women.* Philadelphia: Temple University Press.

Romero, Mary. 1992. *Maid in the U.S.A.* New York: Routledge, Chapman and Hall.

Tucker, Susan. 1988. *Telling Memories Among Southern Women: Domestic Workers and Their Employers in the Segregated South.* Baton Rouge: Louisiana State University Press.

Woll, Harold, and Bruce Dana Phillips. 1976. *The Labour Supply for Lower-level Occupations.* NY: Praegar.

5. Fighting Sexual Harassment: A Collective Labour Obligation

Stan Gray

Sexual harassment is a problem commonly experienced by women in the workforce. Surveys in Canada and the United States have shown that upwards of 40 percent of women have encountered it at the workplace. This can produce a "poisoned work environment" which compounds the effect of other forms of anti-female discrimination. A widely publicized case of sexual harassment in Canada provides the core for the analysis in this chapter.

The experience of sexual harassment can damage the health of the victims. As such, it ought to be treated as an occupational health hazard. There are many advantages to defining harassment of women as a workplace health-and-safety issue. For women, it can provide new avenues and new weapons to fight long-standing battles. It also involves re-defining a gender-specific experience of women into a more general class experience. This can impact on the men in labour, for it may lead them to a better understanding of the grievances of working women by seeing the similarities with their own experiences. It may also lead them to develop new methods of joining with working women in what ought to be regarded as a common struggle – "an injury to one is an injury to all."

The health-and-safety framework speaks to the experience of working men who have suffered their own forms of harassment and humiliation at the hands of authority. It should be understood, however, that sexual harassment abuses women in unique ways. It crosses lines of personal intimacy to which male workers are not subjected. Sexual harassment is a specific expression of men's power over women. In its many ugly forms, it can unnerve and terrorize women in ways men do not experience. It leaves emotional scars of a distinctive sort.

---

*With sincerest thanks I acknowledge the assistance of Bonita Clark without whose collaboration I could not have written this chapter.

Although male and female workers' experiences are not the same, they have many parallels. Pointing out the similarities may allow more working men to see how much they have in common with women whose dignity and self-respect are battered on the job. It can also serve to undermine the sexist attitudes which have for so long confused and misdirected working men. Exploited and mistreated on and off the job, many male workers compensate for their own victim status by taking it out on women. This victimizing of women, however, has served to channel their class-based anger along irrational and destructive paths. Like racism, sexism has often served to deflect working men away from their true enemies and the real source of their problems. It has proved harmful to their long-term interests as individuals and weakened their collective strength as part of the labour force.

The hardships of the 1990s recession in Canada have led to increased levels of stress on working people. Everywhere we are seeing more scapegoating of and violence against women. One response to this is to explore and develop strategies which enable the victims of both genders to work together.

The case of Bonita Clark

We can begin by looking at a prominent women's rights case which took place recently in the province of Ontario, Canada. Bonita Clark was hired by the Steel Company of Canada (Stelco) in November 1979. Stelco is a large corporation that operated a male-only hiring policy for its giant works which employed over 12,000 people in the city of Hamilton. An affirmative-action campaign launched by women's and labour groups combined public pressure and legal action. When it succeeded in forcing Stelco to start hiring women, Bonita was one of the first to be taken on.[1] She was assigned to pump-tender duties in Stelco's power houses, given her previous training as a stationary engineer.

From the start, Bonita was subjected to continuous sexual harassment from her supervisors. She was followed around by one particularly obnoxious foreman who had the habit of physically grabbing parts of her upper body. When this eventually became too upsetting to ignore, Bonita reported him. But she had to face some horrible reprisals and harassment as a result. The foremen ganged up on her and tried to isolate and blackball her in the department – becoming uncooperative, spreading malicious rumors and telling co-workers not to talk to her.

Bonita was forced to transfer to another department where she earned less pay and had to endure worse conditions of work. There she was placed under the supervision of a foreman who constantly shouted that he hated women. Under protest, she had to enter the men's washroom to clean it. She had refused to do this because it increased her vulnerability, but was compelled to give in when management formally ordered her to do the work if she wanted to keep her job. When she complained about new incidents of sexual harassment, she was doubly victimized by being arbitrarily laid off work. She had to wage a difficult fight to get reinstated.

Supervisors refused to hear Bonita's complaints about safety hazards, leading in one instance to an explosion which demolished most of the power sub-station in which she worked. Later on, the company refused to provide her with protective equipment that would fit a woman, and she was injured as a result. The sexual harassment made it difficult for Bonita to learn on the job. The aggressive abuse and close scrutiny made her tense, and she often froze – unable to remember things or properly absorb what she was being told. This was made worse by the hope of many supervisors that she would not be able to do the work. They therefore told her as little as possible and often refused to give her information essential to perform the job.

Stelco is a giant, world-class corporation with considerable engineering expertise. However, it could not manage to construct adequate in-plant washrooms for the women who were hired after 1979. The facilities were usually overcrowded, in a state of permanent disrepair, lacking in sanitary supplies and with overflowing toilets. In Bonita's case, she had no access to an in-plant washroom but had to take a long, unpleasant walk outside, through hazardous conditions, to a women's trailer situated across a railway track. Her job involved the constant monitoring of equipment and therefore immediate availability in the event of a problem. Being outside the plant at the washroom was incompatible with her job duties.

The foremen used the washroom issue to get at Bonita, in order to make conditions so intolerable that she would quit and they would be rid of women forever. She was disciplined for not complying with supervisors' contradictory directions on washroom use. She was told to limit her use of the washrooms, and so could only go infrequently. Thus, she regularly had to wash her hands in the polluted sewers to get the tar and oils off. She developed bladder leakages and other problems as a result. She was once taken from the plant straight to the emergency ward of the hospital: she had started to hemorrhage but was not aware of the fact until too late as she had been unable to go to the washroom to check whether the moisture she felt beneath her coveralls was sweat or blood.

One of the most insidious effects of this campaign was the attack on her dignity and self-respect. By 1984, the company had laid off most of the new female workers and decided to increase the psychological assaults on Bonita in order to get rid of her as well. Every request she made to the supervisors, whether about a problem on the job or a safety hazard, was met with hostility and belligerence. This occurred continually, day in and day out. She was assigned to new job duties only to be refused training. She was disciplined for doing things that were tolerated of the men, like using the lab sink or reading a newspaper in the control room. She was insulted when she reported safety hazards from asbestos and silica. When Bonita complained about the pornography on the walls in November of 1984, she was laughed at by her supervisor. He then instructed that she would have to ask permission over the plant intercom when she wanted to go to the washroom in the future.

She was subjected to many other indignities and reprisals over the years at Stelco, too numerous to list here. As Bonita wrote in 1984:

> Stelco is simply waiting for the remaining women to quit – our morale destroyed by the conditions of employment ... My experience leads me to believe supervisory personnel are trying to make working conditions so difficult and uncomfortable, so damaging to one's self-respect and dignity, that one will eventually feel compelled to leave the department.

Working at Stelco had become an ordeal. The sexual harassment had taken its toll on Bonita's health: she couldn't sleep, had indigestion, cried at home, lost a lot of weight.

Like some of the other women hired at Stelco, Bonita had first tried to cope quietly and accommodate herself to conditions. When this failed to work, she began to file grievances and human-rights complaints, using the official channels. These got nowhere, the union dropped each of the grievances and the human-rights commission would not move on the charges.

The company, however, did not ignore Bonita's actions. In 1985, it responded to her complaints by dramatically escalating both the level of general harassment and formal discipline against her. The situation deteriorated to the point where Bonita realized that she either had to make some big new move or quit Stelco. She asserted her position: "I told my foreman that I had no intention of quitting. If I had to fight to survive, I would."

A "poisoned work environment"

And fight she did. In September of 1985, Bonita went public and filed a lengthy set of charges against Stelco. What is interesting here is the novel approach she took, an approach which may prove fruitful in the future for women in similar situations. The complaint listed all the instances of harassment, discipline, intimidation, discrimination and abuse over a seven-year period. It was filed under the Occupational Health and Safety Act, rather than the human-rights code or the labour-relations act. Bonita claimed that Stelco had created a "poisoned work environment" that was a hazard to her health; that the sexual harassment constituted a set of unhealthy working conditions and as such was a violation of the provincial safety legislation.[2]

The complaint had many facets to it. First, it alleged that the sexual harassment endangered her health as it led to headaches, nausea, intestinal ailments, weight loss and other symptoms. It ought to be treated no differently than exposure to other workplace hazards. If cleaning solvents can cause headaches and nausea, so can sexual taunts and grasping supervisors; sexual coercion can cause sleep loss and stomach problems just like exposure to leaded paints and other toxins. One of the body's responses to generalized stress is the production of anti-inflammatories. This may lead to decreased production of white blood cells which are an essential part of the body's immune system. The result can be a greater susceptibility to infectious diseases. While at Stelco, Bonita suffered from constant infections of her lungs and urinary tract, something she did not experience before or after working at Stelco. In addition, her specialist wrote that the body's stress response may well have been at the root of Bonita's infertility during this period.

Second, Bonita stated that there was a systematic pattern to the abusive treatment she received from supervisors over the years. This had to be considered apart from the individual incidents. It constituted the creation of a negative or poisoned work environment that made in-plant life unbearable for her and other women. The health hazard this posed included, first, the stress generated by the harassment and abuse, and, second, the potential harm caused by the lack of proper facilities for women, including protective equipment and adequate washrooms.

Finally, the complaint listed the many health-and-safety hazards she had reported which were not gender-specific, including exposure to carbon monoxide, danger from noise, hot metal cars, and chlorine; the unsafe handling of asbestos and silica dusts; and improper facilities for controlling explosive gases.

Ontario's safety law prohibits discipline against or intimidation of employees for reporting safety hazards. Bonita's complaint stated that she was the object of management threats and reprisals for reporting workplace hazards, which included both gender-specific complaints (for example, sexual harassment) and others (such as explosive gases). In other words, the harassment of women was presented not only as a hazardous condition in itself but also as a management reprisal for reporting other harmful conditions.

The complaint demanded a far-ranging series of remedies. These included a declaration by the tribunal that sexual harassment of women constituted a violation of the safety regulations, the enforcement of a policy on sexual harassment and pornography, the construction of indoor washroom facilities for women, a wholesale revision of the plant rules and safety regulations to meet the needs of women, and the disciplining of managers responsible for Bonita's mistreatment.

The Bonita Clark case stretched out over three years and attracted a great deal of public attention. She was represented by Mary Cornish, a labour lawyer and prominent women's-rights advocate. A network of labour activists helped sustain the case. Fund-raising appeals were launched by the women's movement and union federations.[3] The support was motivated by the precedent-setting nature of the complaint. Were sexual and gender harassment to be covered by the safety legislation, it would considerably strengthen women's hand in their fight for decent treatment. For instance: (i) they could invoke the right to refuse unsafe work, something which is granted in a number of jurisdictions in Canada; (ii) the safety legislation could be used to prosecute companies which tolerated harassment and environments detrimental to women; (iii) women's issues would become part of the regular agenda of the plant health-and-safety committees; (iv) women could call in government safety inspectors to order an end to objectionable conduct and conditions; (v) sexual harassment would be considered a compensatable injury under the workers compensation laws (and precedents now exist in Ontario, where women have won compensation for time taken off work as a result of workplace harassment). These new methods and forums would not replace the other avenues such as women's committees and human rights complaints; rather, they would complement them.

In defining harassment as a hazard, one doesn't have to prove that it has already caused the woman ill health, only that it has the *potential* to do this. The same applies to other hazards such as asbestos dust or shaky scaffolding: it is not necessary to wait until the worker is already injured or sick before declaring the problem a hazard. It only has to pose a threat to, or carry the possibility of harming, a worker to be so classified. Thus, if harassment is known to be potentially harmful to health, it can be considered a health hazard and covered by the safety legislation.

This approach has other benefits. By defining sexual harassment in a collective context, as the responsibility of the employer to maintain a safe work environment, it takes the issue beyond the context of individual relations between a woman and her harasser(s). Such a context has always served to make things difficult for and humiliating to women who complain. This new definition would make sexual harassment an adverse condition of work for which the employer is responsible, regardless of what the history of relations was between the specific individuals at issue. It would clearly hold employers liable for any poisoned work environments. If enforced, all of this would pressure employers to control harassing supervisors and to adapt working conditions to the needs of women employees.

This focus would clearly give women workers new weapons to wield and create new mechanisms of government enforcement. It would also make it easier for a union to take up women's complaints as standard trade-union issues. In unions dominated by men, it has always been difficult for women to have their concerns prioritized. This is in large part because traditional sexist attitudes have blinded many union men to the injustices experienced by their sisters in the shop. Defining sexual harassment as a health hazard helps to overcome this by taking it out of the realm of interpersonal relations and placing it squarely within a collective context: the harmful working conditions created by the employer. As such, the union has a clear obligation to its members so affected. It also has corrective actions available: for example, the grievance procedure, negotiating forms of protection in collective agreements, shop-floor actions, filing workers compensation claims, and raising issues at health-and-safety committees.

As to the difficult problem of co-worker harassment, the new definition would provide more satisfactory union responses because there exists a traditional way of dealing with the problem. The union would not try to be neutral and treat the harasser as a member whose right to union protection was equal to that of the harassed woman, as some unions have done. Rather the union would deal with him as unions have traditionally treated individualist members who insist on breaking the collective norm by working below the shop rate or violating the safety rules. On the shop floor and in the union hall, the membership would collectively pressure individuals who behave in a way that is harmful to other members.

Sexism and class experience

But there is more. Looking at anti-female harassment as a poisoned work environment can be a big step toward overcoming sexist attitudes amongst men in the workforce. From the beginning, many of us noticed that Bonita Clark's case was receiving a remarkably positive response from male industrial workers in Hamilton and elsewhere. This was partly because they admired someone who stood up to the monster corporation in a bold and daring manner; but it was also because of the unique way Bonita defined her experiences, a way that made many factory men see women's issues in a different light.

The complaint framed some of women's gender-specific grievances in terms of typical working-class experiences. It pointed to management's undermining of a worker's dignity and self-respect, and it labelled that as a poisoned work environment destructive of health. To do this is to address a concern close to the hearts of male workers, for it expresses a universal experience of class relations. It is something common to secretaries and stevedores, miners and mailhandlers, riveters and receptionists. (See Romero, Chapter 4 in this volume, for a discussion of struggle against similar class relations in a non-organizational setting.)

Working men are degraded and humiliated on the job in ways that are similar to the women's experiences described above. Some of it stems from their *powerlessness* in the shop, where management controls the work process and wage workers are simply objects to be used and abused in the drive for greater production. Their feelings, talents and health count for nothing compared to the pounding economic logic of the assembly line or the blast furnace, to which they must accommodate themselves or leave. They are subjected to perpetual speed-ups and job reorganizations designed to pump more production out quicker. The stress and tension which all this generates is often inhuman and unbearable – a work environment that is truly harmful to health, both mental and physical.

Related to this powerlessness is the *authority structure* which management installs in order to keep the system going. Working men are under the thumb of bosses and resent the disrespect and abuse they receive which is so much a part of everyday life on the shop floor. They are continually pushed and harassed by foremen, sometimes just to produce faster and sometimes to break their independence. Many industrial workers seethe against the bosses' bullying and complain of stress and tension. The poisoned work environment in an auto or steel plant often gets so foul and hateful that it is a struggle to turn up in the morning. Many end up taking pills and addicted to alcohol, unable to sleep, suffering migraines and upset stomachs, constantly feeling tense and irritable.

Some workers respond to this by becoming militant unionists – fighting to survive, in the words of Bonita Clark. Many choose to fight back in the shop in different ways. Others bow and scrape to the boss and later drown their tension in alcohol. Some scapegoat the less powerful by taking it out on the women, in their homes and elsewhere. Some combine all of these responses.

Although sexual harassment of women and class exploitation are qualitatively different, as pointed out above, there are enough similarities between class and gender experiences that working men can see the common interests they have with their sisters. Working in a plant is often a systematic assault on one's integrity as a person. How many self-respecting men feel that their dignity disappears the minute they enter the plant gate? How many have felt the degrading sting of coercion and intimidation? How many workers have become the object of supervisors' needling and harassment, designed to break their independence and undermine their integrity as human beings? How many have felt humiliated by the favours they had to give the boss to keep their jobs or gain promotion?[4]

Placing harassment in the context of a health-and-safety hazard clarifies the trade-union issues that are at stake. A working atmosphere that upsets employees, makes them tense, unable to eat and sleep, constantly on edge, induces headaches and weight loss, is an unsafe condition. It really doesn't matter whether this is caused by harassing supervisors or by exposure to lead fumes, by carbon monoxide gas or by continual speed-ups. In either case, the workplace is causing damage to health. And if the workplace atmosphere becomes so terrible that one is forced off work for a while in order to cope and recover, the compensation board ought to provide remuneration in the same way as when a knee injury or lung infection forces a worker off.

If this relation between occupational stress and health is plain to see, it is also easy to see when it is happening to women workers. The work environment can just as easily be poisoned by sexual and gender abuse as it can be by toxic substances: one can get headaches from breathing styrene vapour and from foremen who molest you; one can be nauseated by sexist derision as well as from pesticide dusts; one's personal equilibrium can be rattled by the sexual bullies or by ethylene oxide gas; one's sleep can be disrupted because of being exposed to sexual intimidation or to benzene emissions. In the above examples, an unhealthy workplace is victimizing employees, whatever the specific cause. The union's job is to force the employer to clean up the hazardous environment.

Solidarity

Defining sexual harassment as a health-and-safety hazard can help male workers see the common interests they have with their sisters against the boss. They are both subjected to a similar kind of degrading treatment, dished out by the same employer who is benefitting from their hardships. There is no good reason why workers of both sexes cannot unite as brothers and sisters to protect each other against something detrimental to their well-being. However, like race, gender divisions run deep, and one finds a wide diversity of responses within the workforce and within unions to gender issues. In some instances these divisions are handled very well, with solidarity all round. In other cases, the reverse is true. And with something this complex, class solidarity can take a very long time to develop, with many contradictory processes erupting along the way. The suggestion to frame sexual harassment in terms of health-and-safety hazards is simply one way to help workers and unions get a better grip on this issue than they have in the past.

The sexism that develops among working men is often at odds with their class consciousness and sense of solidarity. They have learned to survive in the face of superior forces by uniting against the boss. Part of this unity has been the insistence on the principle of equal treatment regardless of individual differences such as colour, size, age, religion, race, strength, and sex. The seniority system is one embodiment of this principle of intra-class equality and is the bedrock of union contracts.

Where unions have sometimes fallen down is when their equality principles developed a gender blindness or a double standard that tolerated the unequal and abusive treatment of their women members. This has been reinforced by the prevalence of traditional sexist attitudes and practices on the part of male members, often coexisting with union militancy. This is a battle which has to be waged, in part, within the male workforce by the non-sexist men in labour. I worked for eleven years at a Westinghouse factory in Hamilton, Ontario, where

I was union steward and safety representative. Elsewhere I have described the battles we engaged in to integrate women as equals on the shop floor (Gray 1987). One of the lessons that came out of that lengthy struggle was the need constantly to counterpose the class-based principles of equal treatment – as they are embodied in the seniority system, for example – to the chauvinist attitudes towards women held by many of our co-workers. The struggle was full of contradictions and setbacks but we found that, when pushed to the wall, class solidarity would usually triumph over individualist male chauvinism. We forged a better union as a result.

The same applies to fighting sexual harassment. To define this as a hazardous working condition or a poisoned work environment is to bring out what is common to the male and female workers. And to allow the boss to get away with victimizing women employees is to undermine the collective standards in health-and-safety and other areas, standards which protect everyone in the shop: "If you let them do it to the women, then nothing is going to stop them doing it to you" – the men. Pushing the issue in this manner may more easily elicit the solidarity responses of working men. It can help to provide common ground in an area that has divided workers for a long time.

Of course, Canadian women have not achieved what they have by waiting for the men to help them out. Rather, they effectively organized themselves and created new centres of power in the workforce and within unions. They built their own struggles and networks and forced through changes in the face of considerable opposition from employers and others. They used the power of their numbers in the electoral arena and the power of the law in the judicial arena. In doing all this and more, they have enriched the world of labour and taught some valuable lessons to everybody.

Still, the battle against sexist abuse in the workplace is one that concerns all of labour. The men have to take up that battle, first, in order to assist their sisters. Women are a part of the membership which the union is supposed to represent and protect. Women should not have to fight these battles on their own. And this obligation holds whether there are many or few women in the union: the labour movement was built on the premise that an injury to one is an injury to all. Second, men in labour also have to take up that battle in order to liberate themselves from the destructive effects male chauvinism can have for their collective strength and for themselves as individuals. Sexism has often served to confuse and misdirect working men. Some have attempted to compensate for their own powerlessness by exercising power over other individuals in the community. Robbed of their dignity and self-respect by a society which treats them like dirt, they get a false sense of manhood by lording it over the women. They play the foreman at home and oversee the wife and children. They try to restore their damaged dignity by controlling and victimizing women. Such men develop petty egos and false ideas of strength, seeking to regain their lost self-respect in ways that abuse others –

pushing women around, for example, and getting the edge over other men.

In the shop, such men have been individualist and competitive when what is needed is solidarity and a collective approach. They try to dominate and bully other workers. Such chauvinist attitudes have also led many male workers to self-destructive practices. There are workers who insist on proving their "manhood" by ignoring the safety rules at work. Like reckless driving, doing dangerous jobs somehow establishes one's masculine superiority. Male bragging and strutting often covers a deep-seated insecurity and fear of the authorities; it substitutes for seriously standing up to the employer – the real power holding them down. One often finds that macho men are the worst in currying favour with the bosses and ratting to them about other workers. When such chauvinists do fight the boss, it is often in a manner that is personalistic, competitive and petty – easily controllable and ultimately harmless to the boss, a lot of bark but little bite. I have also observed that companies recruit their foremen from amongst the most sexist of the males: their aggressiveness, egotistic ambition, and eagerness to backstab make them good supervisory material.

Factory labourers have often developed a male-oriented workplace culture, a traditional function of which has been to express community and solidarity with each other against the bosses. It celebrates their technical skills and physical strength, which they proudly contrast to the phoney and shallow polite society that lives off their daily sweat. This same shop-floor male bonding, however, has expressed hostility and vulgarity towards women. One's manhood is somehow confirmed in the baiting and degrading of women – in the mutual enjoyment of pornography, for example, or in the harassment of female employees.

Sexism has led many men to side with the bosses against their working-class sisters, and thereby undermine the quality of their trade unionism. Male-dominated unions have tolerated female job ghettoes and dual seniority lists. Men have sometimes fought to maintain the workplace as an all-male preserve, denying women jobs and seniority rights. They have often resisted equal pay and equal opportunity for women workers. On many occasions, male workers have scrapped their union principles of seniority and equal treatment in order to preserve their exclusive men's club at the workplace.

Sexism also drives men to establish competitive and power relations with others in their own community. It has been a source of weakness in the union hall as well as on the shop floor. If nothing else, male chauvinism is authoritarian and operates by intimidation. The boss mentality has led many union leaders to become petty tyrants, tightly controlling what ought to be open and democratic organizations. These labour patriarchs thereby stifle the true strength of a union, which is an active and mobilized rank and file.

Finally, sexism represents the opposite of solidarity and mutual respect. Sexist practices and culture have served to undermine the unity of working people and corrode the collective strength of labour. Like racism, sexism has deflected many men away from fighting their real enemies and from seeing the real source of their problems. It has made it easier for the corporations to get the upper hand and thereby drive down the working standards and living conditions of the whole labouring community.

As the recession takes its ever more devastating toll, employers and government try to divide workers against each other. They encourage the scapegoating of women and of people of other races, regions, colours and countries. In the face of all this, it is ever more important to stress what unites us while respecting these differences. Dropping the crutch of sexism will enable more workers to stand up as full human beings and fight to change the conditions that have kept them down. One big step in that direction is for more men to define sexual harassment as creating a hazardous working environment and to perceive their own interest in struggling against it. In fighting for the liberation of their sisters, working men will be fighting for their own liberation as well.

Postscript on the Clark case

As for Bonita Clark, she became a leader in the steel plant, elected by her co-workers as steward and safety representative. She became so adept at using the health-and-safety legislation to the advantage of the shop workers that management soon labeled her "Bill 70 Bonita," after Ontario's new safety law.

When her harassment case was launched, she became the object of respect and admiration throughout the steel mills and the community. Stelco dragged the case on for three years, hoping to win a war of attrition. Bonita's testimony on the witness stand was dramatic and stunning, as she recounted the horrible details of her seven-year ordeal. Stelco's lawyer cross-examined her for twelve full days, trying unsuccessfully to discredit her story. She was followed on the witness stand by a supportive male shop steward whose evidence was an eye-opener. He gave first hand testimony on the sexist hate campaigns instituted by the foremen, directly corroborating Bonita's evidence from his own experience. A settlement was eventually reached, with Stelco installing in-plant washrooms for women and negotiating a policy against sexual harassment. As lay-offs were devastating the Hamilton plant, Bonita took a financial settlement and has gone on to complete high school, college and is now in law school, training to become a human-rights lawyer.

Notes

1. Stelco's workforce was comprised primarily of a mixture of Canadian-born whites with workers of Italian, East European and British origin. Bonita Clark is a white woman from a mixed ancestry that includes native (aboriginal) members, as well as immigrants and Canadian-born.
2. The comprehensive complaint under the safety legislation was the primary avenue for Bonita's charges. For technical reasons, she also filed a parallel complaint under the labour relations act, maintaining her original charges under the human-rights code.
3. Bonita's own union, Local 1005 of the United Steelworkers of America, refused to pay for the case, as its leadership was split down the middle on the issue. While the Grievance Committee endorsed and signed the lesser charges under the labour relations act, the Local's Health and Safety Chairman refused to sign the main complaint under the safety legislation. The majority on the executive was hostile and would not allow the Local officially to support or represent Bonita at the hearings for any of the complaints. The reason for this was the male chauvinist attitudes rampant in many of the leadership, who were also concerned to maintain their friendly relations with Stelco management. These considerations overode any sense of obligation to one of their members victimized by the company.

A year and a half after the charges were laid and well after the case had become a popular one, the Steelworkers District Office endorsed a fund-raising appeal. Like the Local, however, it refused to sign the safety charges, represent Bonita or have the union cover her costs, including her time off from work to attend the hearings. Somewhat hypocritically, the District Office made its first offer to pay her future legal fees in 1988 *after* she had already made a settlement with Stelco – motivated in part by Bonita's financial destitution caused by three years of fighting the case by herself.

4. "The name of the game on the shop floor is humiliation: all workers are forced to endure degrading conditions, equally damaging to their health, to their pride. The guys are also treated like dirt by the foremen, and have to fight the same kind of thing I do." (Bonita Clark)
5. Stelco was compelled to opt for a settlement for a number of reasons. First, the dramatic facts brought out in weeks of testimony had put it in a very bad light both before the tribunal and the public. Second, the corporation was afraid that either the labour board or human-rights tribunal might eventually impose some form of anti-discrimination monitoring that would restrict its management prerogatives in the future. As for Bonita, the case had dragged on for three years without an end in sight. Her union was still refusing to sign the charges or pay for her lawyer, and the fund-raising efforts had not collected enough to continue. Finally, she faced an uncertain future at the plant because of lay-offs, even should she ultimately win the case.

References

Gray, Stan. 1987. "Sharing the Shop Floor." In *Beyond Patriarchy: Essays by Men on Pleasure, Power, and Change*, edited by M. Kaufman, pp. 216–34. Toronto: Oxford University Press.

6. Ethnic Identity and Feminism: Views from Leaders of African American Women's Associations

Bette J. Dickerson

Equity expectations and demands will very likely continue to generate competition, polarization and conflict among the various ethnic segments and between the genders in American society. One result is a growing demand on the leaders of women's voluntary associations to address and attempt to solve increasingly complex social problems because "when it comes to 'saving the world,' or a part of it ... women are the catalysts through whom the critical mass for social change will be achieved" (Aburdene and Naisbitt 1992: 265).

Patterns of ethnic and gender oppression in the United States present unique challenges to the capacity of African American women's associations to be catalysts of social change. In a "double bind" due to the dual disadvantages of ethnicity and gender, relatively little attention has been paid to the perspectives on the intersection of ethnicity and feminism that African American women hold. Hochschild asserted that this information vacuum was "the biggest blind spot in existing sociology" (1973 cited in Wilcox 1990a: 65). Herein lies a significant challenge to those who claim an interest in ensuring the equality of women of all ethnic groups in the United States.

Separating the influence of ethnicity from that of gender is often difficult, but by excelling in the face of these dual barriers, many African American women leaders provide models of tenacity, determination, and survival for both sexes of all ethnic groups. As models, these women furnish some hope for success in reducing ethnic and gender cleavages and conflicts. Yet, collaborative efforts with such individuals and the groups they lead remain a relatively under-utilized resource in the continuing struggle against those structural obstacles which emerge from institutional discrimination.

---

* This chapter is based on an essay developed for the Delta Research and Educational Foundation project, "Models for Community Appplication: Experiences from African American Women's Associations."

African American women have tended to develop their own women's-rights agendas within their own associations, distinct from those of European American women (Smith 1985; Giddings 1984). However, their perspectives on the intersection of their understanding of ethnicity with their feminist views have not received sufficient empirical analysis because most of the contemporary research on feminism has centered on the experience of European American women. This has, however, left a major gap in our understanding of African American women's orientation toward feminism (Wilcox 1990b). The need for clarity is critical if the capabilities of African American women leaders and the groups over which they have authority are to be effectively mobilized to address the critical social problems stemming from racism and sexism.

The purpose of this chapter is to explore the views of leaders of African American women's associations regarding ethnic identity and feminism, and to achieve a better understanding of the constructed realities of ethnicity and gender within which these women function. Such information is particularly important because the success of the feminist movement may depend on its ability to become more inclusive, to understand better and respond to diversity, and to develop more effective collaboration on programs and advocacy. After a brief discussion of the important place of voluntary associations in African American communities, I attempt to close the gap in understanding the intersection of ethnic identity and feminism among African American women through an analysis of the views of leaders of African American women's associations.

Voluntary associations in the African American community

Voluntary associations develop out of the shared interests and concerns of individuals and are "social groups organized for the purpose of reaching one or more goals through cooperative, normatively integrated activity" (Lopata 1964: 120). They are at the very core of democratic freedom, occupying a stratum between the individual and the state, between primary groups, such as the family, and politically organized or recognized powers, such as government. Because of their capacity to advance group issues and interests through collective resources and effort, they are primary agents of group mobilization in society (Dickerson 1986; and, for an analysis of the failure of government policies to respond to poor families, see Brewer, Chapter 7 in this volume). Community functions performed by socializing agents such as voluntary associations include: (i) socialization, which refers to the transmission of basic values and behavioral patterns to the individual members; (ii) social control, which is the structural arrangement for influencing members toward behavioral conformity; (iii) social participation, which refers to those structures which facilitate incorporation into the organization by virtue of opportunities for participation in its life; and (iv) mutual support, which describes the process of care and exchanges for help among the members of a group, especially in times of stress (Warren 1972 cited in Blackwell 1975:17)

The existence of racial-group polarization, categorical group treatment, and social-mobility constraints in the United States have led to greater solidarity, commonality of beliefs, and "racial common fate identification" among African Americans. "Racial common fate identification" means that one has made a conscious decision to identify with a group with which one shares a common history, kinship, and destiny. This belief in group fate undergirds the belief held by African Americans that a collective effort is most effective in bringing about social change (Jackson 1991). The subordinate status of African Americans, the belief in group fate, and the "ingroupness" which flows from frequent patterns of association, create the need for and the conditions of group-based resource mobilization. One outcome is that African Americans have tended to hold memberships in voluntary associations more often than other ethnic groups in the United States (Dickerson 1986).

Historically, African American women's associations have been a primary source of leadership development for women. Such associations have been vital to the advocacy and action taken on both ethnic and women's issues (Noble 1978; Giddings 1984; Davis 1981). They comprise formalized mechanisms through which the relationships, interaction, support, energy, resources, plans, projects, and philosophies of female leaders and their predominantly female followers work collectively toward meeting needs and achieving goals (Davis 1984). Concerted mutual action to achieve common goals was a unifying characteristic of the first African American women's associations, and accountability to the African American community was essential to their survival (Giddings 1984). Such associations provided settings for social intercourse, recreation, cooperative assistance, solace, and work on the problems which affected African Americans (Giddings 1984; Noble 1978). And they provided opportunities to learn and apply the skills needed for survival in the face of racist and sexist oppression, such as how to mobilize and organize and how to be effective leaders *and* followers. These "how to" features of African American women's associations shared the potential to develop means of empowerment through mutual cooperation (Johnson 1980).

An African American women leaders study

This chapter is based on information from a session of the workshop "Leadership Models for Community Applications: Experiences from African American Women's Associations," held in the spring of 1992. The workshop was part of the The African American Women's Associations Leadership Project which was developed and implemented by the Delta Research and Educational Foundation through a grant from the W.K. Kellogg Foundation. The project was designed to bring together women leaders from African American women's associations for four objectives: to provide new insight into leadership development among African American women, to examine traditional models and definitions of leadership, to identify challenges to traditional assumptions based upon their own leadership experiences, and to generate information for actual use in addressing community problems.

One of the workshop sessions, "Influences of Gender and Race," is the source of the information discussed in this paper. The workshop was designed as an inductive inquiry in which participants engaged the learning experience with minimal pre-given structure or expectations. A set of guiding questions moved the discussion toward the general theme and the specific topics. Additional questions and insights emerged out of the workshop session which was guided by a mini-lecture and followed by round-table discussions. A series of simulation exercises were used to initiate the group conversations and to stimulate critical reflections on individual experiences.

The participants and the participatory research strategy

The sample consisted of the twenty-two leaders of African American women's associations, representing eleven associations, participating in The African American Women's Organization Leadership Project.[1] Each leader completed a pre-workshop survey which requested data on the respective association's history, membership, structure, and current programs as well as personal thoughts on and experiences of leadership. The survey data revealed that, together, these associations encompassed over one million members, many possessing international chapters. Despite the breadth of missions and programmatic activities, all share a commitment to improving the quality of life of people of African descent and to contributing to the overall welfare of the larger society.

Fifteen of the leaders indicated that their associations have influence over African American females between the ages of 12 and 14. Nine indicated that their associations have an extensive influence over African American males. Half indicated that their associations have extensive influence over Black civil rights groups, while the remaining half claimed to have moderate influence. Thirteen indicated that their influence on low-income African American women is extensive. Although led by, predominantly composed of, and organized to address the needs of women, some of the associations admitted men as affiliate or associate members, or existed as auxiliary associations to African American associations predominantly composed of men. Although their programs targeted concerns and groups of people of African descent, some have members of other ethnic groups. In some cases, the participating groups are organizational members of formal African American alliances purposefully established for the collaborative attainment of specific shared goals (National Leadership Forum, National Pan-Hellenic Council).

The leaders of African American women's associations were especially knowledgeable, insightful, and perceptive regarding the dynamics of their respective associations. All were involved in service to their communities, broadly or narrowly defined, and were representative of the diversity of personal backgrounds, organizational missions, and programmatic activities reflected in African American women's associations. It was not unusual to find interlocking memberships and leadership (for example, members of one group who also hold membership or leadership positions in one or more of the other associations). And fourteen of the leaders responded that their associations prepare members to be leaders and consist of individuals who serve in a variety of leadership capacities in other associations and communities.

A participatory action research design was best suited for addressing the project objectives because members of the group under study were expected to be actively involved with the professional researchers throughout the process of searching for information and ideas to guide future actions. This research approach contrasts sharply with more conventional approaches in which researchers serve as experts, designing the project, gathering the data, interpreting the findings, and recommending action (Whyte 1991).

The workshop convenors acted less as disciplinary experts and more as facilitators to ensure optimum involvement and open contributions in order to mobilize as much relevant expertise as possible from each participant. We discussed with the participants what we were trying to find out about leadership in African American women's associations and also consulted with them about how to interpret the findings. We engaged in dialogue with the participants, listening and sharing individual and common experiences, insights, and emotions about leadership.

As the project's Leadership Theory Consultant, one of my responsibilities, prior to the workshop, was to review the scholarly literature on the characteristics and practices of leadership by African American women in organizational settings. I found that topics needing further study included: definitions and dimensions of leadership, demographics of African American women leaders, leadership selection, influences of gender and race, leadership roles and responsibilities, leadership empowerment for participation in social change, and developing, nurturing and rewarding leadership. The use of workshop facilitating techniques, simulation exercises, and workbook materials transformed the scholarly treatments of the topics into forms appropriate to a participatory workshop setting. In addition, a series of self- and group-affirming litanies that stimulated critical reflection and initiated group conversations were read in unison at the beginning and end of each day.

Throughout the workshop, the leaders were encouraged to respond openly and critically to previous study findings and to share in identifying factors affecting leadership. The participants thus became active co-researchers in the inquiry process as all participated fully in this reciprocal, reflexive group conversation in a collaborative effort to better understand African American women's leadership experience. In this context, "reflexive" refers to the understanding that "all manner of describing, analyzing, questioning, criticizing ... are ... tied to the social settings ... in which they are situated" (Wolf 1979 cited in King and Mitchell 1990: 10). Through the group-conversation method, the participants and the workshop facilitators together became more critically aware of the collective experience through the reflexive examination of their own reality.

The group-conversation method, a qualitative strategy which centers social inquiry in the perspectives and experiences of the participants, relies on "talkin' and testifyin'," key educative and spiritual elements in the African and African American community (King and Mitchell 1990). These traditional oral communicative forms have served very important, interactive and spiritual functions in African life and socialization. The spoken word in African community life has always been the major means for communicating history, values, and ideas. The role of the spoken word as a principal cultural transmitter continues to flourish among people of African descent. Through factual story-telling, individuals became documents in themselves – sharing past experiences so that their lessons could be understood and appreciated in preparation for the future (Leslie 1991). Speaking and listening to each other's stories generates knowledge about the collective condition and produces insights needed to understand and effectively respond to the collective condition. This oral-data-collection approach engages participants in a mutual search for collective understanding and affirms the communality of the African American experience. It is empowering in its aim to contribute to social problem-solving by creating the conditions necessary for the research-ers to learn, with the participants, about what "we" do and to reflect on why "we" do it in preparation for what "we" will do (King and Mitchell 1990).

The participants were divided into five small groups to reach consensus in their views and obtain responses to the research questions. The group conversation, which lasted three hours, was structured so that participants sat in a circle and took turns responding to the five questions. Comparisons were drawn between personal experiences of leadership and the literature selections. This permitted participants to compare their personal experiences to the collective "Black Experience" as reflected in the literature and to consider the extent to which the literature reflected their experiences. The small group responses were then presented to the full group for consensual endorsement.

Along with participants' views on leadership, the following questions were among those examined in the workshop and are the focus of this paper:

1. What are African American women's association leaders' definitions of and perspectives on ethnic identity, feminism, African feminism movements?
2. How do the leaders perceive their leadership roles and responsibilities to ethnic identity, feminist, and African feminist movements?
3. What do the leaders perceive to be their primary responsibility among competing ethnic identity, feminist and African feminist issues?
4. Which of the following do the leaders consider to be the primary factor for which they are held accountable by their followers: their stance against racist or against sexist oppression?
5. What are the leaders' perspectives on developing coalitions and alliances with predominantly European American feminist associations?

Views of leaders of African American women's associations

Leadership

In contrast to influencing through the exercise of informal persuasion, leaders of voluntary associations have the authority through legitimated and institutionalized channels to influence and, in many cases, to determine action. Thus, the leader role deserves special attention because the process of group mobilization is greatly affected by the leadership phenomenon. Since organizational leaders can, and do, make a difference, it would be unwise to treat the leadership role as "just" another role within the group, having no particular conceptual interest.

One definition of leadership is the "process of influencing the activities of an organized group in its efforts toward goal setting and goal achievement" (Stodgill 1950 cited in Holloman 1984: 110). The idea of "power to influence behavior" dominates traditional understandings of leadership, but the understandings offered by leaders of African American women's associations focused on "collective responsibility." A leader: "empowers others to exert creativity in completing goals of the organization and, as a result, the organization continues to gain strength and build stronger leaders for tomorrow; and continues to *bring someone else along.*"

The leaders perceived themselves as responsible to both their respective organizations and to the larger community: "We are social activists with a continuing and changing social agenda determined by the needs of our communities and our organizational base." Reflecting two factors identified in an assessment of African American leadership – the leader's recognition of unmet social needs and the persistence of inequity in the distribution of opportunities (Thompson 1963) – the participants also felt that leaders must "remain in touch with the present environment; and remain aware of community service needs."

One function of the leadership role in associations includes maintaining a reciprocal relationship with the members. Groups which are oppressed, exploited, and alienated from those societal institutions that determine their quality of life require a specific kind of leadership. According to Hamilton (1981), such leaders face the formidable task of meeting goals of social change and redistribution of power and resources while leaders of dominant groups strive to manage resources and opportunities in order to maintain the status quo. Thus, for leaders of African American women's associations, "Primary responsibilities are predetermined by the organizational goals and the problems dictated by society."

Members are aware of and motivated by a problem, policy, condition, or need which influences the quality of life. Therefore they respond to and voluntarily follow the direction determined by (or mutually arrived at with) leadership, provided leaders identify and respond to the problems and needs and develop, implement, and evaluate probable solutions (Burns 1978). When faced with competing ethnicity and gender issues, the leaders considered the mission of the group which hired or voted for them. They felt that, ultimately,

> [leaders of African American women's associations] are held accountable to their followers for their stance against racist oppression ... Although the racist oppression stance would be priority, leaders would certainly sensitize their members to the feminist struggle and sexist oppression. This will enable them to focus on those feminist issues which most affect them as African American women.

Another function of the leadership role is to establish coalitions and alliances when necessary. For many African American women leaders, the creation of such networks has been as important a survival strategy as establishing self-reliance imperatives (Terborg-Penn 1987). Coalitions are those short-term working associations based on specific short-term goals. An alliance, on the other hand, is a long-term ongoing unity based on common interests and common basic principles (Karenga 1989). The leaders felt that coalitions were important for addressing major social issues which affect large segments of the population but said that relatively few *alliances* had been formed out of issue-specific coalescing: "[We] build coalitions with feminist associations focusing on issues revolving around the socioeconomic [for example]; however, few alliances have been formed on this issue [of racist oppression]."

Karenga (1989) found that for most African American associations alliances are usually ingroup first (that is, among the same racial/ethnic group) and then extended among others whose long-term goals and principles coincide with those of the ingroup. For alliances to be effective, clear principles must be established and observed: (i) mutual respect for each people's political, economic and cultural interests; (ii) non-interference in each other's internal affairs; (iii) a clear conception of each other's interests; (iv) independent power bases; (v) a clear conception of possibilities and problems in unity; (vi) clear and concrete goals around which to unify; (vii) a clear statement and agreement on principles of cooperation; and (viii) a clear statement and agreement on methods of cooperation and struggle (Karenga, 1989). Some of the principles are implicit in the following comment:

> Focus on certain issues can be different, for example latchkey children. [This] is not such a problem for them [European American women]. There exists a different ranking of what the specific issues should be. The particular focus on some issues can be different (for example, latchkey children) but the overall issue could still be the major agenda item.

The failure to distinguish between "alliance" and "coalition" has created situations in which too much was assumed about the relationship between coalition partners, leaving the respective associations vulnerable to joint actions not mutually beneficial, and to withdrawal of expected support at crucial times (Karenga 1989). "All too frequently, coalitions involving Black people have been only at the leadership level, dictated by terms set by others, and for objectives not calculated to bring major improvements in the lives of the Black masses" (Carmichael and Hamilton 1967: 59–60). This is problematic in at least two ways: it has led to a confusion of patronage with coalition or alliance; it has tended to encourage denial and reductive translation of African Americans' contribution to their own struggle (Karenga 1989). Thus the experience of leaders of African American women's associations has been that:

> [Our] level of involvement [when developing coalitions] is restricted. Planning is usually defined by European American feminist associations. They make you think that you are part of the process but you really are not ...

> Generally we have not been included on their [European American feminist associations'] agenda. They have defined it for us. Their agenda is not necessarily our agenda. If we have an idea that is worthwhile feminist groups will snatch it and run it [without including us].

Ethnicity
Milton Gordon (1964 cited in Davis 1992: 147) describes ethnicity as a "shared feeling of peoplehood," "a special sense of both ancestral and future-oriented identification" and an "indissoluble and intimate identity" with

a given group. Ethnic groups are social groups whose members tend to interact with one another and share a consciousness of kind. Real or presumed ancestry is the criterion by which an individual's group membership is decided, and central to an ethnic group's self definition is a sense of a common history which sets it apart from others (Alba 1990). Identifying with a specific ethnic group implies particular beliefs, attitudes, or history with which others of that group can identify (Mays 1986). Thus social and historical developments play a primary role in the determination of ethnic identity. Given the amalgamation that forms their ethnic make-up, the leaders of African American women's associations could select among the various identities associated with their backgrounds, and even create new ones if they wished. However, they consciously prioritized the choices, selected their African heritage and felt that other African American women would make the same choice: "Looking at question one and Black women's analysis of their ethnic identity, there were strong feelings that for the most part Black women identity with their African heritage, not with their Indian or their white heritage." Despite national trends which reduce the structural connections among persons of the same ethnic background, ethnic identity serves as a basis of solidarity when its salience for the individuals is great. The leaders of African American women's associations proudly acknowledged their common ethnic background and its relevance to many social situations and asserted: "We identify with being of African origin."

Most of the African American women's associations were founded as solidarity ethnic groups. These groups consist of self-conscious members who interact with each other to achieve common purposes. The solidarity notion implies not simply the recognition of some distinction between ingroup and outgroup but an awareness of something shared by members and a requirment of their mutual cooperation. It is the awareness of being bound together by a common fate, of suffering discrimination in common; an awareness of shared interests, such as furthering the advancement of the group and thus its individual members; and the valuing of a heritage the group wishes to perpetuate (Alba 1990). The leaders acknowledged the existence of a distinct African American ethnic group within the larger pluralist society: "We do not see African Americans as competing with other ethnic identities ... because of our uniqueness."

According to Alba (1990), in order for ethnic identity to have social, as opposed to merely personal significance, it must be linked to activities which have an ethnic character. African American women's associations link ethnic identity and behavior. For example, the leaders considered organizational observances of events such as Martin Luther King, Jr.'s birthday, Black History Month, and Kwanzaa very important. They provided examples of organization-sponsored activities to illustrate the high levels of ethnic identity. These included:

the naming of our associations (for example, National, Black, Women), special events regarding our history (for example, historical exhibit of black nurses, African ceremonies), attention to Black books and literature (sponsorship of book fairs, especially for children), ethnic foods and dances at our affairs ...

Throughout the group conversation, there were references to "our community," and experiences were shared in which the needs of the community were often more important than those of the individual. According to Blackwell (1975: 16) the concept "community" refers

to the role of shared values in creating a sense of identity with a particular group that may or may not live within the same geographic boundary. People are brought together in community because they happen to share common interests and values. They have accepted sets of definitions of situations, life experiences, or other conditions that give them a uniqueness apart from others whose views, values, and experiences are dissimilar.

When probed, the leaders presented a generalized belief in a distinct ethnic group consisting of African Americans. The ethnic group identification of leaders of African American women's associations can, therefore, be influential in shaping their ideologies. An ideology based on ethnic identity consists of a "consciousness of kind," a collective sense of community and identity. This demonstrates that, despite class diversity, African Americans still find themselves in what Thomas C. Shelling aptly describes as "the same boat together" (1960 cited in Blackwell 1975: 16) which maintains a sense of ethnicity and community.

Feminism
According to Webster's Dictionary, feminism is a doctrine for the attainment of social, political, and economic rights for women equal to men. The concept is also used to refer to the social "movement to end sexism and sexist oppression" (hooks 1989: 23). Some have expanded the definition to encompass the struggle for total liberation which must exist as part of the larger struggle to eradicate domination in all its oppressive forms. Hooks (1981: 195) states that "to be 'feminist' in any authentic sense of the term is to want for all people, female and male, liberation from sexist role patterns, domination, and oppression."

Despite the fact that relatively few African American women are in the forefront of feminist associations, African American women have been found to support feminist goals (Reid 1984). Using data from a national survey of African Americans in 1980, Wilcox explored the determinants of feminism among African American women. His findings indicated strong support for feminism among African American women. The leaders of African American women's associations agreed that the "goals of feminism are generally acceptable" and considered the primary goal to be "to end the sexist oppression of women." They felt they demonstrated their feminism by the fact that "we are continuing to assert our [woman] leadership in our communities, first, and emerging as [woman] leaders in the larger community."

The role African American women should take in the feminist movement, however, has long been a matter of debate, and a recurring theme is the relative lack of participation by African American women. Tensions have been created because many African American women feel European American women have been partners in the racist oppression of both African women and men. Such feelings were reflected in the leaders' response: "Feminism is not or never has been a choice for the African American women. Until we are treated equally according to race we cannot deal [fully] with the issue of gender."

The matter is confounded by the evolution of the United States' women's movement, which has historically been the preserve of European American women. European American suffragists, for example, excluded African American women from playing a major role in the struggle for sexual equality despite the fact that African American women had long been fighting for both ethnic and gender equality (Davis 1981; Giddings 1984). The contributions of African American women to the women's rights movement have been generally overlooked or marginalized, at best. "The domination of white women in the feminist struggle is less a sign of black female disinterest than an indication that the politics of colonization and racial imperialism have made it historically impossible for black women in the U.S. to lead a women's movement" (hooks 1981: 161). The critical importance of ending this domination has begun to be accepted among European American feminists, as the narrative by white feminist Kathryn Ward (Chapter 12 in this volume) illustrates.

Black feminism

Some African American women feel that "feminism is really 'a white female thing that has nothing to do with black women'" and advocate a separate Black feminist consciousness (hooks 1989: 179). King (1988: 58) states that "the assumption that the family is by definition patriarchal, the privileging of an individualistic world-view, and the advocacy of female separation are often antithetical positions to many of the values and goals of black women and thus are hindrances to our association with feminism." Among the leaders of African American women's associations there was resistance to the term "feminism." They perceived and asserted differences between African American women and European American women in needs, values, and relationships with men. Their attitudes were captured in the following group response:

> [We] do not buy into the process or version of white women's movement [that is, to] separate from men. It was felt that for some African American women

the word "feminism" connotes [either] "not being feminine or loving other women" [lesbianism].

Some scholars argue that African American women's political and economic status provides them with different experiences which offer a distinct point of view that is not available to women of other ethnic groups. Collins (1989: 770), for example, states that "living life as an African-American woman is a necessary prerequisite for producing Black feminist thought because ... thought is validated and produced with reference to a particular set of ... epistemological conditions." As to the uniqueness of the experience of leaders of African American women's associations, compared to their European American counterparts, they felt they were frequently perceived as being stronger – as having more insights; as having the impetus for change; required to fight both racism and sexism; and as nurturing leaders compelled to assist in the development as males and females of their peers, family members, and the community's youth.

While African American women arguably can develop both a racial and a feminist consciousness because their own experiences are different from those of white feminists, they may seek to develop a uniquely Black feminist perspective (Wilcox 1990a). This view was supported by the leaders of African American women's associations who voiced a need for "efforts to determine our own 'word' instead of accepting one with so much baggage [attached to it]."

Black feminist scholars are having an impact on this hitherto European American-dominated area, with perspectives which exhibit multiple influences. The very concept of feminism, for example, is often qualified to allow for specific race/ethnicity and cultural considerations, and the result, Black feminism, is the combination of Black womens' and feminist concerns. A concept preferred by some is "womanist," defined as "a black feminist, or feminist of color ... committed to survival and wholeness of entire people, male and female ... [but who] loves herself" (Walker 1983: xi–xii). Significantly, this conception acknowledges the dual allegiance to both Black liberation and to women's emancipation. After considering the definitions of womanist and feminist, the leaders of African American women's associations found the meaning of "womanist" more acceptable and felt that "more African American women's groups subscribe to this concept, even to the point of denying our gender oppression."

In Filomina Steady's comprehensive introduction to *The Black Woman Cross-Culturally* (1981), she states that Black feminism includes such components as female autonomy and cooperation, the centrality of children, and multiple mothering and kinship. Steady also incorporates the socioeconomic and class factors which contribute to Black women's oppression, exploitation, and marginalization, as well as their self-reliant responses. The foundation is the need to liberate Black peoples from neo-colonialism and other forms of race and class oppression, coupled with a respect for certain features of traditional African cultures. The leaders reviewed and accepted the many facets of the term "Black feminism" as specified by Davies and Graves (1986: 8–11):

a. The recognition of a common struggle with African men for the removal of the yokes of racist domination and exploitation. It is not antagonistic to African men but, rather, challenges them to acknowledge the unique aspects of women's subordination.
b. The recognition that certain gender inequities and limitations existed before colonialism and that colonialism reinforced them and introduced others.
c. The recognition that African women have addressed the problems of women's position in society historically and that there have existed, in some societies, structures which gave women equality prior to the colonial and post-colonial period.
d. An examination of African societies for institutions which are of value to women and does not simply accept European American women's agendas.
e. Respect for African women's self-reliance and the tendency for cooperative work and social organization and the historic fact that African women have seldom been financially dependent but instead accept income-generating work as a fact of life. It rejects, however, the often accompanying exploitation and discrimination.
f. The interconnectedness of race, class, and gender oppression.
g. African women telling their own story.

The leaders acknowledged that a feminist consciousness was vital to the critical examination of the status of African American women and to their role in US society. They felt this consciousness was particularly essential because of the fine line they tread between collective responsibility to combat group oppression and the denial of one's personal oppression: "[We] tend to put our gender issues on the back burner."

The leaders of African American women's associations also felt that the very survival of the African American community depended on a serious assessment of the status of African American women. However, just as Gray (Chapter 5 in this volume) makes the case for solidarity between *working class* women and men, they considered it vital that such analysis occur in conjunction with African American men. As they put it, "[We] must deal with [these] issues in our communities with our men," thereby affirming Angela Davis's assertion, "We must strive to 'lift as we climb'... and indeed all of our brothers must climb with us" (1989 cited in Collins 1990: 158).

Conclusions

Residing in a society stratified by ethnicity and gender, African American women weave their way through a labyrinth of discriminatory obstacles. This chapter has explored perspectives on ethnicity and gender held by African American women leaders in formal organizational settings, a group ignored by previous researchers (Collins 1990). The methodology attempted to narrow the distance between the researcher and the subjects. The research model was based on the wisdom, knowledge, and direct experience of the leaders themselves without any need for ratification by outside experts.

The group did not consider ethnicity and gender as a dichotomous, either/or issue, but rather as intersecting structures used for oppression. At the center of their analysis was the shared view that racism *and* sexism are both powerful determinants of African American women's status in American society.

Ethnicity still shapes African American life in the United States and heightens the level of "racial common fate identification." Although the effects of ethnic discrimination are deeply felt and constantly challenged, for the leaders of African American women's associations racism is not a solely personal problem. Their struggle is for ethnic group survival, cultural retention and transmission, and ethnic group empowerment. Thus the systemic, structural dimensions of ethnicity must be considered when examining African American women's feminist consciousness, and the significance of ethnicity should not be obscured when creating the feminist coalitions that are crucial for institutional transformation.

The leaders of African American women's associations may not have labelled themselves as "feminists", but when feminist issues were discussed, consensus prevailed around the significant contribution of sexism to their subordinate status and the need for equity. They expressed high levels of support for and had involvement in pro-feminist issues and were trying to realize many of the general goals of feminism within their specific ethnic context. The leaders refuted the generally held assumption that, by focusing on racial oppression, they place less emphasis on sexism.

The vision of feminism which the leaders of African American women's associations share is one which unites women and men. In their view, it is essential for African American women to work with African American men, as equal partners, in addressing feminist issues and in bringing shared perspectives to the debates on issues such as sexual harassment and gender roles in family life. They recognize the challenges and obstacles to the intense dialogue required but feel the task should no longer be avoided because ethnic group survival is at stake.

Finally, the leaders of African American women's associations envision a more inclusive definition of feminism which understands, acknowledges, and respects cultural diversity. The following litany used during the project workshop aptly captures the essence of their motivation and determination:

> We look forward to the future in faith and hope, working for the day when we and all our sisters no longer have to fit a stereotype, but are free to use all our gifts to share in all of the benefits of human life and work. We believe that all the forces for good, love, peace, and justice and all the creative powers of the universe work with us to achieve that vision.

Notes

1. The following associations were represented:

Alpha Kappa Alpha Sorority, Inc. An international public-service organization founded in 1908 whose program emphases include education, health, economics, the Black family, the arts, and the world community.

AME Women's Missionary Society An international religious organization established to help women and youth grow in the knowledge and experience of God, founded under the aegis of the African Methodist Episcopal Church that was founded in 1796.

Chi Eta Phi Sorority Inc. An international organization of professional nurses founded in 1932 to: (i) develop a corps of nursing leaders; (ii) encourage continuing education; (iii) conduct continuous recruitment for nursing and health professions; (iv) stimulate close and friendly relations between members; and (v) develop working relationships with other professional groups.

Delta Sigma Theta Sorority, Inc. An international public-service sorority founded in 1913 to develop programs which address issues in the areas of economics, education, international awareness and involvement, physical and mental health, and political awareness.

The Links, Inc. An international organization founded in 1946 and committed to educational, civic and intercultural activities through its program facets: The Arts, Services to Youth, National Trends and Services, and International Trends and Services.

National Association of Colored Women's Clubs A national organization founded in 1896 and dedicated to "raising to the highest plane home life, moral standards and civic life of the Black race" and to be "a potent force in the development of social institutions in the Black community and in the woman suffrage and other political movements."

National Association of Negro Business and Professional Women Clubs, Inc. An international organization founded in 1935 to: (i) improve the quality of life in the community; (ii) create an atmosphere in which Black women are able to bring about meaningful change in their public and private lives; (iii) present positive models to young women in their community; (iv) share skills and knowledge with others; and (v) explore alternative ways for women to meet the multiple challenges of today's world.

The Young Adult Club of the National Association of Negro Business and Professional Women Clubs, Inc. — See the immediately preceding organization statement.

National Black Women's Health Project An international organization founded in 1984 and committed to improving the overall health status of Black women through self-help and advocacy programs.

Progressive National Baptists Convention Women's Department An international organization founded in 1962 to address educational, social, national and international issues with a deep Christian emphasis that focuses on women's concerns.

Sigma Gamma Rho Sorority, Inc. An international public-service organization founded in 1922 to encourage academic achievement, nurture talents and promote community involvement.

Zeta Phi Beta Sorority, Inc. An international organization founded in 1920 to promote education by: encouraging the highest standards of academic achievement; supporting worthwhile college and community projects; providing training, scholarships, counseling services and grants; and by implementing improvement in every area of community life through programs and volunteer services.

References

Aburdene, Patricia, and John Naisbitt. 1992. *Megatrends for Women*. New York: Villard Books.
Alba, Richard D. 1990. *Ethnic Identity: The Transformation of White America*. New Haven: Yale University Press.
Aptheker, Herbert. 1971. *Documentary History of the Negro in the United States*. Vol. 1 . New York: Citadel Press.
Blackwell, James E. 1975. *The Black Community: Diversity and Unity*. New York: Harper & Row.
Burns, James McGregor. 1978. *Leadership*. New York: Harper & Row.
Canady, Hortense. 1985. "Black Women Leaders: The Case of Delta Sigma Theta." *The Urban League Review* 9: 92–95.
Carmichael, Stokely, and Charles Hamilton. 1967. *Black Power*. New York: Random House.
Collins, Patricia Hill. 1989. "The Social Construction of Black Feminist Thought." *Signs* 14: 745.
Collins, Patricia Hill. 1990. *Black Feminist Thought*. Boston: Unwin Hyman.
Davis, Angela Yvonne. 1981. *Women, Race, and Class*. New York: Random House.
Davis, King E. 1984. "The Status of Black Leadership: Implications for Black Followers in the 1980s." In *Contemporary Issues in Leadership*, edited by William E. Rosenbach and Robert L. Taylor, pp.192–208. Boulder: Westview Press.
Davis, Richard A. 1992. "Black Ethnicity: A Case for Conceptual and Methodological Clarity." *The Western Journal of Black Studies* 16: 147–51.
Dickerson, Bette Jeanne. 1986. *Demographic Characteristics Affecting the Voluntary Organization Memberships of Black Americans*. Ann Arbor: University Microfilms International.
Dumas, Rhetaugh Graves. 1980. "Dilemmas of Black Females in Leadership." In *The Black Woman*, edited by La Frances Rodgers-Rose, pp.203–15. Beverly Hills: Sage Publications.
Giddings, Paula. 1984. *When and Where I Enter: The Impact of Black Women on Race and Sex in America*. New York: Bantam Books.
Hamilton, Charles V. 1981. "On Black Leadership." In *The State of Black America*, edited by Robert Hill, pp.1–59. New York: The National Urban League.
Hill-Davidson, Leslie. 1987. "Black Women's Leadership: Challenges and Strategies." *Signs* 12: 381–5.
Holloman, Charles R. 1984. "Leadership and Headship: There is a Difference." In *Contemporary Issues in Leadership*, edited by William E. Rosenbach and Robert L. Taylor, pp.109–16. Boulder: Westview Press.
hooks, bell. 1981. *Ain't I a Woman: Black Women and Feminism*. Boston: South End Press.
hooks, bell. 1989. *Talking Back: Thinking Feminist, Thinking Black*. Boston: South End Press.
hooks, bell. 1991. *Yearning: Race, Gender, and Cultural Politics*. Boston: South End Press.
Hope, Richard O. 1980. "Patterns of Black Leadership." In *Black Organizations: Issues on Survival Techniques*, edited by Lennox S. Yearwood, pp. 115–33. Lanham, Md.: University Press of America.
Jackson, James S., ed. 1991. *Life in Black America*. Newbury Park, Calif. Sage Publications.
Johnson, Audreye E. 1980. "Black Organizations: The Extended Kinship for Survival." In *Black Organizations: Issues on Survival Techniques*, edited by Lennox S. Yearwood, pp. 103–13. Lanham, Md.: University Press of America.
Karenga, Maulana. 1989. *Introduction to Black Studies*. Los Angeles: University of Sankore Press.
King, Deborah K. 1988. "Multiple Jeopardy, Multiple Consciousness: The Context of a Black Feminist Ideology." *Signs* 14: 42–72.
King, Joyce Elaine and Carolyn Ann Mitchell. 1990. *Black Mothers to Sons: Juxtaposing African American Literature with Social Practice*. New York: Peter Lang.
Kurlander, Gabrielle and Jacqueline Salit. 1990. *Independent Black Leadership in America*. New York: Castillo International Publications.

Leslie, Annie R. 1991. "How Single Black Mothers Socialize Daughters to Participate in the Black Ethical Tradition through Brer Rabbit Storytelling." Paper presented at the Association of Black Sociologists, Cincinnati, Ohio.

Lopata, Helena Z. 1964. "The Function of Voluntary Associations in An Ethnic Community: 'Polona'." In *Contributions to Urban Sociology*, edited by Ernest W. Burgess and Donald J. Bogue, pp.203-23. Chicago: University of Chicago Press.

Mays, Vickie M. 1986. "Identity Development of Black Americans: The Role of History and the Importance of Ethnicity." *American Journal of Psychotherapy* XL: 582-93.

Neverdon-Morton, Cynthia. 1989. *Afro-American Women of the South and the Advancement of the Race, 1895-1925*. Knoxville: University of Tennessee Press.

Noble, Jeanne. 1978. *Beautiful, Also, Are the Souls of My Black Sisters: A History of the Black Woman in America*. Englewood Cliffs, N.J.: Prentice-Hall.

Olsen, Marvin E. 1978. *The Process of Social Organization: Power in Social Systems*. New York: Holt, Rinehart and Winston.

Randolph, Suzanne. 1992. *New Models of Leadership for Community Applications: Lessons from African American Women's Associations*. Paper prepared for the Delta Research and Educational Foundation. Washington, D.C.

Randolph, Suzanne. 1992. *Facing the Rising Sun: Leaders in African American Women's Associations Respond to Changing Communities*. Paper prepared for the Delta Research and Educational Foundation. Washington, D.C.

Reid, Pamela Trotman. 1984. "Feminism Versus Minority Group Identity: Not for Black Woman Only." *Sex Roles* 10: 247-55.

Rodgers-Rose, La Frances. ed. 1980. *The Black Woman*. Beverly Hills: Sage Publications.

Rosenbach, William E., and Robert L. Taylor, eds. 1984. *Contemporary Issues in Leadership*. Boulder: Westview Press.

Smith, Robert C. 1985. "Leadership in Negro and Black: Retrospect and Prospect." *The Urban League Review* 9: 8-19.

Terborg-Penn, Rosalyn. 1987. "African Feminism: A Theoretical Approach to the History of Women in the African Diaspora." In *Women in Africa and the African Diaspora*, edited by Rosalyn Terborg-Penn, Sharon Harley, and Andrea Benton Rushing, pp.43-63. Washington: Howard University Press.

Terborg-Penn, Rosalyn, Sharon Harley, and Andrea Benton Rushing, eds. 1987. *Women in Africa and the African Diaspora*. Washington: Howard University Press.

Thomas, Bettye C. 1980. "The Role of the Black Woman in the Development and Maintenance of Black Organizations." In *Black Organizations: Issues on Survival Techniques*, edited by Lennox S. Yearwood, pp.103-13. Lanham, Md: University Press of America.

Thompson, D.C. 1963. *The Negro Leadership Class*. Englewood Cliffs, N.J.: Prentice-Hall.

Tocqueville, Alexis de. 1954. *Democracy in America*. New York: Vintage Books.

Tucker, C. Delores. 1980. "The A.B.C.'s of Black Organizational Survival." In *Black Organizations: Issues on Survival Techniques,* edited by Lennox S. Yearwood, pp. 129-33 Lanham, Md.: University Press of America.

Walker, Alice. 1983. *In Search of Our Mothers' Gardens*. San Diego: Harcourt Brace, Jovanovich.

Walters, Ronald. 1985. "Imperatives of Black Leadership: Policy Mobilization and Community Development." *The Urban League Review* 9: 20-41.

Whyte, William Foote, ed. 1991. *Participatory Action Research*. Newbury Park, Calif.: Sage Publications.

Wilcox, Clyde. 1990a. "Black Women and Feminism." *Women and Politics* 10: 65-84.

Wilcox, Clyde. 1990b. "Race, Gender Role Attitudes, and Support for Feminism." *The Western Political Quarterly* 43: 113-21.

Woodson, Robert L. 1985. "Leading from Our Strengths." *The Urban League Review* 9: 46-54.

Yearwood, Lennox S., ed. 1980. *Black Organizations: Issues on Survival Techniques*. Lanham, Md.: University Press of America.

7. Race, Class, Gender and US State Welfare Policy: The Nexus of Inequality for African American Families

Rose Brewer

This chapter is about the United States welfare state and African American family inequality. It is a sociological analysis of the welfare state, race, class, gender and the family which is both critical and historical in perspective. Although the growing literature on the state and public policy in sociology indicates its sociological significance (Wilson 1980 and 1987; Dickinson and Russell 1986; Zaretsky 1976), little of the existing work on state form and state practice tackles the welfare state in the context of the multiple inequalities which shape American society with a specific focus on African American families. A major gap in the literature is the small amount of theorizing about state formation and change in the context of the interaction of race, class and gender.

Although racial, gender, and class inequalities have been examined from the perspectives of social roles, organizational structure, and social attitudes, few if any analyses have looked at these inequalities in the context of state theory, political economy, and the welfare state simultaneously. Even the new scholarship by Black feminists (see Collins 1986 and 1990; Barkley-Brown 1989) is developed largely on the basis of the everyday. The intersection of everyday life with structural phenomena is under-theorized. Thus there is a crucial need to interrogate these levels of social reality.

Indeed, in examining race, class and gender simultaneously, it is evident that they are pointedly expressed in the social positioning of Black Americans. Blacks "have not made it," as it is aptly put by Lieberson (1980). By any indicator – occupational, educational, political – African Americans are still heavily marginalized and excluded from equal participation and equal rewards in American society. Racism in its advanced form is alive and well (Baron 1985). Class differences do exist, and they suggest that a segment of the Black population is somewhat well articulated into the labor market (Wilson 1980). Nonetheless the working-class poor and very poor have increased. Moreover, poverty is increasingly concentrated in female-headed households (Brewer 1988). These structural realities have profound consequences for African American family formation and change. Most critically, family formation is increasingly around women and children. Nearly 60 percent of all African American children are born to single women (Brewer 1988). Unfortunately, most of these families are poor. They illustrate the convergence of Black women's and men's disadvantage under late capitalism. Marriage is difficult to forge under these conditions. Thus families are often built around consanguineal kin networks.

Although family inequality can be demographically delineated, the *why* of persistent inequality remains. Why the persistent poverty of Black women, men, and children – families – in the United States? I would say the answer cannot be given in a single term. A robust explanation involves teasing out the confluence of a number of social forces. The crux of my argument is that African American family inequality is not due singularly to race or class or gender but to their complex interplay. These complexities must be much better understood in order to create social policy and social change that will make a difference in the lives of African Americans.

Where to begin?

I believe Grubb and Lazerson depict an essential truth in the following assessment of family policy:

> Because the issues of race are so stark, they make clear the essential challenge of family policy: the most appropriate approach to racial issues within family policy is to ignore issues of the family altogether and to concentrate instead on the most obvious and pernicious forms of discrimination – in employment, in education, in housing, and in access to political power (1982: 262–3).

They alert us to the idea that in a society in which resources are so starkly distributed along racial lines, policy makers are in trouble if they do not place systemic discrimination at the center of their analyses. I believe this admonition is especially important for analysts who are trying to make sense out of the changing African American family. Moreover, I would take the Grubb and Lazerson analysis a step further. Under conditions of advanced capitalism, crucial to policy analysis is an explication of the intersection of race, class, and gender. The separate literatures and research practices which characterize race, class and gender studies are partial perspectives. But these deeply rooted inequalities are also highly embedded in one another. Racial inequality shapes and takes form through class and gender relations. A thorough understanding of African American families requires comprehension of those social relations internal to it and the social structure in which it is embedded. This point is central to the current discussion.

Indeed, the policy debate on Black families has been too much dominated by conservatives who lay the burden of family crisis on the Black community. They see declining median family incomes, teen pregnancy, and poor female heads of households as examples of the so-called internal pathology of African American families. Thus conservatives in the United States have traditionally resisted the idea that the state has a role to play in the family – for example, to promote a social wage. They have resisted state minimum-income policies, public-sector jobs, and a liberal social safety net. Conservatives do not, however, pass up the opportunity to use the state for moral purposes and to constrain sexual expression. The moral agenda of the Far Right has been infused into a broader discussion of sexuality and "family values." This has been transferred to those families which don't conform to the "nuclear family" model by characterizing them as culturally defective and morally lax.

Unfortunately, structural critiques of inequality have not dominated or been at all prominent in the recent public-policy debates or public-policy initiatives on families. Take as an example the "Family Policy Act", a conservative policy proposal. Critics showed, in a close examination, that this act was rooted in a narrow and unrealistic conception of American family life (Currie and Skolnick 1988). The proposed legislation based its policy recommendations on a family form which is found less and less in the United States today: a full-time homemaker with a husband in the workplace. A structural analysis would be more inclined to explain the fact of impoverished, female-headed, single-parent households as a growing family form by acknowledging the truncated participation in the labor force of African American men and the race/gender wage and occupational inequality of African American women (Amott and Matthaei 1991). Thus a structural analysis of Black family changes is related to broader political-economic and cultural changes. The deindustrialization of the economy has left little or no work for African American men and women. Traditional nuclear family formation under such profound economic disjuncture is very difficult.

Baron (1985) makes the crucial observation that progressives must come to terms with the state in advanced capitalist orders. The welfare state is an especially awkward proposition given the tendency of some radicals to view welfare simply as an example of regulating the poor. Yet we must come to grips with race, state, and economy in interplay if we are to understand the African American family experience today. Given this, my starting points are two. First, I assert that discussions of African American families are cast too narrowly. In academic and social-policy debate, the Black family is treated as a unit separate and apart from broader social dynamics. It is viewed as a personal sphere in which interpersonal dynamics determine its form and structure. Although Zaretsky (1976) challenged the notion of the personal in isolation from the political economy, many analysts still continue to use the personal pathology notion of the Black family twenty-five years after the

Moynihan report. Thus the racial, class, and gender dynamics of the broader American social structure are overlooked. We need to understand these dynamics in the context of economic and state restructuring.

We also need to understand the interplay between interpersonal dynamics and the broader social structure. Black family resistance and cultural creation are key here. Although a fully elaborated discussion of interpersonal dynamics and cultural creation is not possible in this essay, it is important to keep these issues in mind. Structural inequality is not simply imposed. Resistance and response reshape structural realities in cultural context. My point here is that a structural analysis alone is not enough. However, it is a good starting point for conceptualizing African American families and the state and it will be the focus of this discussion.

Second, I argue that the intersection of racial, class and gender inequality is the crux of African American families' crises. The challenge is to center our analyses in multiple articulations of social structure: gender, class, and race. Yet, explicating the intersection of class, race, and gender, even among Marxist feminists, is in its infancy (Sacks 1989; Glenn 1985; Matthaei 1988). No doubt, especially in the context of advanced capitalist society, class and gender inequality powerfully intersect with race to create a complex dynamic of social inequality. This has monumental implications for Black families and Black family policy.

Like class, racism remains a powerful social force for families. Historically, and under current conditions of advanced racism (Baron 1985), the forging of family bonds has been difficult for African people in the US. Today, racial formation, the re-creation of race as a central organizing principle of American society (Omi and Winant 1987), takes the sophisticated form of institutionalization and cultural hegemony. The social reproduction of racial inequality persists even as formal racial divisions collapse. For example, Black families remain exceedingly wealth- and income-poor in this social order. Inherited family wealth and property advantages whites. A good deal of this "white" wealth has come from the persistent disadvantaging of African Americans. Thus, the fusion of class and race inequality is a key marker of neo-racism.

Consequently, more complicated racial/class interactions appear to be at play. Wilson (1980 and 1987) makes a powerful argument that within the African American community there is a significant split between a middle class living outside impoverished inner cities and a poor and working poor population marginalized within them. The inner city population, thus, is left more vulnerable under conditions of advanced capitalism. These class and race issues are complicated by gender/race realities. The configuration of gender relations – the social construction of maleness and femaleness – means African American women and men are socially located somewhat differently under conditions of advanced racism and capitalism. For example, the significant representation of African American women in service work today means that these women contribute to social reproduction through public tending and caring. Jobs such as nurses' aides, cafeteria workers, and others in geriatric and mental hospitals are disproportionately occupied by poor Black women (Simms and Malveaux 1986). Such jobs cannot provide a family wage but represent highly exploitable labor arrangements.

This contrasts with the experience of poor African American men whose labor-force participation has stood at 46 percent for some years (Model 1990). Unemployed or opting out of low-waged work, men enter the irregular economy. This work is often intermittent or risky. Family formation is complicated by this economic marginalization of Black men. Welfare becomes the state structural backdrop to the political economy of Black men's irregular labor. Marriage is less desirable for both women and men under these systemic realities. The inequality in which Black families are situated is a complex interplay of race, class and gender forces. Accordingly, we need to understand more about the social constitution of Black family life under conditions of advanced capitalism.

Economic transformation, advanced capitalism, and the restructuring of the state: the context for the social construction of Black families

The key problems for African Americans in an advanced capitalist order such as the US are clear cut: too few jobs, too much poverty, too many Black children suffering. Let me now turn more directly to the issue of economic restructuring, for it is there that I anchor the changing social-structural realities of Black families in the United States.

The emergence of capitalism and the emergence of racism coincided quite closely. These systems of oppression, in turn, are mutually reinforcing and deeply embedded within one another. (See Shulman and Darity 1989; Omi and Winant 1987; Wilson 1980 and 1987; and Baron 1985 for recent accounts of this relationship.) What is happening today? I say that the current economic, political, and social crises affecting large numbers of people in the Black community should be understood in the light of continued racial discrimination in the labor market – segmentation of American labor markets – and the restructuring of the current economy – the global division of labor in an international labor force and the new international division of labor by gender. In the latter case, capital mobility strikes at the heart of economic decline in urban areas through the process of deindustrialization and the division of labor internationally (Bluestone and Harrison 1982).

Moreover, reindustrialization, when it has occurred, has not led to the demise of particularistic tendencies within new growth regions. Growth remains heavily uneven within the United States. This means that race plays a key role in new growth regions (Brewer 1988). At the same time, there is a new social structure of accumulation in the making. As World War II expansion came to an end, fueled by the oil crisis of the early 1970s, it was imperative for the system to generate new ways of assuring corporate profit. Thus, the new structure of accumulation was reflected initially in dramatic cutbacks in the – largely male – industrial working class. More specifically, the shaping of a minimalist welfare state is a key part of this general crisis of accumulation in post-World War II capitalism (see Gordon et al. 1982 for support for this view).

The economic role for government and the maintenance of a hegemonic military posture to protect American corporations' opportunities to invest abroad had all begun to decay as the post-World War II accord came to an end. The post-World War II wave of global capital accumulation was exhausted in the seventies, and American and British structural weaknesses became more severe. The contradictions inherent in the Keynesian welfare state have meant that its development has always been political. This dynamic became more marked in the seventies. The current crisis stems from the deterioration of a social structure of accumulation (Gordon et al. 1982). Moreover, the channeling of class and racial conflict into contestation over governmental policy has produced a dramatic increase in the role and cost of the state. The restructuring of the Welfare State in the United States occurred in this political-economic context.

State practices during the decade of the 1980s supported high levels of military spending and a minimalist role for government social spending – shifting this onto individual states. But it proved to be a contradictory state restructuring. Social spending was gutted, but corporate support, primarily through military spending, remained at record levels (Currie and Skolnick 1984). Although not overtly implicated in social spending, the infrastructure of the social welfare state remained constant through perks for the upper middle classes and continued tax support and supplements for the rich. Along with tax breaks and social security, guaranteed mortgages and highways are instances of middle-class and upper-class welfare subsidization by the state.

While the American social welfare state may not have been dismantled, it was being changed. Blacks figured poorly in this equation because they are disproportionately represented in those sectors of state spending which were being cut back or eliminated; they possess little wealth, and are heavily marginalized from the private sector (Beverly and Stanback 1986). There is a blurring of lines between social and economic markets. And the preference for private enterprise over public intervention has reasserted itself. Blacks in declining cities and deindustrialized areas, confronting massive unemployment, are the first and most vulnerable point of attack on the social wage (Beverly and Stanback 1986).

Indeed, there are two welfare states. One supports the income of households, and the other supports the profitability of firms. These might be called social wage and state capital, respectively. Each is composed of some combination of government contracting, subsidies, transfer payments, and public production net of taxes. It is the welfare state for business which has received less attention, and this dimension of state intervention in the private market has received relatively little scholarly analysis. Nonetheless, it is quite significant. Reich (1983) estimated that government support for private firms in the United States, including subsidies, tax expenditures, loan guarantees, and low-interest financing, amounted to almost 14 percent of GNP in 1980.

The conservative strategy for the stimulation of growth focuses on dismantling the welfare state for households. The argument is that higher levels of public spending for transfer payments to households depress economic growth. Recent research suggests that this is not the case, however. Block (1987) shows how transfer payments to support household income stimulate economic growth over several years, while transfers to sustain firm profitability do not. Contrary to the conventional wisdom of the conservatives, transfers to households do appear to stimulate growth, whether due to increased household spending or labor adaptation to technological change. Cuts in this form of government support for household income are unlikely to stimulate economic growth. They simply "place the costs of public policy failures to achieve growth on the least powerful victims of economic downturn" (Friedland and Sanders 1985: 421).

Of central importance to the process is state legitimization. O'Connor (1973) argued that the state must try to maintain or create the conditions in which profitable capital accumulation is possible. However, the state must also try to maintain or create the conditions for social harmony. A capitalist state which openly uses its coercive forces to help one class accumulate capital at the expense of other classes loses its legitimacy and hence undermines the basis of its loyalty and support. But a state which ignores the necessity of assisting the process of capital accumulation risks drying up the source of its own power – the economy's surplus production capacity and the taxes drawn from this surplus (and other forms of capital). The state must involve itself in the accumulation process. But it must either mystify its policies by calling them something they are not, or it must try to conceal them, according to O'Connor. If the welfare state is implicated in capital accumulation, why has so much emphasis been placed on social welfare spending, especially on Black AFDC recipients? This question is central. It brings together issues of economy, polity, and ideology in an analysis of the Black poor. In order to answer it, the emphasis must shift somewhat, from accumulation to legitimization.

Legitimization refers to the maintenance of an atmosphere of consent and support. Ideology involves beliefs as well as practices that help solidify a new social structure of accumulation. As an assault on the social wage occurs across race, class, and gender, one way to maintain legitimization is to step up the level of rhetoric on the so-called undeserving poor. This has been the key strategy of neo-conservatives and neo-liberals. The other strategy is to mystify the support given to corporations and upper-income groups. Both strategies are key to the creation of the minimalist social welfare state. Thus, rhetoric is high regarding the imperative of work for the poorest sectors of the social order, while the state camouflages subsidies to corporate coffers.

Increasingly, so-called "feminist" ideology cross-cuts economic and state issues: poor women are expected to work, even if they have small children. Fox-Genovese (Chapter 14 in this volume) asks us to look hard at the universalizing and essentializing tendencies of feminist public policy. What young African American women contribute to social reproduction is done under horrendous conditions. But the fact remains that their work at trying to survive is intensified through the expectation of forced (public) wage work. African American women's labor in the form of household labor and social reproduction is unrecognized in much of the liberal-feminist policy agenda.

This omission represents the contradictory and flawed legacy of liberal feminism. This ideology overlooks the privileged position of two-earner families compared with single-parent households. Poor Black women must do everything, but their work at making a home and rearing children is devalued. Despite the fact that they accomplish such domestic work under trying circumstances – substandard housing, few of the amenities enjoyed by the upper middle class, and highly strained resources – Black women's reproductive labor is viewed as inessential to society's sustenance and to social reproduction.

Neo-liberal and conservative policy makers have conveniently appropriated an element of liberal feminist thinking – women's access to paid labor – and use it to the detriment of women who are living on the edge. Yet, abstracting women's work from a broader critique of patriarchy and capitalism illustrates the cooptability and the contradictions of a liberal feminism that is rooted in an unreflective notion of women's work and other public policies more generally (see Fox-Genovese, Chapter 14 in this volume). Clearly the contradictions of race and class in the context of gender must be figured into feminist thinking on women's work and public policy.

In sum, the issues discussed around public policy, welfare reform and Black poor families are rooted in processes of economic transformation and restructuring. And the ideology of the welfare state is embedded in issues of state legitimation and capital accumulation.

Restructuring family policy in the interest of African American families

An explication of the intersection of gender, race, and class should be the cornerstone of an emancipatory perspective for forging new Black family policy. Progressive social policy must be predicated on the notion that class and gender inequality are highly implicated in the dilemmas confronting African American families. For example, initiatives in social policy, such as workfare, are targeted at the Black female poor. Workfare serves the two-fold purpose of retracting the social welfare state as well as creating a class of highly exploitable labor. If there is work for young Black women to be coerced into, it is work at the bottom. These women take on the least desirable, lowest-paid jobs of the service economy. A move away from a policy analysis based solely on young black women's so-called "cultural predilection to have children" (see Mead 1986; Klaus 1986; and Murray 1984) to one which emphasizes the interplay of structure and culture is crucial to the forging of progressive social policy.

Given the economic assault on Black families (the median income of which was 56 percent of that of white families in 1989 and is currently falling), public policies must express economic democracy and sensitivity to the race and gender structure of the labor market. Social policy must be viewed in the context of economic reorganization (Wilson 1987). Data show that business and corporate decisions can be highly damaging to communities, especially inner-city minority communities (Brewer 1983). Decisions to move plants to suburbs or out of the country altogether gut areas of economic development and growth possibilities. This has been the African American economic legacy of the past twenty-five years. The availability of low-paid service work has not resolved the economic dilemma.

Indeed, understanding gender, race, and class in intersection illustrates that these multiple inequalities are the linchpin of Black women's poverty specifically, and African American family poverty more generally. As Black *women,* we are likely to be in a narrow range of female jobs, thus sharing a fate with women across racial-ethnic and class lines. As *Black* women, we are likely to be the last hired, first fired and performing the least desirable work in women's jobs: dirty, dangerous, temporary (Simms and Malveaux 1986).Ending *race/gender* discrimination on the job should be an essential feminist/progressive policy issue.

African American family policy and the state

The idea that the state should develop strategies which affect the lives of families is the crux of the family policy issue. Nonetheless, there has been widespread resistance to visible public action on families, which means that families are *inadvertently* shaped politically (Zinn and Eitzen 1987). The resistance exists largely because families in the United States have been viewed as part of the private sphere, autonomous and exempt from governmental tinkering. The resistance also occurs because families are racially typed. In fact, economic, political, and social forces have always impinged upon families. Zaretsky (1976) has argued forcefully that there would not have been an American family without state intervention. Yet we still mystify the role of the state in shaping family dynamics.

Nonetheless, as has been pointed out in this chapter, the years since World War II have been absolutely essential in framing the family/state interplay, and the last twenty-five years have been especially strategic because they coincide with state response to racial crisis in this country (Piven and Cloward 1971). Although explicit family policy is mystified, it is evident that the state has "some kind of family policy" (Grubb and Lazerson 1982). In this context, what I refer to as the restructuring of the American economy and state undergirds the need for a structural analysis of African American families and changed theoretical lenses for scholars who are studying Black families in the United States. The assumptions of an earlier historical moment have to be refined and reinterpreted in the light of current realities. In short, we need holistic analyses of Black families. More specifically, I mean spelling out the full range of relations within the Black community: embedding economic and political discussions in the context of gender with the various ideologies and social constructions which constrain people of color in US society. I fully believe we must ground analysis of contemporary Black families in the US in critical perspectives of economy and state, not simply culture.

Although family compositional changes are the subject of much current policy debate on African Americans, the response, the "what's to be done," varies according to ideological position. I believe renewed political struggle, new alliances, and revitalized coalitions are crucial to what eventually becomes possible: cutbacks, workfare or economic transformation. Indeed, at minimum, progressive family policy for African Americans involves the following:

1. Economic transformation: economic democracy and equity policy
Corporate decisions marginalize various groups from economic participation and gut communities of economic viability. Since many African American families are in trouble or are suffering because of corporate and multinational level decision-making, national and state level planning should be undertaken to ensure economic justice for all groups. The deindustrialization policy which is the center of the post-World War II economic crisis in the United States must be addressed head-on. Is there going to be corporate responsibility toward issues of race, class and gender inequality? Democratic planning in the interests of the masses of American people is key to this recommendation.

2. A full-employment economy in the nation and the state
Clearly, from a progressive perspective, the issue is not simply one of finding

low-paid work for the welfare population, as presented in the Family Security Act and welfare reform, but one of addressing the employment needs of a broader group of unemployed and working poor people – many of whom are underemployed at extremely low wages. Full employment cuts across racial-ethnic lines and would include the majority of families in the nation. Who stands to benefit from economic democracy embodied in a full- employment agenda? There is still too little work with too little pay, and this has an adverse effect on all families.

3. Racial/gender pay equity, solidary wage policy, and the strong enforcement of affirmative action and anti-discrimination laws in the workplace

Black women suffer from race, gender and class inequality. However, poverty is present nationally among fully employed women whether Black, Native American, Asian, Chicana/Latina or white. And poverty is especially present among female-headed households. Indeed, the concerns of female-headed families which are impoverished are crucial to forging progressive family policy. Real education and retraining come as a key part of employment initiatives, and a solidary wage policy which will raise the wages of all low-paid work should be introduced into the public debate on wage equity.

Because a near majority of Black families with children under the age of eighteen are headed by women who are generally the sole wage earners, large numbers of Black families suffer because of occupational segregation and the resulting low wages of the mothers/sisters/aunts/grandmothers who head them. Since Black women participate in the labor force in great numbers, disproportionately concentrated in low-paying female jobs and too often unemployed, decent jobs and employment for all are essential.

4. Local community development and cooperative enterprises

An imperative in creating economic democracy involves using the strengths of the communities to buttress families (Simms and Malveaux 1986). Thus, beyond national and state polices for economic democracy, cooperative economic development emanating out of Black communities is in order. Buying apartment buildings, credit unions, food coops, etc., are essential initiatives which go considerably beyond the idea of "Black (Asian, Native American, or Hispanic) capitalism." It means support of collective work and responsibility on the part of ethnic groups. It also means that new politics and forms of political struggle are in order.

When one turns to the question of the achievement of these policy changes, new grounds for political struggle are called for. Historical alliances which are organized exclusively on issues of class or race or gender must be superseded by alliances that focus on the simultaneity and relational nature of these inequalities. Emancipatory strategies which center on alliances reflecting the multiple social locations of women, racial-ethnic groups, and working people must be created for generating shared agendas across differences. As Fox-Genovese points out (Chapter 14 in this volume), the model of autonomous individualism is proving incapable of meeting women's needs. Such an organized political struggle goes beyond existing Democratic and Republican party politics. Localized struggles which center on issues of health, jobs, and schools must be embedded in an awareness of gender, race and class and their complex interrelationship. Struggle should proceed from this recognition. Spawning a broad-based economic and political democracy is central to policies which will make a difference for African American families and countless others. This is the struggle for the socially just society.

Clearly, with a new Democratic administration in office, potential exists for placing on the current centrist platform the complexities around race, class and gender raised in this essay. This means that Clinton and the Democrats will have to be more nuanced in the attention they give to the complexities of economic, racial and gender inequality.

Conclusions

I have argued here that at the center of the current turmoil engulfing broad sectors of the Black population and African American families is the operation of the economy, the state (particularly in its "welfare" form), advanced racism, and the distinctive situating of African American men and women in the context of gender inequality. A key part of economic restructuring has been state restructuring. The squeeze for Blacks under current reprivatization is profound due largely to their extremely vulnerable position in the private sector. The operation of the economy and the state are implicated in the structuring of racial divisions and the imposition of occupational inequality which characterize contemporary Black life in the US. Blacks can be marginalized or excluded from the economy and other institutions as long as capitalism generates a surplus population and there is a segment of white labor which protects its interests. Indeed, many Blacks will be "out" as long as race and the racialization of gender and class can channel the brunt of the costs of economic and state restructuring to African Americans.

America's social welfare state is conservative, some say non-existent. The tremendous cutback of transfers to the working poor, who make up the lower level of the service economy, presents a case in point. Clearly, other strategies are needed. Indeed, the cultural strengths and innovations of African Americans must be part of new emancipatory strategies. Taking seriously and buttressing the strengths of Black communities is vital, and this will involve African American women's organizations (see Dickerson, Chapter 6 in this volume). The challenge for feminists/progressives is to forge a social-justice agenda into the twenty-first century.

References

Amott, Teresa and Julie Matthaei. 1991. *Race, Gender and Work*. Boston: South End Press.
Barkley-Brown, Elsa. 1989. "African American Women's Quilting." *Signs* 14 (4): 921–29.
Baron, Harold. 1985. "Racism Transformed: the Implications of the 1960s." *Review of Radical Political Economics*, 17(3): 10–33.
Beverly, Creigs C., and Howard J. Stanback. 1986. "The Black Underclass: Theory and Reality." *The Black Scholar* 17: 24–32.
Block, Fred. 1987. "Rethinking the Political Economy of the Welfare State." In *The Mean Season,* edited by Fred Block, Richard A. Cloward, Barbara Ehrenreich and Frances Fox Piven, pp.109–60. New York: Random House.
Bluestone, Barry, and Bennett Harrison. 1982. *The Deindustrialization of America: Plant Closings, Community Abandonment, and the Dismantling of Industry*. New York: Basil Books.
Brewer, Rose M. 1983. "Black Workers and Corporate Flight." *Third World Socialists* 1 (Fall): 9–13.
Brewer, Rose M. 1988. "Black Women in Poverty: Some Comments on Female-Headed Families." *Signs* 13: 331–9.
Collins, Patricia Hill. 1986. "Learning from the Outsider Within." *Social Problems* 33: 514–32.
Collins, Patricia Hill. 1990. *Black Feminist Thought*. New York: Unwin Hyman.
Currie, Elliott, and Jerome Skolnick. 1988. *America's Problems*. Boston: Little Brown.
Dickinson, James, and Bob Russell. 1986. *Family, Economy & State*. Toronto: Garamond Press.
Friedland, Roger, and Jimmy Sanders. 1985. "The Public Economy and Economic Growth in Western Market Economies." *American Sociological Review* 50 (4): 421–37.
Glenn, Evelyn Nakano. 1985. "Racial Ethnic Women's Labor: The Intersection of Race, Gender and Class Oppression." *Review of Radical Political Economics* 17(3): 86–108.
Gordon, David, Richard Edwards, and Michael Reich. 1982. *Segmented Work, Divided Workers*. Cambridge: Cambridge University Press.
Grubb, W. Norton, and Marvin Lazerson. 1982.*Broken Promises*. New York: Basic Books.
King, Deborah. 1988. "Multiple Jeopardy, Multiple Consciousness: The Context of a Black Feminist Ideology." *Signs* 14 (1): 42–72.
Klaus, Mickey. 1986. "The Work Ethic State." *The New Republic* 195 (July): 22–33.
Lieberson, Stanley. 1980. *A Piece of the Pie: Black and White Immigrants since 1880*. Berkeley: University of California Press.
Matthaei, Julie. 1988. "Political Economy and Family Policy." In *The Imperiled Economy: Through the Safety Net,* edited by Robert Cherry, pp. 141–48.New York: The Union for Radical Political Economics.
Mead, Lawrence. 1986. *Beyond Entitlement*. New York: The Free Press.
Model, Suzanne W. 1990. "Work and Family." In *Immigration Reconsidered,* edited by Virginia Yans-McLaughlin, 130–59. New York: Oxford University Press.
Murray, Charles. 1984. *Losing Ground*. New York: Basic Books.
O'Connor, James. 1973. *The Fiscal Crisis of the State*. New York: St Martins.
Omi, Michael, and Howard Winant. 1987. *Racial Formation in the United States*. New York: Routledge & Kegan Paul.
Piven, Frances Fox, and Richard Cloward. 1971. *Regulating the Poor*. New York: Vintage.
Reich, Michael. 1983. *Racial Inequality in the U.S.* Berkeley: University of California Press.
Sacks, Karen. 1989. "Toward a Unified Theory of Class, Race, and Gender." *American Ethnologist* 16: 534–50.
Shulman, Steven, and William Darity, Jr., eds. 1989. *The Question of Discrimination*. Middletown: University of Connecticut Press.
Simms, Margaret C., and Julianne M. Malveaux, eds. 1986. *Slipping Through the Cracks: The Status of Black Women*. New Brunswick: Transaction Publishers.
Wilson, William J. 1980. *The Declining Significance of Race*. Chicago: University of Chicago Press.
Wilson, William J. 1987. *The Truly Disadvantaged*. Chicago: University of Chicago Press.
Zaretsky, Eli. 1976. *Capitalism, the Family, and Personal Life*. New York: Harper and Row.
Zinn, Maxine Baca, and D. Stanley Eitzen. 1987. *Diversity in American Families*. New York: Harper and Row.

Part III

Reproduction of and Challenges to Gender Relations: Cases and Comparisons at the National Level

Mona Danner and **Lucia Fort** are doctoral candidates at the American University, Washington DC, where **Gay Young** is Assistant Professor; the latter's most recent book is *Women at the Center: Development Issues and Practices for the 1990s*.

Nüket Kardam is a member of the Political Science faculty at Pomona College. She is the author of *Bringing Women In: Women's Issues in International Development*.

Maria Sagrario Floro teaches Economics at the American University, Washington DC. She is the co-author of *Informal Rural Credit Markets and the New Institutional Economics* and is co-editing a book *Women's Work in the World Economy*.

Christine Obbo is Associate Professor of Anthropology at Wayne State University and author of *African Women*.

8. Gender Inequality around the World: Comparing Fifteen Nations in Five World Regions

Lucia Fort, Mona Danner, and Gay Young

In this chapter, we describe patterns of gender inequality in fifteen countries selected purposefully from five regions of the world: Sub-Saharan Africa, the Middle East, Asia, Latin America, and Western Europe/North America. Our cross-national assessment of gender inequality seeks to determine the extent to which relations in the gender system can be observed empirically across a group of specific nations. In addition, we are interested in setting our findings in context by uncovering the broad historical, cultural, political, and economic forces which condition the gender systems of the individual countries under investigation. Thus, we pose the questions: what are the features of gender inequality that are common to all or most nations in our sample, and what patterns are unique to each region or country? And, in the latter case, how can we account for these variations?

In this analysis we employ a specific definition of gender inequality: the departure from parity in the representation of women and men in various dimensions of social life. We first elaborate our understanding of gender inequality as a multidimensional concept. Then, using data compiled by the United Nations Statistical Office, circa 1980, we assess gender inequality through twenty-one social indicators which compare the situation of women to men. The values for the indicators provide some "facts" on the situation of women relative to men in the fifteen countries. Finally, our discussion of the findings addresses the contextual and unique aspects of the countries studied, allowing us to introduce new ideas about the forces working to reproduce or to transform gender systems.

Concern for the human rights of women prompts our research. All nations in the study are parties to the United Nations Convention on the Elimination of All Forms of Discrimination Against Women. In force since 1981, the Convention comprises a bill of rights for women, and prescribes actions that states-parties should take to eliminate discrimination and achieve equal rights for women. Our indicators, which are developed from official statistics, provide a baseline for assessing progress toward the equitable treatment of women in the fifteen nations.[1]

The concept of gender inequality and its operationalization

We begin with the assumption that there exists a socially constructed status quo of female disadvantage in all nations of the world (Chafetz 1990). This gender stratification system is structured to reproduce itself, and the macro-level gender division of labor is the key element in that process. Gender social definitions result from and reinforce the gender division of labor. Justifying the unequal distribution of (non-domestic) opportunities and rewards, they operate both to restrict and to double women's work. Despite forces for "stability" of the male advantage in the gender system, macro-structural changes (for example, in demographics, technology, the economic system) can expand women's roles and their access to resources. Ultimately, those changes can translate into policies, programs, and laws that partially ameliorate women's disadvantage.

Understanding gender as a basic organizing category that leads to different outcomes for women and men in the attainment of socially valued resources provides the starting point for specifying dimensions of gender inequality. With this framework in mind, we conceptualized gender inequality as the departure from parity in the representation of women and men in five key dimensions of social life: physical well-being, family formation, education, economic activity, and public power. Each dimension is integrally connected to the others, and all are implicated in the gender division of labor (Young et al. 1994).

We developed our empirical indicators of gender inequality using the United Nations Women's Indicators and Statistics (WISTAT) microcomputer database released in 1988. WISTAT contains data collected for or by the UN and its family of agencies. These statistics have been disaggregated by sex as well as by age groupings in many cases. Using circa 1980 data from WISTAT, we computed twenty-one variables that measure gender inequality in the five dimensions noted above. The Appendix to Table 1 presents the twenty-one indicators of gender inequality with their definitions.

Seventeen of these variables indicate the situation of women relative to men. With one exception (mean age at first marriage), these variables are ratios – the number of women per 100 men[2] – and control for the sex/age distribution of the population. The other four measures are connected to women's child-bearing capacity (total fertility, use of contraception, the presence of trained attendants at birth, and infant mortality). While not direct comparisons of women and men, they suggest the extent of women's personal autonomy and the degree to which societies value their female members.

Some particular indicators included in the analysis need further explanation. We specify the age group 15–24 in some variables as this represents a pivotal time in terms of the alternatives available to women and chosen by women: more education or participation in the labor force as alternatives to marriage and motherhood. We also calculated gender ratios among teachers because, especially in Third World countries, teaching opens avenues to women for subverting some of the mechanisms that reproduce gender inequality – the devalued status of this occupation in advanced industrial countries notwithstanding. Finally, women's representation in the various sectors of economic activity is important because the empowerment which accompanies economic activity varies by sector – industry being the most advantageous sector for women according to some analysts (Joekes 1987).

In order to assess gender inequality globally, we selected three nations from each major region of the world.[3] We grouped the nations by geographical region under the assumption that those in each region share similarities. Focusing on the general features of cases, we undertook the systematic analysis of similarities and differences among countries within and across regions (Ragin 1989). Moreover, the countries we chose to analyze are among the more than one hundred nations which have signed the United Nations Convention on the Elimination of All Forms of Discrimination Against Women. Since we developed our indicators from data collected at about the time the Convention went into force, what follows represents an empirical assessment of the base from which the fifteen nations began their efforts to comply with the Convention and end gender discrimination in all its forms. Table 1 presents the findings for our indicators of gender inequality for the fifteen nations grouped by region. We begin our discussion with the African continent.

Sub-Saharan Africa

Much analysis of Africa rightly begins with an admonition regarding diversity (Duley and Edwards 1986; Hay and Stichter 1984; Oboler 1985; Robertson 1984; Parpart and Staudt 1989; Staudt and Glickman 1989). The countries we examine represent three of the five distinct regions of the continent south of the Sahara: Kenya in Eastern Africa, Mali in the Sahel Appendix to Table 1: definitions of social indicators of gender inequality and Ghana in Coastal West Africa.[4] These nations underwent varied colonial experiences and processes of state formation; their levels of urbanization and degrees of ethnic diversity differ, as do their relations to the world economic system. Nonetheless, the general tendencies of gender inequality are markedly similar. Since colonialism, African women's traditional, pre-colonial options and powers have been eroding and, with independence and development, women have been systematically excluded from new opportunities. Moreover, while women have borne the brunt of the

Table 1. Social indicators of gender inequality for 15 nations

	Africa			Middle East		
	Ghana	Kenya	Mali	Iraq	Syria	Egypt
Physical well-being						
Sex ratio						
Age 5–14	100	100	100	96	96	93
Age 15–24	101	100	112	95	91	93
Age 25–44	104	102	114	96	99	98
Infant mortality[b]	98	80	180	77	59	100
Births attended[c]	73	10	14	60	37	24
Family Formation						
Age at marriage	ND	–5	–10	–4	ND	–5
Total fertility rate[d]	7	8	7	7	7	5
Use of contraception[e]	10	7	ND	ND	20	24
Education						
Illiteracy, age 15–24	ND	ND	118	ND	ND	167
Enrollment						
First level	78	89	52	90	78	69
Second level	60	68	36	49	60	60
Achievement age 15-24						
No schooling	ND	194	118	ND	ND	137
Entered 2nd level	ND	71	22	ND	ND	66
Teachers						
First level	72	45	25	92	117	89
Second level	27	ND	ND	67	30	45
Economic activity						
Labour force part'n, 15–24	74	70	21	25	26	14
Labour force part'n, all ages	69	71	20	23	18	10
Sector of activity						
Agriculture	89	112	90	309	221	41
Industry	83	28	207	36	41	81
Services	141	84	159	43	68	203
Public power						
Seats in legislative body	ND	2	4	13	9	4

Notes
[a] Figures indicate the number of women per 100 men in a category unless otherwise noted.
[b] Infant deaths per thousand live births.
[c] Reported as % of all births.
[d] Total number of children that would be born to a woman who survived her child-bearing years–using age-specific fertility rates.
[e] Reported as the % of women of child-bearing age who use any form of contraception.

c. 1980 data[a]

Asia			Latin America			Europe & N.America		
China	Indonesia	Japan	Brazil	Mexico	Peru	Canada	Italy	Sweden
94	99	95	99	97	97	95	95	95
93	101	97	99	97	97	98	96	96
91	104	99	100	102	98	99	100	95
39	84	6	71	53	99	9	13	7
ND	31	100	73	ND	44	99	100	100
−3	−4	−4	−3	−3	−3	−2	−4	−2
2	4	2	4	5	5	2	2	2
71	27	62	ND	39	41	ND	78	78
373	176	ND	85	133	291	ND	ND	ND
85	85	93	95	95	93	94	90	93
69	ND	95	114	88	85	96	88	104
379	185	ND	86	ND	ND	80	109	ND
75	68	ND	117	ND	ND	99	98	ND
59	49	133	367	163	150	257	669	456
33	ND	36	ND	48	ND	72	139	88
99	49	97	46	46	44	83	72	92
81	45	59	37	37	32	65	44	76
111	94	149	41	45	54	45	114	50
77	99	67	65	95	69	42	65	35
70	114	116	196	191	177	147	133	171
21	0	4	5	11	5	10	11	31

Appendix to Table 1: definitions of social indicators of gender inequality.

Physical Well-being

Sex ratio is the number of females per 100 males, controlling for the sex ratio in the population, for each age group: *Age 5–14, Age 15–24, Age 25–44*.

Infant mortality is the number of infants who die before reaching one year of age per 1000 live births.

Births attended by health staff is reported as a percentage of births recorded where a recognized health service worker was in attendance.

Family Formation

Age difference in years at first marriage is the difference in the singulate mean age at marriage for women and men. (This is a relative, not ratio, measure.)

Total fertility rate is the number of children that would be born to a woman who survived her child-bearing years and bore children at each age in accordance with prevailing age-specific fertility rates.

Use of contraception is reported as the percentage of married women of childbearing age who use, or whose husbands use, any form of contraception.

Education

Illiteracy, age 15–24 is the number of illiterate women per 100 illiterate men for that age group, controlling for the sex ratio in the population.

Enrollment, all ages is measured by two indicators: *First level* is the number of females per 100 males who are enrolled in primary school, controlling for the sex ratio in the population. *Second level* is the number of females per 100 males who are enrolled in secondary school, controlling for the sex ratio in the population.

Achievement is measured by two indicators for the 15–24 age group: *No schooling* is the number of women per 100 men who have never attended school, controlling for the sex ratio in the population. *Entered second level* is the number of women per 100 men who have started secondary school, controlling for the sex ratio in the population.

Teachers is the number of female teachers per 100 male teachers, controlling for the sex ratio in the population, at the *First level* and at the *second level*.

Economic Activity

Labor force participation is the number of women per 100 men who are counted as economically active, controlling for the sex ratio in the population, for two age groups: *Age 15–24* and *All other ages*.

Sector of economic activity, all ages is the number of economically active women per 100 economically active men, controlling for the sex ratio in the population, who work in the following sectors: *Agriculture, Industry, Services*.

Public Power

Seats in legislative body is the number of female members per 100 male members in the national legislature, controlling for the sex ratio in the population.

economic crisis in Africa (as well as its "cure"), they still continue to devise strategies to exploit the few opportunities that do exist and (re)gain some autonomy (Leonard 1989). Their struggle has not been made easier by the implicit assumptions driving development planning – that technological change is gender-neutral, that women's interests are subsumed by men's, that women play only a marginal part in the development process. In Africa, these false beliefs served to double women's workload, shift the control of profits from their labor to men, and exclude them from vocational training and agricultural extension services (Parpart 1989).

African women's material resources, family/household relations, and public power interconnect in particular ways (Oppong 1983 and 1988; Guyer 1989; Robertson and Berger 1986; Staudt 1986; Barrett 1987). European systems of gender inequality were superimposed on a system of separate and unequal but connected and interdependent spheres of activity. Colonialism institutionalized male advantage and devalued or reallocated the resources that women used to maintain relative autonomy in their own sphere. The traditional reciprocal rights and obligations in households, based on generation and gender, took the new form of senior men controlling the labor of women and junior men. As beneficiaries of development programs and with resources to raise capital or use for collateral, it is men who engage in cash-crop production. Yet, virtually all African women work to support themselves and their children, raising most of the food their large families eat and earning cash through small-scale retailing and trade. As women's activities shift towards the market, women and men have been redefining rights and obligations to one another and to kin. This influences ongoing bargaining over the flow of resources as they generate income from different sources and put it to different uses. Parenthood, more than marriage, has been the cornerstone of African families, and labor migration and the cash economy have served to reduce the economic interdependency of wives and husbands.

A key element in women's economic survival strategy is their associations and networks. African women's rich tradition of cooperating in groups is more vital when women must earn money to buy food and clothing, and off-farm employment opportunities are limited. Moreover, except for the educated elite, women are incorporated into the urban economy in ways that reflect their disadvantage relative to men in terms of training and experience; that is, in personal services and as "micro-entrepreneurs." Obbo (Chapter 11 in this volume) elaborates all of these issues – from men's control of cash crops and the profits from women's labor to women's unequal share of the burdens of parenthood and structural adjustment programs – in Uganda.

The shift in power from village and lineage to nation-state has moved politics further from women's actual spheres of influence. Of course, women must still contend with policies of state, but turning to the findings in Table 1, the values for public power indicate that the presence of women in positions of formal power in these African countries is among the lowest. The findings for other dimensions further illuminate African women's lack of power. For example, the sex ratios for the three countries form what can be called an "impoverished" pattern in which women are left behind (through men's death or migration). Poverty and inadequate health care do take their toll, and overburdened, undernourished women give birth to babies which do not survive. Yet, in these countries with high fertility rates and limited use of contraception, motherhood and work go together.

The values for the labor-force participation ratios should be interpreted with caution for Mali, in particular. The unpaid household production of food and cloth by village women in Mali does not "count." Neither does production for the informal exchange economy which is key to women's economic survival. In terms of what is counted, Ghana's pattern – women dominating in services – reflects women's economic options in urban areas; rural women in Kenya appear central to agricultural production; and in Mali, both the small industrial sector (primarily needle trades) and the limited service sector engage many more women than men.

Education data are reported incompletely for these countries. In the light of analysis which suggests that the content of formal education in Ghana is economically dysfunctional for girls (Robertson 1984), it is ambiguous whether the low values in the table really do mean that girls in Mali are highly disadvantaged educationally. Women are not well represented as teachers due to the general pattern of limited educational and training opportunities for African women, an obstacle to greater productivity throughout the continent. Overall, the disparity between women and men in Ghana, Kenya, and Mali can only act as a brake on socioeconomic development in the three countries.

The Middle East

One way to approach the analysis of the situation of women in the Arab Middle East is to cast it as part of the conflict between a traditional, religion-based ideology regarding social organization and the actual social relations emerging in the process of economic development in the region. However, this broad assessment of Egypt, Iraq, and Syria comprises complexities that require elaboration.

The "Muslim woman question," which is a manifestation of the "lag" between new economic relations and traditional values, has less significance for peasant and Bedouin women than for urban women. Moreover, its importance for urban women varies for the poor, the middle class, and the elite (Mohsen 1985; Rassam 1984; Stowasser 1987a and 1987b; Mernissi 1987). Reactions against women's increased public participation (particularly in urban life) have come from fundamentalists/traditionalists of both rural society and the urban lower middle class. Key is their belief that the "Westernization" of women will lead to the loss of all cultural authenticity because women are not capable of properly choosing which new cultural elements to take on and which old ones to throw off (Mernissi 1987).

Reforms in personal status codes strengthened the rights of Arab women as individual members of the community, particularly in Egypt and Iraq. Yet contradictions remain between the constitutionally granted public rights and duties for women and the Personal Status Laws. Indeed, states have taken care to include elements of Shari'a (Islamic law) in their reforms (Rhoodie 1989; Mueller 1985; Hussein 1985; el Saadawi 1988; Hijab 1988). Control of women's sexuality anchors the integrated view in Islamic ideology of women and their place in society. The meaning of veiling is less clear; it is both symbolic of sexual oppression and empowering – enabling a woman to go out in public when and where she wishes and still keep her reputation intact (Fernea 1985: 215–23; Mernissi 1987; Ahmed 1988; Abu-Lughod 1986). But the so-called modesty code also has practical consequences in terms of women's economic dependency on men.

Where the peasant economy has undergone dislocation, men have become more independent and women more dependent in relation to the family/household. Urbanized women are also losing traditional productive activities through the ongoing transformation of the male breadwinner ideology, but urbanization places constraints on the ability of the family/household to support its women; thus, older daughters and wives must seek employment. The household and the state assume women have a dual role but view women's paid work – mainly in the informal sector and in (stereotyped) services – as secondary (Chamie 1985; Assam et al. 1985; Rugh 1985; Ibrahim 1985; Hoodfar 1988). Changed economic relations have been slow to bring about lower fertility, in part because women derive much of the limited power they enjoy from maternal relations. However, evidence shows that increasing educational opportunities for girls leads to reduced fertility; and, at least for women in the middle and upper classes, more education leads to improved employment opportunities (Al Kadhi 1985; Chamie 1985; El Sanabary 1985).

The findings in the table for Egypt, Iraq, and Syria reveal aspects of the interconnections among marriage/motherhood, education, and paid work. First, however, note that sex ratios depart most from parity in the 15–24 age range. Rather than an artifact of male labor migration, this disparity is more an indicator of the degree to which women are withdrawn from public view during the years when modesty and maternity are central.

Low ratios of labor-force participation in part reflect the nature of women's productive activities – unpaid and informal. When women are counted they are overrepresented in agriculture – in Iraq and Syria – and also in services – in Egypt. The relatively high rate of women in industry in Egypt reflects their domination of the needle trades. (This number would be higher still if it included women involved in domestic outwork.) Women's limited participation in the formal labor force is consistent also with high fertility rates in all three countries.

Teaching young children is a major public role for women; participation in legislative bodies is not, unfortunately. Near parity exists between women and men as teachers at the first level and, in Iraq, boys and girls enroll at about the same rate. In all three countries, however, girls and women are underrepresented at the second level as students and teachers, and young women's attainment is lower (although illiteracy and achievement data are poorly reported). Women's situation in education offers a clear example of Middle Eastern women's more general struggle for full participation in public life.

Asia

As part of the most diverse geographic area in the world, the Asian countries on which we focus – China, Japan, and Indonesia – are too disparate to allow us to speak meaningfully about women in the "region." Following World War II, all three countries reformed their laws to increase women's freedom in matters of marriage and to guarantee legal rights. Still, gender inequality remains rampant in social and private life. The undiminished preference for sons in China presents one clear example; in Japan, men enjoy much greater educational and employment opportunities; and purdah, while not widespread, still restricts women in some parts of Indonesia. Gender inequality continues to exist partly because of the particular cultural heritage of each country. Japan and China share a common patriarchal tradition in Confucianism, and the dominant religion in Indonesia is Islam. Both religions emphasize hierarchical authority and women's inferiority and, thus, subservience to men. Cultural traditions alone do not explain gender inequality, however; changing economic relations are also critical.

Indonesia epitomizes the diversity of Asia. It comprises more than 13,000 islands spread over 3,500 miles of ocean, ten major ethnic groups, three hundred smaller ones, and over two hundred distinct languages. Despite its wealth in natural resources, the country is poor and economic inequality is extreme. The agricultural export economy superimposed by Dutch colonizers on the indigenous tradition of the joint teamwork of husbands and wives in subsistence production served to disadvantage women – although somewhat less than in other colonies. Encouraged by the military government, recent Indonesian industrial development, which employs mainly young single women (much like that of Taiwan or South Korea), is foreign-dominated and export-oriented. Overall, social class inequalities interact with gender to ensure that the poorest women work the hardest only to achieve the least return for their labor (Enloe 1983; Hull 1979; Locher-Scholten and Niehof 1987; Stoler 1977; Wolf 1988).

The labor of women has provided a key element of Japan's economic success. Women work long hours in poorly paid positions with few benefits and minimal job security, and employers keep their costs down through the discriminatory practice of hiring women for low-skilled, high-turnover jobs

(Brinton 1992). Moreover, although companies maintain loyalty to (and thereby elicit loyalty from) male employees, they commit little to their female employees. After marriage, women invest heavily in the role of "good wife and wise mother," taking complete control of the household while their husbands work long hours. Since other forms of public participation are unlikely, women are closely involved with their children, especially their education (Pharr 1977; Sugisaki 1986; Lebra et al. 1976; Bingham and Gross 1987).

China's numerous and tumultuous plans, campaigns and revolutions since 1949 were aimed at reforming ideology as well as political-economic structures. The 1950s' policies which established rural communes in order to collectivize the means of production have been reversed since 1978, through the modernizing efforts in all sectors within China. As a result, the rural household has re-emerged as a center of production. Whether this has increased women's household bargaining power because their labor is critical, or reduced their relative independence as they are re-subsumed in a household system dominated by men, is unclear. However, despite the socialist revolution's important changes in traditional practices towards women, patriarchal attitudes remain firmly entrenched within the household as well as in society at large (Gates 1989; Croll 1985; Davin 1987; Stacey 1983).

The values in Table 1 reveal no patterns that hold for all three nations. No other region, for example, has a wider range of representation of women in legislative assemblies. Certain of the variations make for noteworthy comparisons however – beginning with sex ratios. Patterns for Japan and Indonesia reflect affluence ("weaker" males benefit from increased resources) and poverty ("stronger" females manage to survive under adverse conditions) respectively, while the increasing disparity in Chinese sex ratios reveals the effects of pervasive preference for males in all facets of life. China's deliberate policy of slow population growth, even before the advent of the one-child policy in 1978, resulted in a profile of fertility and contraceptive use similar to that found in Japan and other industrial nations. Japan's low fertility rate, however, is probably achieved not only through the practice of contraception but also through the widespread use of abortion (O'Kelley and Carney 1986).

In both Indonesia and China, girls enroll in elementary school at the same relative rates not far from parity with boys. However, young women are not realizing the same educational outcomes as young men. Women's illiteracy and lack of schooling are approximately two to four times higher than men's, and teaching, even at the first level, remains a male-dominated occupation. In Japan, the traditional view of women as better than men at dealing with children leads to their over-representation as first-level teachers. Yet, although Japanese women have achieved near parity in second-level enrollment, they are not trusted to prepare students for college and, consequently, are under-represented as secondary teachers.

Chinese women, whose labor in agriculture is critical, participate in the workforce throughout their lifespan. The labor-force participation of Japanese women, however, is highest prior to marriage and motherhood. And, while they share the service sector fairly equally with men, women's labor in agriculture continues to be important in this advanced industrial society. Only in Indonesia do women approach parity with men in the industrial sector, which is small and dominated by labor-intensive export-processing work. However, the nearly equal representation of Indonesian women in all economic sectors illustrates the inadequacy of looking simply to accounts of women's economic activity for assessing their situation, not only in Indonesia but throughout the world.

Latin America

In contrast to Asia, the countries of Latin America are part of a fairly homogeneous region. Diversity among the countries (different colonial experiences, ethnic composition and level of industrialization) and within them (variations in racial-ethnic background, rural/urban and regional origin, and age and class) notwithstanding, they share characteristics of historical heritage, sociocultural tradition, and economic structure.

Late industrialization and underdevelopment have been concomitant with Latin America's subordinate incorporation into the world economic system. Most of the population of the region lives in burgeoning cities, and young, unmarried women compose the largest category of rural to urban migrants. Moreover, the need to maintain the competitive advantage of low-cost commodities and cheap labor has implications for processes of employment as well as household economic strategies – both of which bear on the position of women (Nash 1983; Cunningham 1987; Leahy 1986; Fernandez-Kelly 1983a and 1983b; Scott 1986; United Nations 1986; Schmink 1986). The patriarchal family interacts with and supports the international gender division of labor as well as the region's integration into the world capitalist system, as illustrated, for example, by Mexico's export-processing industrialization.

The legacy of colonial domination still shapes the sociocultural context of these countries. The introduction of Catholicism exacerbated the hierarchical organization of society, and the practice of slavery with its caste divisions gave rise to racism, which is still prevalent. In addition, the patriarchal family, cornerstone of social organization, comprises rigidly differentiated gender roles that intensify the subordination and exploitation of women.

Even today, the family is central to the identity and survival of the individual, and women's primary identity is that of wife/mother. Indeed, the relatively high rates of fertility and low rates of contraceptive use in all three countries presented in Table 1 attest to the centrality of women's mothering and the resistance to women's control of their own sexuality. Moreover, their domestic subordination is extended into the public domain (Leahy 1986; Patai

1988; Deere and Leon de Leal 1982; Chant 1987; De Vos 1987; Schmink 1981 and 1986).

In the 1970s, the regimes of the region maintained stability and social peace either by military coercion, as in Brazil through the early 1980s, or by cooptation through corporatist structures, as with the PRI (Partido Revolucionario Institucional) in Mexico and the military government in Peru from 1968 to 1975 (Patai 1988; Nyrop 1981 and 1983). In both cases, women were routinely excluded from participation and representation in government (Leahy 1986; Deere 1986; Jaquette 1976). The findings for women's representation in legislative assemblies underline this exclusion, although the situation appears less pronounced in Mexico where the ruling party has included a women's section.

As the poorest of the three countries, Peru lags behind Brazil and Mexico in the values for infant mortality, presence of trained midwives at birth, and illiteracy. The education indicators for Brazil suggest that it is leading the way to equality. But the anomalous pattern of high ratios of secondary-level enrollment and achievement for females can be attributed to the "tracking" of women into public secondary vocational schools which offer teaching degrees. The outcome is evidenced by the ratio for teachers at first level.[5]

Most economically active women in the region work in the service sector, and their main employment category is that of domestic worker (Chaney and Garcia-Castro 1989; Leahy 1986). Other categories include "feminine professions" – like teaching, nursing and social services – associated with the state, low-level and low-wage jobs in food services and retailing, and white-collar clerical jobs (Leahy 1986; Schmink 1986; Scott 1986; United Nations 1986; Joekes 1987; Humphrey 1984 and 1987).

Low ratios of women to men in agriculture, still an important source of employment in the region, reflect the displacement of women from this sector (and their undercount) (Recchini de Lattes and Wainerman 1986; Deere and Leon de Leal 1982; Patai 1988).[6] Women's increasing participation in industry is evidenced by the relatively high ratios in all three countries. Especially in Mexico, young, unmarried women are employed in export-processing plants as part of the international gender division of labor; older, married and less- educated women make up the workforce of decaying textile industries (Leahy 1986; Fernandez-Kelly 1983b; Schmink 1986). The relatively low ratios of young women-to-men's labor-force participation drop even lower as women get married and have children. However, since Latin American women's work in the informal sector remains invisible in these counts, their involvement in productive work is vastly under-represented. Clearly, the problem of measuring women's economic activities is acute throughout the developing world.

Western Europe and North America

While the nations within our sample of Western Europe and North America are not a single geographic region, they share broadly the same general Western European heritage and level of development. Canada, Italy, and Sweden also share similar patterns of gender relations and the same large-scale trends, for example in demographics and family organization. These trends are closely related to the massive entrance of women into the labor force, with concomitant implications for change in the gender system, including educational achievement, family structure, and fertility.

The family in Italy is a key societal institution and provides economic as well as emotional and social services. Because of the rigid division of labor by sex within a social organization that is both patriarchal and Catholic, women are solely responsible for childcare, housework, and bureaucratic tasks for the family. Nevertheless, in the 1970s, a vocal feminist movement forced the Italian state and society to recognize women's rights within marriage and their right to control their fertility, and is currently pressuring for changes in the educational and employment policies towards women. Nonetheless, the rigid gender roles which consign women to the home following marriage or childbirth, together with tracking in professional education, result in high female unemployment and underemployment. Thus, women's formal labor-force participation is low and continues to fall throughout the life-cycle. Women work primarily in the feminine professions, mainly teaching, but also in personal services, low-level white-collar jobs, and as self-employed retailers (small shopkeepers). After marriage, women often continue to work in their homes as part of the "gray economy" – unofficial and unreported industrial outwork – primarily in the textile and clothing industries (Balbo and May 1974; Sgritta 1988; Colombo et al. 1988; Shinn 1987).

The situation of women in Sweden follows from the prevailing state–society relations. In contrast to Italy, Sweden's social corporatist approach accepts and actually facilitates changes in family relations through policies encouraging women's employment in the formal economy. The state is actively involved in mediating the impact of the market economy and of patriarchal tradition through progressive social insurance and childcare programs. The Swedish state has advocated equality between women and men since the 1960s and is well known for promoting policies supportive of working parents. However, legislation banning sex discrimination in employment was not passed until 1980, and Sweden's labor force remains highly segregated, with women performing the lowest paid and lowest status jobs. Women still retain primary responsibility for the home, and their opportunities are limited also by differences in educational choices: boys study science and technical subjects while girls pursue the liberal arts and social sciences (Wistrand 1981; Heom and Heom 1988; Ruggie 1981; Cherlin and Furstenberg 1988).

In Canada, women comprise most of the clerical workers in the white-collar sector – the largest employment sector in this post-industrial economy – and they remain relegated to low-level, low-skilled jobs, with lingering income disparity relative to men (Marchak 1974; McDonald 1977; Ornstein 1983; Fox and Fox 1987). Moreover, women are tracked into a limited range of professions and careers with higher unemployment or underemployment than men (Turrittin et al. 1989; Fox and Fox 1987). Women also carry the burden of household and childcare tasks without adequate support from public welfare policies and programs, reflecting the prevailing view that their employment is secondary (Erwin 1988; Ram 1988; Meissner 1977). In addition, Canada is experiencing the feminization of poverty as more women assume sole custody and financial responsibility for dependent children (Abowitz 1986; Ram 1988). And, since a large proportion of Canada's population is made up of immigrants, many women suffer multiple subordination due to ethnicity and immigrant status as well as social class and gender (Denis 1986; Ornstein 1983).

Looking at the findings in Table 1, both the social value and the individual autonomy of women appear highest in this region where infant mortality is low and contraceptive use is widespread. Note that the sex ratios take on an "affluent" pattern in which males, more vulnerable at many points in the lifecycle, benefit from the greater resources available in advanced industrial nations. The three nations are approaching educational parity and, in some cases, women appear advantaged educationally. The table values suggest that there is considerable tracking of women into teaching young children, particularly in Italy.

Clearly the economies of advanced industrial societies incorporate women most readily into the service sector. Teaching is an example of the importance to women of the public sector in providing service employment. In Canada and Sweden, women's participation in agriculture and industry is low relative to men's. In Italy, however, women predominate in the proportionately small agricultural sector because they are left in charge of family farms when men migrate to work in urban areas. Italian women's recruitment into labor-intensive assembly of soft goods partially explains Italy's ratio for women in industry – the highest in the group. All other things being fairly similar in terms of the indicators of gender inequality, the higher values for the ratios of labor-force participation and representation in legislative assemblies give the edge to Sweden as the nation closest to gender equality.

Conclusions

Our analysis does little to undermine the assertion that social inequality based on gender exists in all nations. In the five dimensions of social life, we find patterns indicating that inequality in the gender system is continually reproduced. The broad regularities that we see in the indicators follow.

In the dimension of physical well-being, at least for women's function as *child-bearers,* the more affluent nations devote more resources to women. However, comparing sex ratios at the extremes of wealth and poverty suggests that males in affluent nations benefit disproportionately from the greater resources available for health care in general.

Whether intentional and aimed at the gender system or not, actions taken by states which impact the macro-structures of society shape gender social relations in families, education, and the economy. First, the findings in the dimension of family formation reveal a trend toward lower fertility and wider contraceptive use with higher levels of economic affluence. However, the indicators also reveal the mark of the state (in China) and the interplay between economic change and normative forces (in Islamic and Catholic nations). Second, movement toward parity in education is also associated with higher economic levels. Nonetheless, ideology certainly influences who may teach whom and who may learn what at what level. Also noteworthy is the inconsistency with which information about education is reported.

Third, in spite of problems with what counts as economic activity, in all countries the representation of women in the formal (counted) labor force is greater between the ages of 15 and 24 than across all ages. We attribute lower labor-force participation in general to women's investment in marriage and motherhood. Unfortunately these data reveal nothing about women's involvement in income-generating activities in the informal sector, which is often where women turn in order better to accommodate work and childcare. Nor do they measure the intensity of women's work, that is, the overlapping of women's productive and reproducitve activities (see Floro, Chapter 10 in this volume).

When women *are* counted, we can discern patterns in their sector of economic activity. In over one third of the cases – parts of the Middle East and Africa, Asia including Japan, and Italy – women remain important in agricultural production, usually under the most difficult circumstances and often as unpaid family workers. At the same time, the consequences of urbanization are clear; in eleven of the fifteen nations women dominate the service sector (by almost two to one in Latin America). Although there is variation, this "women's sector" is typified by personal services and low-level government jobs. Finally, the countries closest to parity in industry (Ghana, Egypt, Indonesia, Mexico, China, and Mali with a vast overrepresentation of women) have small industrial sectors and/or large concentrations of labor-intensive assembly activities usually for export. The need remains for clearer understanding of the consequences for Third World women of work on the global assembly line.

As for public power, in all nations the deplorable representation of women in national-level positions of political decision-making limits their influence on policies that affect their lives. Two nations where the state has actively addressed the gender system (with mixed consequences for women) lead the group in the formal political inclusion of women: the Scandinavian social democracy of Sweden, and the People's Republic of China. Such public participation appears to be necessary but not sufficient for women's control over their personal existence.

We recognize that the experience of gender inequality is not the same for all women within a nation. Disaggregating data by sex and age does not reveal the subordinations imposed by race, ethnicity, region, rural or urban origin, or social-class differences. And that broaches a host of political data-collection issues. But in this analysis we have focused largely on women's numerical representation (relative to men's) in key dimensions of social life because we believe that, while not the only factor, numbers do matter in analyzing and challenging gender inequality. The recognition of women's presence in social life is critical to fulfilling and protecting their human rights. The numbers we have presented here illuminate the distance all nations still have to move before women and men are treated as equals in society.

Notes

1. We recognize the serious problems present in the reporting and collecting of official statistics. However, we know of no better database than WISTAT in terms of several criteria – number of cases, variables measured, comparability, and reliability/validity. Thus, we present the analysis in the light of three points.

First, we call on those who are discomfited with our data (or our findings) to work to improve the quality of the indicators measured so that others can produce a more accurate picture of the situation of women relative to men. The Institute for International Research and Training for the Advancement of Women (INSTRAW) and the United Nations Statistical Office represent channels through which it is possible to work on these concerns.

Second, we use these (limited) data in a preliminary way. We uncover evidence of women's disadvantage in every nation, and believe it is appropriate to expose the pervasiveness of gender inequality – in the way we are able to measure it.

Finally, we acknowledge the need for other methods of data collection and other types of studies (quantitative and non-quantitative) to complement the picture provided by our indicators. And, without question, the involvement of scholars from other countries is essential for full understanding of gender inequality cross-nationally.

2. We recognize the standard practice among demographers of using 100 women as the base for such calculations. Since our whole purpose is to compare the situation of women relative to men, we have chosen to use 100 men as the base for the ratios.

3. The countries selected had to meet two criteria to be included in the analysis: to be among the approximately one hundred states-parties to the UN Convention on the Elimination of All Forms of Discrimination Against Women, and to report sufficient statistics to allow us to compute indicators in the five dimensions of social life on which we focus. African nations presented the most difficulty in regard to the latter (although some industrialized countries were eliminated on these grounds as well).

4. Although we considered countries in the central and southern regions, no countries in those regions – which had signed the Convention – report data as completely as do the three we analyze. For a discussion of data on women in Africa, see Jeanne S. Newman, *Women of the World: Sub-Saharan Africa* (Washington, DC: Bureau of the Census, 1984).

5. Other reasons for the unexpected findings in education for Brazil are (i) differences in reporting and definitions – which schools and which geographical areas; and (ii) the fact that only a very small proportion of the age-eligible population of both sexes is enrolled in the second level (Nyrop 1983; Patai 1988).

6. The undercount in women's work applies also to the statistics for labour-force participation, which do not reflect home production and trade, outwork for manufacturing firms, and services provided within the informal sector.

References

Abowitz, Deborah A. 1986. "Data indicate the Feminization of Poverty in Canada, Too." *Sociology and Social Research* 70(3): 209–13.

Abu-Lughod, Lila. 1986. *Veiled Sentiments*. Berkeley: University of California Press.

Ahmed, Leila. 1988. "Arab Women: 1995." In *The Next Arab Decade*, edited by Hisham Sharabi, pp.202–20. Boulder: Westview Press.

Al Kadhi, Ann Bragdon. 1985. "Women's Education and Its Relations to Fertility: Report from Baghdad." In *Women and the Family in the Middle East*, edited by Elizabeth Warnock Fernea, pp.145–47. Austin: University of Texas Press.

Assam, H., J. Abu Nasr and I. Lorfing. 1985. "An Overview of Arab Women in Population, Employment and Economic Development." In *Women, Employment and Development in the Arab World*, edited by J. Abu Nasr and N. Khoury, pp.5–37. Berlin: Mouton.

Balbo, Laura, and Marie P. May. 1974. "Woman's Condition: the Case of Postwar Italy." *International Journal of Sociology* 5(4): 79–102.

Barrett, Minna. 1987. "Women's Income-Generating Initiatives in Kenya." *African Urban Quarterly* 2: 435–42.

Bingham, Marjorie Wall, and Susan Hill Gross. 1987. *Women in Japan: From Ancient Times to the Present*. St Louis Park, Minn.: Glenhurst.

Brinton, Mary C. 1992. *Women and the Economic Miracle: Gender and Work in Postwar Japan*. Berkeley: University of California Press.

Chafetz, Janet S. 1990. *Gender Equity*. Beverly Hills: Sage.

Chamie, Mary. 1985. *Women of the World: Near East and North Africa*. Washington: US Department of Commerce.

Chaney, Elsa M., and Mary Garcia-Castro, eds. 1989. *Muchachas No More: Household Workers in Latin America and the Caribbean*. Philadelphia: Temple University Press.

Chant, Sylvia. 1987. "Family Structure and Female Labor in Querétaro, Mexico." In *Geography of Gender in the Third World*, edited by Janet Henshall Momsen and Janet G. Townsend, pp.277–93. Hutchinson: State University of New York.

Cherlin, Andrew, and Frank F. Furstenberg. 1988. "The Changing European Family, Lessons for the American Reader." *Journal of Family Issues* 9(3): 291–97.

Colombo, Daniela, Luigi Frey, and Renata Livraghi. 1988. "The Response of Public Authorities to the Needs Expressed by Women." In *Women and Economic Development, Local, Regional and National Strategies*, edited by Kate Young, pp.74–110. Oxford: Berg/UNESCO. Croll, Elizabeth. 1985. Women and Rural Development in China: Production and Reproduction. Geneva: International Labour Office.

Cunningham, Susan. 1987. "Gender and Industrialization in Brazil." In *Geography of Gender in the Third World*, edited by Janet Henshall Momsen and Janet G. Townsend, pp.294–308. Hutchinson: State University of New York.

Davin, Delia. 1987. "Gender and Population in the People's Republic of China." In *Women, State, and Ideology*, edited by Haleh Afshar, pp.111–29. Albany: State University of New York Press.

Deere, Carmen Diana. 1986. "Rural Women and Agrarian Reform in Peru, Chile and Cuba." In *Women and Change in Latin America*, edited by June Nash and Helen Icken Safa, pp.189–208. South Hadley, Mass.: Bergin and Garvey.

Deere, Carmen Diana, and Magdalena Leon de Leal. 1982. *Women in Andean Agriculture: Peasant Production and Rural Wage Employment in Colombia and Peru.* Washington, D.C.: International Labor Office.

Denis, Ann B. 1986. "Adaptation to Multiple Subordination: Women in the Vertical Mosaic." *Canadian Ethnic Studies* 19(3): 61–74.

De Vos, Susan. 1987. "Latin American Households in Comparative Perspective." *Population Studies* 41: 501–17.

Duley, Margot I., and Mary I. Edwards. 1986. *The Cross-Cultural Study of Women.* New York: The Feminist Press.

el Saadawi, Nawal. 1988. "The Political Challenges Facing Arab Women at the End of the 20th Century." In *Women of the Arab World*, edited by Nahid Toubia, pp.8–26. London: Zed.

el Sanabary, Nagat. 1985. "Continuity and Change in Women's Education in the Arab States." In *Women and the Family in the Middle East,* edited by Elizabeth Warnock Fernea, pp.93–110. Austin: University of Texas Press.

Enloe, Cynthia H. 1983. "Women Textile Workers in the Militarization of Southeast Asia." In *Women, Men, and the International Division of Labor,* edited by June Nash and Maria Patricia Fernandez-Kelly, pp.407–25. Albany: State University of New York Press.

Erwin, Lorna. 1988. "Real Women, Anti-feminism, and the Welfare State." *Resources for Feminist Research* 17(3): 147–9.

Fernández-Kelly, María Patricia. 1983a. "Mexican Border Industrialization, Female Labor Force Participation and Migration." In *Women, Men, and the International Division of Labor,* edited by June Nash and María Patricia Fernández-Kelly, pp.205–24.Albany: State University of New York Press.

Fernández-Kelly, María Patricia. 1983b. *For We Are Sold, I and My People: Women and Industry in Mexico's Frontier.* Albany: State University of New York Press.

Fernea, Elizabeth Warnock, ed. 1985. *Women and the Family in the Middle East.* Austin: University of Texas Press.

Fox, Bonnie J., and John Fox. 1987. "Occupational Gender Segregation of the Canadian Labor Force, 1931 – 1981." *Canadian Review of Sociology and Anthropology* 24(3): 374–97.

Gates, Hill. 1989. "The Commoditization of Chinese Women." *Signs* 14: 799–832.

Guyer, Jane. 1989. "Dynamic Approaches to Domestic Budgeting: Cases and Methods from Africa." In *A Home Divided,* edited by Daisy Dwyer and Judith Bruce, pp.155–72. New Haven: Yale.

Hanson, Norwood. 1958. *Patterns of Discovery.* London: Cambridge University Press.

Hay, Margaret, and Sharon Stichter, eds.1984. *African Women South of the Sahara.* New York: Longman.

Heom, Britta, and Jan M. Hoem. 1988. "The Swedish Family: Aspects of Contemporary Developments." *Journal of Family Issues* 9: 397–424.

Hijab, Nadia. 1988. "Democracy, Development, and Human Rights: Can Women Achieve Change Without Conflict?" In *The Next Arab Decade,* edited by Hisham Sharabi, pp.45–52 Boulder: Westview Press.

Hoodfar. 1988. "The Nonpooling Household: A Challenge to Theory." In *A Home Divided: Women and Income in the Third World,* edited by Daisy Dwyer and Judith Bruce, pp.120–42. New Haven: Yale.

Hull, Valerie J. 1979. *A Woman's Place...: Social Class Variations in Women's Work Patterns in a Javanese Village.* Yogyakarta, Indonesia: Population Studies Center, Gadjah Mada University.

Humphrey, John. 1984. "The Growth of Female Employment in Brazilian Manufacturing Industry in the 1970's." *Journal of Development Studies* 20(4): 224–47.

Humphrey, John. 1987. *Gender and Work in the Third World, Sexual Divisions in Brazilian Industry.* London: Tavistock Press.

Hussein, Aziza. 1985. "Recent Amendments to Egypt's Personal Status Law." In *Women and the Family in the Middle East,* edited by Elizabeth Warnock Fernea, pp.229–32. Austin: Univers- ity of Texas Press.

Ibrahim, Barbara Lethem. 1985. "Cairo's Factory Women." In *Women and the Family in the Middle East,* edited by Elizabeth Warnock Fernea, pp.293–9. Austin: University of Texas Press.

International Women's Rights Action Watch (IWRAW). 1988. *Assessing the Status of Women: A Guide for Reporting Using the Convention on the Elimination of All Forms of Discrimination Against Women.* New York: The Development Law and Policy Program, Columbia University.

Jaquette, Jane. 1976. "Female Political Participation in Latin America." In *Sex and Class in Latin America*, edited by June Nash and Helen Icken Safa, pp.221–47. New York: Praeger.

Joekes, Susan P. 1987. *Women in the World Economy, an INSTRAW Study*. New York: Oxford University Press.

Leahy, Margaret E. 1986. *Development Strategies and the Status of Women*. Boulder: Lynne Rienner.

Lebra, Joyce, Joy Paulson, and Elizabeth Powers, eds. 1976. *Women in Changing Japan*. Boulder: Westview Press.

Leonard, Ann, ed. 1989. *Seeds: Supporting Women's Work in the Third World*. New York: The Feminist Press.

Locher-Scholten, Elsbeth, and Anke Niehof, eds. 1987. *Indonesian Women in Focus: Past and Present Notions*. The Netherlands: Foris Publications.

Marchak, Patricia. 1974. "Women, Work, and Unions in Canada." *International Journal of Sociology* 5: 39–61.

McDonald, Lynn. 1977. "Wages of Work." In *Women in Canada* (Revised Edition), edited by Marylee Stephenson, pp.181–91. Don Mills, Ontario: General Publishing.

Meissner, Martin. 1977. "Sexual Division of Labour and Inequality: Labour and Leisure." In *Women in Canada* (Revised Edition), edited by Marylee Stephenson. Don Mills, pp.160–80. Ontario: General Publishing.

Mernissi, Fatima. 1987. Beyond the Veil (Revised Edition). Bloomington: Indiana University Press.

Mohsen, Safia. 1985. "New Images, Old Reflections: Working Middle-Class Women in Egypt." In *Women and The Family in the Middle East*, edited by Elizabeth Warnock Fernea, pp.56–71. Austin: University of Texas Press.

Mueller, Eric. 1985. "Revitalizing Old Ideas: Developments in Middle Eastern Family Law." In *Women and the Family in the Middle East*, edited by Elizabeth Warnock Fernea, pp.224–28. Austin: University of Texas Press.

Nash, June. 1983. "The Impact of the Changing International Division of Labor on Different Sectors of the Labor Force." In *Women, Men, and the International Division of Labor*, edited by June Nash and María Patricia Fernández-Kelly, pp.3–38. Albany: State University of New York Press.

Nash, June, and María Patricia Fernández-Kelly. 1983. *Women, Men, and the International Division of Labor*. Albany: State University of New York Press.

Nash, June, and Helen Icken Safa. 1986. *Women and Change in Latin America*. South Hadley, Mass.: Bergin and Garvey Publishers.

Nyrop, Richard F., ed. 1981. *Peru, A Country Study*. Washington, D.C.: American University, Foreign Area Studies.

Nyrop, Richard F. 1983. *Brazil, A Country Study*. Washington, D.C.: American University, Foreign Area Studies.

Oboler, Regina Smith. 1985. *Women, Power, and Economic Change: The Nandi of Kenya*. Stanford: Stanford University Press.

O'Kelley, Charlotte, and Larry Carney. 1986. *Women and Men in Society*. Belmont, Calif.: Wadsworth.

Oppong, Christine, ed. 1983. *Female and Male in West Africa*. London: George Allen and Unwin.

Oppong, Christine 1988. *Sex Roles, Population and Development in West Africa*. Portsmouth, N.H.: Heinemann.

Ornstein, Michael D. 1983. "Class, Gender, and Job Income in Canada." *Research in Social Stratification and Mobility* 2: 41–75.

Parpart, Jane. 1989. Women and Development in Africa. Lanham, Md.: University Press of America.

Parpart, Jane L., and Kathleen Staudt, eds. 1989. *Women and the State in Africa*. Boulder: Lynne Rienner.

Patai, Daphne. 1988. *Brazilian Women Speak*. New Brunswick: Rutgers University Press.

Pharr, Susan J. 1977. "Japan: Historical and Contemporary Perspectives." In *Women: Roles and Status in Eight Countries*, edited by Janet Zollinger Giele and Audrey Chapman Smock, pp.219–55.New York: Wiley.

Ragin, Charles. 1989. "New Directions in Comparative Research." In *Cross-National Research in Sociology*, edited by Melvin Kohn, pp.57–76. Newbury Park, Calif.: Sage Publications.

Ram, Bali. 1988. "Reproduction: The Canadian Family in Transition." *Journal of Biosocial Issues* 20(1):19–30.

Rassam, Amal. 1984. "Arab Women: the Status of Research in the Social Sciences and the Status of Women" and "Toward a Theoretical Framework for the Study of Women in the Arab World." In *Social Science Research and Women in the Arab World*, UNESCO, pp.1–13 and 122–38.London: Frances Pinter.
Recchini de Lattes, Zulma and Catalina H. Wainerman. 1986. "Unreliable Account of Women's Work: Evidence from Latin American Census Statistics." *Signs* 11(4) : 740–50.
Rhoodie, Eschel M. 1989. *Discrimination Against Women*. London: McFarland.
Robertson, Claire C. 1984. *Sharing the Same Bowl: A Socioeconomic History of Women and Class in Accra, Ghana*. Bloomington: Indiana University Press.
Robertson, Claire, and Iris Berger, eds. 1986. *Women and Class in Africa*. New York: Holmes & Meier.
Ruggie, Mary. 1981. "Public Day Care in Britain and Sweden: A Sociological Perspective." In *Women and World Change*, edited by Naomi Black and Ann Baker Cottrell, pp.159–79. Beverly Hills: Sage.
Rugh, Andrea. 1985. "Women and Work: Strategies and Choices in a Lower Class Quarter of Cairo." In *Women and the Family in the Middle East*, edited by Elizabeth Warnock Fernea, pp.273–88. Austin: University of Texas Press.
Schmink, Marianne. 1981. "Women in Brazilian Abertura Politics." *Signs* 7(1) 115–134.
Schmink, Marianne. 1986. "Women and Urban Industrial Development in Brazil." In *Women and Change in Latin America*, edited by June Nash and Helen Icken Safa, pp.136–64. South Hadley, Mass.: Bergin and Garvey.
Scott, Alison MacEwen. 1986. "Women and Industrialization: Examining the 'Female Marginalisation' Thesis." *Journal of Development Studies* 22(4): 649–80.
Sgritta, Giovanni. 1988. "The Italian Family, Tradition and Change." *Journal of Family Issues* 9(3): 372–96.
Shinn, Rinn S, ed. 1987. *Italy, A Country Study*. Washington, D.C.: American University, Foreign Area Studies.
Stacey, Judith. 1983. *Patriarchy and Socialist Revolution in China*. Berkeley: University of California Press.
Staudt, Kathleen. 1986. "Stratification: Implications for Women's Politics." In *Women and Class in Africa*, edited by Claire Robertson and Iris Berger, pp.197–215. New York: Holmes & Meier.
Staudt, Kathleen, and Harvey Glickman, eds. 1989. "Beyond Nairobi: Women's Politics and Policies in Africa Revisited." *Issue: A Journal of Opinion* XVII/2.
Stoler, Ann.1977. "Class Structure and Female Autonomy in Rural Java," *Signs* 3: 74–89
Stowasser, Barbara Freyer. 1987a. "Religious Ideology, Women, And The Family." In *The Islamic Impulse*, edited by Barbara Freyer Stowasser, pp.262–96. London: Croom Helm.
Stowasser, Barbara Freyer. 1987b. "Liberated Equal or Protected Dependent?" *Arab Studies Quarterly* 9: 260–82.
Sugisaki, Kazuko. 1986. "From the Moon to the Sun: Women's Liberation in Japan." In *Women in the World, 1975–1985*, edited by Lynn B. Iglitzin and Ruth Ross, pp.109–24. Santa Barbara: ABC-Clio.
Turrittin, Anton H., Paul Anisef, and Neil J. Mackinnon. 1989. "Gender Differences in Educational Achievement: A Study of Social Inequality." *Canadian Journal of Sociology* 8(4): 395–419.
United Nations Department of International Economic and Social Affairs. 1986. *World Survey on the Role of Women in Development*. New York: United Nations Publications.
United Nations Statistical Office. 1988. *Women's Indicators and Statistics Database*. New York: United Nations.
Wistrand, Birgitta. 1981. *Swedish Women On the Move*. Edited and translated by Jeanne Rosen. Stockholm: Swedish Institute.
Wolf, Diana L. 1988. "Female Autonomy, the Family, and Industrialization in Java." *Journal of Family Issues* 9: 85–107.
Young, Gay, Lucia Fort, and Mona Danner. 1994. "Moving from 'the Status of Women' to 'Gender Inequality': Conceptualization, Social Indicators and an Empirical Application." *International Sociology*, 9 (1).

9. The State, Gender Policy, and Social Change: An Analysis from Turkey

Nüket Kardam

How do international norms, recommendations and rules get "translated" into domestic political culture at the national level? Are they automatically implemented, are they transformed in the process of implementation, or are they not heeded at all? What sorts of domestic political conflicts result? These questions have not yet received the attention they deserve. The International Relations literature has often treated states as "black boxes", leaving the domestic politics of compliance aside. What has not been sufficiently explored is the interaction between international norms and rules, on the one hand, and the particular domestic setting of a country, on the other. The chapter by Fort et al. (Chapter 8 in this volume) demonstrates how patterns of gender inequality differ in fifteen nations which all signed the United Nations Convention on the Elimination of All Forms of Discrimination Against Women. I will argue that international norms and rules may be very influential in prompting policy changes in a particular country, but whether these policy changes are more than words on paper, whether there is any content to them and, if so, what kind of content, depends upon relationships between the state and society.

A certain level of international pressure and the desire to avoid embarrassment at an international arena may prompt state representatives to go along with decisions taken at international conferences. For example, Tekeli (1990) found that the more links a state has to international organizations which are sensitive to women's equality, the more progressive policies on women it tends to devise. But international organizations still cannot enforce compliance. According to Oran Young (1989), the lack of well-entrenched and properly financed supranational organizations in international society ensures that international regimes must rely heavily on the ability and willingness of individual members to elicit compliance with key provisions within their own jurisdictions. Young goes on to say: "While trade restrictions are hard enough to verify and police, it is not easy even to imagine how to implement a regime requiring the individual members to take effective steps to control the forces causing habitat destruction within their jurisdictions" (1989: 371). To propose that states make changes regarding women's roles and status creates deeper problems than just those of verification and policing. Issue areas which propose changes in the relationship between the national state and its subjects are especially sensitive, for as Krasner (1985: 118) points out, prevailing international norms and practices place few inhibitions on a state's discretionary control over its own subjects.

I will focus here on the norms and rules regarding women which are formulated at the international level and the extent of compliance with these norms by national governments. I use the Turkish response to these norms as a case study to illustrate my arguments.

The international agenda on women and the Turkish response

The international women's movement succeeded in placing women on the agenda, as witnessed by the conferences held under United Nations auspices since the early 1970s and by the many women's units set up within international development agencies and within governments (Kardam 1991; Staudt 1990). The aim of the international women's movement has been to influence a number of international regimes, covering development, natural resources, science and technology, human rights and the environment, towards changing their norms and rules to include women.

The nature of the international women's movement is reformist. As Jaquette (1981: 8ff) points out: "While U.N. women's conferences, and their mix of liberal and socialist feminists, NIEO [New International Economic Order] advocates and others spent considerable time identifying and debating the source of women's subordination, from male prejudice to international capitalism, their solutions are limited to practical, incremental bureaucratic reform and women's pressure activity."

The essence of a women-in-development approach was defined as ascertaining what women actually want and do within a society and providing them with opportunities, skills and resources to enhance that participation. The WID strategy rests on creating more rational and even-handed planning which takes into account the gender division of labor, fair returns for labor, and the equitable infusion of new opportunities and resources to all members of a given community (Staudt 1985). The vague, ambiguous nature of demands such as "more equitable development for women" exemplifies this approach; yet, it is this reformist strategy that also made it possible for governments with different ideological orientations to agree to sign the Nairobi "Forward-Looking Strategies for the Advancement of Women" at the United Nations Conference in 1985.

In order to ensure the implementation at the national level of the "Forward-Looking Strategies for the Advancement of Women" adopted at the 1985

Conference, one of the recommendations stipulated that governments set up appropriate units to deal with women's affairs:

> Appropriate machinery with sufficient resources and authority should be established at the highest level of government as a focal point to ensure that the full range of development policies and programmes in all sectors recognizes women's contribution to development and incorporates strategies to include women and to ensure that they receive an equitable share of the benefits of development. (United Nations 1986: 33)

What does this mean at the national level? Alvarez (1990) points out that, in the past, international feminist solidarity successfully brought pressure to bear on the international development establishment, indirectly pushing Third World states to open up some political space, however minimal, for the articulation of progressive gender discourses and policies. However, as the following account of the Turkish response to the stipulation articulated above will show, there is no way to understand what this means without an analysis of how gender discourses function in the relationship between state and society. The demand for "more equitable development for women" is devoid of meaning unless one clarifies what it means for particular people and why it is defined the way it is.

In April 1990, the Turkish government introduced a bill to set up a Directorate for Women's Status and Problems which was publicly proclaimed to be a response to and in accordance with the Nairobi Conference recommendations. In the Turkish case, the interpretation of "equitable development for women" provoked fierce battles among groups and organizations competing for social control. Women's issues had not been so fiercely disputed since the 1930s when Mustafa Kemal Ataturk established his hegemony over the gender discourse in Turkey. Why is it that in the 1980s and 1990s the seemingly innocent bill to set up a unit for women's affairs within the government created such furor? In order to understand these events, it is necessary to link international events with the domestic context and to place gender discourses within the context of state–society relations.

Before I probe these issues further, it is useful to define what is meant by the state. I will adopt the definition of the state found in Michael Bratton's work (1989: 408–9): "The state is an organization within the society where it coexists and interacts with other formal and informal organizations from families to economic enterprises or religious organizations. It is, however, distinguished from the myriad of other organizations in seeking predominance over them and in aiming to institute binding rules regarding the other organizations' activities." Third World states, as Migdal (1988: 27) points out, struggle to achieve certain goals: "The central political and social drama of recent history has been the battle pitting the state and organizations allied with it (often from a particular social class) against other social organizations dotting society's landscape." Within this context those who make the rules acquire social control. In relatively new states, rules of the game are not necessarily agreed upon. State elites try to penetrate society, regulate social relationships, extract resources with varying degrees of success. For example, the seemingly inconsequential conflict in Mustafa Kemal's Turkey over what kind of hat men should wear was, in fact, about who had the right and ability (religious elites or bureaucratic elites) to make rules.

State leaders do not necessarily achieve predominance for the state: "The most subtle and fascinating patterns of political change and political inertia have resulted from the accommodation between states and other powerful organizations in society. Such accommodations could not have been predicted using existing models and theories of macro-level social and political change" (Migdal 1988: 31). What this perspective shows is that political life is not simply a struggle over the allocation of resources, or the competition of interest groups, but is also a struggle over the rules of the game and the underlying ideology. Thus, the best way to understand the nature and extent of the Turkish response to the Nairobi recommendation is to perceive it as a battle over the rules of gender discourse between the Turkish state and society.

State–society relations and the gender discourse in Turkey

Alvarez (1990) suggests that rules over women's status and behavior form part of the structural and ideological grid upon which state power is based. Cagatay and Soysal (1990) point out that those groups vying for political power offer different gender policies than the ruling groups; this is one of the major ways opposition groups distinguish themselves from the discourse of the rulers. The Turkish case illustrates both theoretical points well.

From its establishment in the 1920s up to the 1980s, the Turkish state controlled the rules over what women could and could not do and this hegemony formed one important basis of the newly formed Turkish state's power. The Turkish civil code outlawed polygamy, gave equal rights of divorce to both partners, and granted child-custody rights to both parents in 1926. In 1934, women were granted the vote and could be elected to political office. These policies were devised to achieve international acceptance of Turkey as a "modern" or "Western" state, as well as to achieve domestic control over previously central religious elites which represented Ottoman-Islamic influences (Tekeli 1981). As a result of the state's control of the gender discourse and the state's claim to having bestowed upon women their rights, women's organizations in the 1930s were closed, based on the claim that there were no meaningful demands women could make on the state since the state had already given women their rights.

The hegemony of the Turkish state over the gender discourse was not absolute, however. The rights given to women were not implemented across the board and mostly benefitted elite women. The Turkish state ignored instances of polygamy practiced by clan leaders and landowners; the continuing high number of marriages by religious ceremony only were likewise ignored, despite the law requiring a civil ceremony for a marriage to be legitimate. When the secular, bureaucratic state elites had difficulty penetrating society to achieve compliance with, participation in, and legitimation of new gender rules, they struck a bargain with local strongmen, what Migdal (1988: 32) calls, a "hands-off policy which allowed the strongmen to build enclaves of social control".

While the bureaucratic elites were capable of striking a bargain with the religious elites, they were less interested in engaging in any dialogue with women's groups in society. In fact, up to the late 1970s and 1980s, the women's groups in society followed Ataturk's interpretation of gender issues and expressed gratitude to the secular state for having granted them their rights. The reasons cited to explain the lack of independent women's movements in the Third World, which are generally related to the nature of Third World states and societies, hold true in the case of Turkey as well (Cagatay and Soysal 1990). It is suggested that Third World states favor nationalist ideologies which reject class, gender, and ethnic divisions and espouse some version of "unity" or "a classless society where everyone works for the common good." Studies from many parts of the Third World show that newly independent Third World states have coopted emerging women's movements for the above reasons and as a means of dismantling the old order and of separation from the old order (Massell 1974; Molyneux 1981).

Bratton (1989), writing in the state–society tradition, tells us that conflict arises when a movement or an organization tries to engage the state in political space which the state elites have already occupied and intend to hold. Since the 1980s, it has been clear that the Turkish bureaucratic secular elites are no longer able to dictate the terms of the gender discourse. They share power with elites who support religious conservatism and who have openly begun to redefine the gender discourse along the lines of their values and beliefs. This is far beyond just allowing clansmen to build their own enclaves of social control; it represents an open challenge to the previously accepted definition of gender roles. Although Turkey is a secular state and the religion-based ideology is not as pervasive as in other Moslem Middle East states, the situation of women can still be broadly assessed as Fort et al. have described (Chapter 8 in this volume: p. 140): "as part of the conflict between a traditional, religion-based ideology regarding social organization and the actual social relations emerging in the process of economic development in the region." They also point out that while development brings about women's increased public participation, reactions come from fundamentalists/traditionalists in rural areas, as well as from the urban lower middle class, and this is true in the case of Turkey. Yet urbanization brought about the proliferation of women's groups of various ideological persuasions. In short, in the 1980s, a rising women's movement (composed of liberal, radical and socialist feminist orientations), as well as a strengthening of the position of religious elites, brought women's issues back on the national agenda and started questioning the legitimacy and the adaptability to modern times of "state feminism" as conceived by Mustafa Kemal Ataturk.

The rise of the women's movement in Turkey

The international women's movement which arose in the 1970s inevitably influenced women in Turkey. The late 1970s and 1980s witnessed the emergence of a consciousness of women's issues, especially among the educated women in big cities. In Turkey, the late 1970s were marked by a great deal of social unrest and frequent changes in government, ending with the 12 September 1980 military coup. The new military government outlawed all political organizations at that time, stalling the process of democratization in the country.

Many observers see the Turkish women's movement as the first democratic movement to emerge after the coup (Tekeli 1989). A number of explanations are given for its emergence at that time. As leftist ideologies were repressed and as Marxist women became convinced that a revolution was not likely to bring about gender equality, they turned to socialist feminism. Others argue that when all political parties were closed and all groups which were perceived to be politically active were disbanded and their leaders taken into custody, space for political debate on hitherto unexplored issues opened up. It is also possible that political suppression raised the importance of informal groups, which could continue to meet and discuss issues.

When Turkey returned to democracy in 1982, the new government headed by Turgut Ozal did not feel threatened by the emerging women's movement, partly because it allowed the government to see itself as democratic, and partly because the government did not attach much importance to a few women speaking out on women's rights. Moreover, women's groups themselves did not challenge state authority and, in fact, preferred to have minimal interaction with the state (Tekeli 1989).

What were the strategies and activities of the Turkish women's movement? Alvarez (1990) writes that women's movements are deliberate attempts to push, redefine, and reconstitute the boundary between public and private, between political and personal, and between natural and artificial. The Turkish women's movement began pushing women's issues beyond Kemalist feminism. (I use Kemalist feminism and state feminism interchangeably to mean the gender philosophy and policy established by Mustafa Kemal Ataturk, the founder of modern Turkey.) Tekeli (1990) suggests that one of the first strategies of women's movements is to change discriminatory laws. Although Turkish feminists did not attempt to claim political power themselves, they did try to influence government policy. Two of the civil code items which were recently revised as a direct result of feminist pressure-group activity now grant women the right to work without the permission of their husbands and specify consistent punishment for rape, even if the victim is a prostitute. Besides activities to amend discriminatory civil codes, six thousand signatures were collected and presented to parliament demanding the implementation of the United Nations Declaration of Women's Rights, which Turkey had officially signed. This declaration bound its signatories to accord citizens equal rights regardless of sex.

Other activities of a number of women's groups have ranged from the publication of books, newspapers and journals, to setting up organizations such as the Association for Discrimination Against Women, a Women's Library and Information Center Foundation, Women's Culture House, Mor Cati (Purple Roof) Foundation which assists battered women, and Kadin Cevresi (The Women's Circle). The latter, a service and consultancy company, evaluated the work of women, paid or unpaid, outside or within the home, and organized campaigns and marches to protest against the battering and abuse of women, against forced virginity tests for female civil servants, and against sexual harassment of women on the streets (Sirman 1989). It must be pointed out that these activities were carried out mostly in urban areas by educated, privileged women. At the same time, through pressure "from below," all of these activities extended considerably the more simple, older gender agenda set from above.

The gender discourse which previously lay dormant, except for a few women's organizations following Ataturk's ideology, now ranged from socialist feminism and radical feminism to the proponents of the "female sphere" ideology, who have been called "the turbaned feminists" by the popular press. These groups differed in their ideologies as well as their relationships with the state. More importantly, they were groups of women, not male bureaucrats, who spoke on behalf of women. Their differing perceptions of gender equality provide a means to discern their varying discourses. Socialist feminists argued that gender equality would come with a socialist order accompanied by the dismantling of patriarchal practices, while radical feminists drew attention to how tradition and culture have perpetuated patriarchy and relegated all women to the status of second-class citizens. The "turbaned feminists" maintained that women did not need to claim equality; they were already equal to men – in their separate sphere. They argued that capitalist development, with its accompanying corrupting influence, has worsened women's situation by burdening them with waged work and housework and by turning them into commodities. Finally, the discourse of the Kemalist feminists has emphasized the maintenance of secularism and the upholding of the rights which Ataturk gave women against the onslaught of religious conservatism.

For Tekeli (1990), this wide ideological range of the gender discourse reflects the tremendous social changes Turkey underwent in the 1980s. According to Tekeli, a civil society has grown and matured in Turkey so that neither the state nor the civil society is predominant anymore. This is the result of the tremendous socioeconomic changes Turkey has undergone in the last decade. Urbanization has advanced to the point where half the population now lives in urban areas. Those who work in the agricultural sector are now equal in number to the workers in the industrial and service sectors. Turkish society has become more complex. At the same time, paradoxes abound: "yuppies" and tribe members rub shoulders on the streets; the influence of Westernization and the integration of Turkey into the world market economy clash with the need to maintain Islamic traditions; returning immigrant workers from Europe inevitably change Turkish society as they make their re-entry.

According to Sirman (1989: 15–16), the 1980s was a period marked by new attempts to define and regulate the social order in Turkey through efforts to redefine modes of legitimate participation within the political domain. She suggests:

> In the process, the very identity of the individual as a Turkish citizen was being called into question. This search for new conceptions of democracy and individuality was (and still is) a process that involved all sections of the political spectrum and is indeed productive of new forms of political participation. This search for "democracy" can perhaps be best understood as producing a new balance between the drive toward modernization and individual aspirations for social mobility that will not be unduly disruptive of the social fabric. That such a search also includes a search for female identity has been noted by many observers.

The state elites themselves compete in proposing different discourses on women. The liberal wing of the government promotes a liberal, free-market economy and believes that women's position will improve as economic development proceeds. According to this discourse, women should be given equal opportunity to achieve economic independence. The main opposition party, on the other hand, believes that equal opportunity is not sufficient, that women need to be given special attention, such as in the form of affirmative action quotas, in order to remove discrimination against them. This party has also proposed a ministry for women's affairs. Meanwhile the conservative wing of the government has introduced a discourse called "The Turkish-Islamic Synthesis." This discourse, uncomfortable with the changes occurring in Turkish society, tries to hang on to disappearing institutions and values such as the extended family and fatalism. They claim that industrialization, urbanization, and interaction with other's culture have harmed the "Turkish family" (*Turkish Family Structure* 1989). In particular, women working outside the home have contributed to the disintegration of the family. Women are not considered separately but are called upon to reclaim their domestic roles and help rebuild the traditional family. The state minister, Cemil Cicek, one of the leaders of the conservative movement, cited feminism as one of the major obstacles to the formation of the Turkish-Islamic family, along with the increase in premarital relations and moral degeneration caused by the increased communication, industrialization and tourism in Turkey (Arat 1990). Given the wide range of discourses on women that already existed in Turkish society, then, how was the introduction in parliament of a bill to set up a Directorate of Women's Status and Problems (in accordance with the Nairobi Conference) received? The following account shows that it highlighted existing disputes as well as the lack of genuine communication between the state and groups within society. At the same time, the events which followed the introduction of the bill make it clear that Turkish state–society relations have taken on a much more complex and open character, compared to fifty years ago.

A directorate for women's status and problems?

The bill, introduced in April 1990, was almost immediately withdrawn after much criticism from women's groups and from the deputies of leftist opposition parties. The extent of the controversy, as reflected in the number of public meetings, announcements and newspaper articles connected with this issue, has been extraordinary. The revised bill finally became law on 15 October 1990 after a number of changes and an eight-hour debate in the National Assembly.

Before analyzing the response to the bill, let me first indicate what it proposed to do. This bill sought to establish a directorate under the auspices of the prime minister which would define women's status in social and economic life and offer solutions to what are regarded as women's problems. The directorate was to work "to increase women's level of education, to increase their economic participation in agricultural, industrial and service sectors, to increase women's security in the health, social and legal arena, to improve women's status and to establish their deserved status as equals in social, economic, cultural and political arenas" (*The Turkish Official Gazette*, 20 April 1990: 2).

Introduced by the only woman in the cabinet, Imren Aykut, the Minister of Labor and Social Welfare at the time, it reflects the Nairobi recommendations as well as the liberal free-market philosophy of the Ozal government. Aykut, as a member of the liberal wing of the cabinet, believes in the preservation of Kemalist feminism and believes that increased opportunities for women and their integration into the development process will serve the general goal of free-market-oriented economic growth. The following features of the bill bear witness to this view. The Economic and Social Affairs Unit of the Directorate has the responsibility: (i) to make sure that women participate in all decision mechanisms so that they may be integrated into social life and contribute to development; (ii) to increase employment opportunities for women in order to ensure economic independence; (iii) to ensure women's training and education so that they may compete for jobs in a free-market economy; and (iv) to consider women in all social, economic and political decisions so that they may fully be integrated into the development process. These reforms are the same as those advanced in international forums to bring about change in the norms and principles governing women's role in developing societies. Liberal feminism conforms to the ideals of a free-market economy and demands that women be given equal opportunity, equal access to resources, and equality before the law. In short, the liberal wing of the ruling party in Turkey supports Ataturk's gender policies but takes them a little further and puts them at the service of a free-market-oriented development.

The opposition to the bill did not stem from its general content (although questions were raised about the ambitiousness of the goals) but rather from the use of certain words which evoked religious conservatism and procedures and which implied control of, rather than cooperation with, women's groups. The items listed below were strongly criticized by women's groups and opposition parties (*The Turkish Official Gazette*, 20 April 1990: 2):

> To promote cooperation and coordination among institutions which work in the area of women's affairs, to regulate and support the activities of independent women's associations, to observe all activities of local administrations related to women.
>
> To engage in appropriate activities to protect women's status and to prepare principles, policies, and programs to solve women's problems.
>
> To acquire knowledge on the activities and research of the women's studies units of universities.
>
> To direct the activities of voluntary women's associations in accordance with the national viewpoint to be formulated.

Women's groups protested the bill's intent to regulate the activities of women's associations. As the English-language newspaper *Dateline* observed:

> Several women's associations, among them the Turkish Women Lawyers' Association, The Association for the Promotion of Contemporary Life, the Istanbul University Center for Research into Women's Problems, the Turkish Women's Union, the Soroptimist Clubs Federation, and the Turkish Women's Council, issued a press release in which they objected to the decree in its present

form and proposed amendments. The women's associations objected to what Gultekin Baktir, Chairwoman of the Turkish Women's Union Istanbul branch, called the government's intention to control the activities of the independent women's associations unacceptable. (*Dateline*, 15 October, 1990)

University professors protested the Bill's intent to acquire information about all activities and research on women, claiming this to be a violation of their academic freedom.

The phrase "national viewpoint" which appears in the bill created even more outcry. In Turkey, "national viewpoint" connotes a conservative perspective. (It was a slogan used by a rightist religious party and is widely known to represent a conservative, religious perspective.) This slogan, coupled with the public knowledge that Mehmet Kececiler, one of the conservative state ministers in the cabinet, was involved in the drafting of the bill, raised doubts about the liberal goals of the bill. Meanwhile, state minister Cemil Cicek contributed to the furor by publicly declaring the following:

> Flirting is nothing different from prostitution. Flirting and pre-marital relationships are human beings' rapprochement with animal instincts. According to Law 41 in the constitution, the Turkish family structure is to be preserved. This was not just a natural obligation after 1982, as it became a social obligation ... Industrialism, urbanization and interaction with other cultures brought along social changes. It was the family which was harmed by these changes. We are an old nation, a family nation. At first, the family was confronted by mass communication. Satellites enabled us to watch the world's television programs. A lot of tourists visit Turkey, and they have a certain influence on the Turkish people which is hardly positive. Family values change ... Instead of taking the developments of science and technology, we are imitating the degenerated values of the West. (*Dateline*, 17 November 1990)

Women's groups have vehemently objected to these claims. One of the leaders called Cicek's views "unacceptable". She said: "They are trying to put women behind bars. There are human rights in Turkey, with equality of women and men." A member of the main opposition party, the Social Democratic Populist Party, claimed: "It is useless to try to revive the model of traditional Moslem Turkish women; it is like making rivers flow upstream" (*Dateline*, 17 November 1990). As one University professor pointed out:

> What does national viewpoint mean? As I understand it, national viewpoint has been articulated by Erbakan for twenty years [Erbakan is the leader of the religious conservative party]. Is this Erbakan's national viewpoint? If it is not, since it represents a particular political party's perspective, what is it? Does national viewpoint mean the traditional Turkish family structure where women sit at home, do not work and look after their children? Whose national viewpoint is this? (*Ozbilgen*, 17 May 1990)

While the bill to set up the directorate articulated liberal solutions to women's problems, conservative policies on women were being voiced by the same government. For example, a report of the Commission on the Turkish Family Structure, prepared as a reference document for the Sixth Five Year Development Plan indicates that: "Turkish television should emphasize national programs. In music, literature, and folklore, the Turkish culture should be promoted and a Moslem-Turkish personality should be created" (*Turkish Family Structure* 1989: 36).

According to this report, the Turkish family structure has been disintegrating as a result of rapid cultural changes, and the roles of men and women in the family have begun to alter. However, the report continues, in the Moslem-Turkish family, the father has a sacred role and women are revered as mothers. This report implies that the disintegration of the Turkish family structure is partly due to women working outside the home and proposes ways for women to work in cottage industries in the home. Not by coincidence, one of the conservative state ministers, Cemil Cicek, heads the new Family Research Institute, established in 1989 and entrusted with formulating a national policy on the family.

The discussions revolving around the bill culminated in a revised version which became law on 15 October 1990. The following items compare the two versions as they were published in the *Official Gazette* dated 20 April 1990 and 28 October 1990.

(1) Instead of "To engage in appropriate activities to protect women's status and to prepare principles, policies and programs to solve women's problems", the revised version reads: "To engage in appropriate activities to protect and improve women's status and to prepare principles, policies and programs in accordance with Ataturk's reforms."

(2) Instead of "To acquire knowledge on the activities and research of women's units in universities", the revised version reads: "To use the research and publications produced by women's units in universities."

(3) Instead of "To direct the activities of voluntary women's associations in accordance with the national viewpoint to be formulated", the revised version reads: "To provide information to voluntary women's associations who are members of international organizations on national values as reflected in Ataturk's principle's and reforms."

(4) Instead of "To promote cooperation and coordination among institutions who work in the area of women's affairs, to regulate and support the activities of independent women's associations, to observe all activities of local administrations related to women", the revised version reads: "To promote cooperation and coordination among institutions who work in the area of women's affairs, to request information from them, to support the activities of independent women's organizations and to observe all activities of local administrations related to women."

The revisions respond to most criticisms, by giving up the phrase "regulating women's organizations" and "national viewpoint", and guaranteeing adherence to Ataturk's gender discourse, calming the fears of Kemalist feminists that their rights are in jeopardy. The unit was first set up under the Ministry of Labor and Social Welfare. It is now called the Directorate General on the Status and Problems of Women in the Prime Minister's Office. At this time, it is too early to evaluate this unit's effectiveness. However, the process which led to its establishment yields some important insights about domestic compliance with international norms.

Conclusions

In the 1930s, the implementation of gender policy by a secular bureaucratic elite which brought Turkish women Western women's status served not only to demonstrate to the international community that Turkey was becoming a "Western" nation but also to establish control of gender role definitions within Turkish society. The wish of the state elites to appear "modern" to the international community coincided with their wish to define gender roles in their own terms (as one way to establish dominance over society). In one sense, what we see in the 1980s and 1990s is rather similar: a bill to set up a women's bureau is prepared to impress the international community and to show that Turkey abides by the international norms on women. But the vague statement of norms – that women receive an equitable share of development – which was necessary to elicit international agreement also left both the content and the process of implementation open to discussion. Given the nature of state–society relations in Turkey in the 1980s, the Turkish state could no longer pass a bill quietly to abide by international pressure. Furthermore, the Turkish state no longer could impose one gender discourse on Turkish society because different gender discourses were being discussed and debated, with no overall agreement in sight.

This dispute has to be analyzed and understood within the context of 1980s Turkey. Competing state elites voiced contradictory gender discourses. More importantly, within the same government one sees contradictory gender discourses. The liberal wing promoted women's integration into a liberal capitalist economy and therefore had an interest in preserving Ataturk's gender policies. The conservative wing, on the other hand, espoused patriarchal policies and women's return to the home in an attempt to roll back the impending change that accompanies capitalist development. Meanwhile, Turkish society had become much more complex, varied, and democratically oriented. A women's movement has arisen, although different feminist groups are at odds on many issues. The groups are distrustful and fearful of the state, especially of the possibility of a move away from secularism. Given this context, it is easy to understand how the introduction of a bill ostensibly to implement an international recommendation could become the focal point of the battle between secularism and religious conservatism which had been brewing for some time. The introduction of the bill also highlighted the complexity of civil society and the growth of disparate voices within society. Finally, it revealed the narrowing but still present gulf between the Turkish state and society, which at times prevents communication. In the case of gender issues, real communication between state and society takes a long time to achieve.

The original version of the bill did not help to build trust among women's groups because its top-down approach reflected the attitude of a state that is used to delivering services to people without their participation, regulating their activities and doing much of their thinking for them. As this bill was introduced by the only woman minister in the Turkish cabinet, Imren Aykut, a self-professed Kemalist feminist allegedly on the liberal wing, it was ironical and unfortunate that the bill was opposed by most women's groups. Although personally popular, her government was not. The increasing influence of the conservative wing in her government aroused fears that, alone, she would not be able to withstand their pressure. Moreover, some women would find whatever policy she introduced wrong because they support other political parties. These factors contributed to women's opposition to a bill whose professed *raison d'être* was to implement the recommendation of the Nairobi Forward-Looking Strategies.

The presumed power of the religious conservatives in government along with the absence of communication between the government and women's groups shifted the debate from the bill itself to the much larger issue of secularism versus religious conservatism. The docile and quiet associations of women professionals were threatened by the wording of the bill which promised to "regulate" independent women's associations in accordance with a "national viewpoint" to be formulated. This threat resulted from the increasing influence on government policy of the Conservative Wing of ANAP (The Motherland Party) and from the activities and public statements of the newly established "Family Research Institute" headed by Cemil Cicek, a conservative minister. The reports by the Family Research Institute alarmed most women's groups because they claimed that the Turkish family was degenerating and disintegrating as a result of Western influences and women's employment outside the home.

Many professional women's associations were motivated to protest the bill to set up a women's directorate partly because they realized that the rights given to them by Ataturk could no longer be taken for granted and partly because of the pressure on them from socialist and radical feminists to act. They joined hands with these feminists to protest discriminatory civil codes and the battering of women, and allied themselves with leftist opposition parties at once committed to the preservation of secularism and yet still not open to the democratic participation of women within their own ranks. Meanwhile, radical and socialist feminists remain distrustful of the state, preferring to work within society to change cultural norms and practices that discriminate against women.

In short, the bill to implement the Nairobi recommendations in Turkey illustrated what compliance with international norms really means in a specific domestic context. On the surface, Turkey set up a women's unit within the government; but what does this mean in practice? Perhaps compliance should not be understood in literal terms but, rather, in the way international norms spark and change domestic debate on a particular issue. The Turkish bill provoked and fueled discussion on appropriate gender roles as well as on relations between the state and groups in society. And it highlighted the great deal of disagreement which exists on these issues. As Fort et al. point out (Chapter 8 in this volume), actions taken by states shape gender relations in the family, in education and in the economy. The establishment of a women's unit within the Turkish government is just one more way to acknowledge and increase women's presence in politics so that issues of gender inequality in all spheres of life are publicly debated. But looking at the Turkish case, it is apparent that the extent and nature of compliance with international norms and recommendations cannot be understood in abstraction from the debates specific to a country, located as they are in particular state–society relationships. Ultimately, it is these debates that will define and enforce women's formal rights to participate as equals in the public sphere. Without women's participation in policy-making, gender inequalities cannot be overcome.

References

Alvarez, Sonia. 1990. *Engendering Democracy in Brazil*. Princeton: Princeton University Press.
Arat, Necla. 1990. "A New Identity is Being Produced" (in Turkish). *Cumhuriyet* (Turkish daily newspaper), 20 July 1990.
Bratton, Michael. 1989. "Beyond the State: Civil Society and Associational Life in Africa." *World Politics* 41(3): 407–30.
Cagatay, Nilufer, and Yasemin Soysal. 1990. "Comparative Thoughts on the Process of Becoming a Nation and Feminism" (in Turkish). In *A Women's Perspective on Turkish Women in the 1980s*, edited by Sirin Tekeli. Istanbul: Iletisim Yayinlari.
Dateline. An English-language daily newspaper published by Hurriyet in Turkey.
Jaquette, Jane. 1981. "Copenhagen 1980: Women in Development, Feminism and the New International Economic Order." Paper presented at the annual meeting of the American Sociological Association, August.
Kardam, Nüket. 1991. *Bringing Women In: Women's Issues in International Development Programs*. Boulder: Lynne Rienner.
Krasner, Stephen D. 1985. *Structural Conflict: The Third World Against Global Liberalism*. Berkeley: University of California Press.
Massel, Gregory. 1974. *The Surrogate Proletariat: Moslim Women and Revolutionary Strategies in Soviet Central Asia, 1919–1929*. Princeton: Princeton University Press.
Migdal, Joel. 1988. *Strong Societies and Weak States*. Princeton: Princeton University Press.
Molyneux, Maxine. 1981. "Women in Socialist Societies: Theory and Practice." In *Of Marriage*

and the Market: Women's Subordination in International Perspective, edited by Kate Young, Carol Wolkowitz, and Roslyn McCullagh, pp.167–202. London: CSE Books.

Ozbilgen, Fusun. 1990. "Along the 'National Viewpoint'" (in Turkish). *Cumhuriyet* (a Turkish daily newspaper), 17 May.

Sirman, Nukhet. 1989. "Feminism in Turkey: A Short History." *New Perspectives on Turkey*, 3 (Fall): 1.

Staudt, Kathleen. 1985. *Women, Foreign Assistance and Advocacy Administration*. New York: Praeger.

Staudt, Kathleen, ed. 1990. *Women, Politics and International Development*. Philadelphia: Temple University Press.

Tekeli, Sirin. 1981. "Women in Turkish Politics." In *Women in Turkish Society*, edited by Nermin Abadan-Unat, pp.293–310. Leiden: E.J. Brill.

Tekeli, Sirin. 1989. "The Development of the Turkish Women's Liberation Movement in the 1980s" (in Turkish). *Birikim* 3: 34–41.

Tekeli, Sirin. 1990a. *The State and Gender Equity Policy* (in Turkish). Istanbul: The Turkish Foundation on Social, Economic and Political Research.

Tekeli, Sirin. 1990b. "Women in 1980s' Turkey." In *A Women's Perspective on Turkish Women in the 1980s*, edited by Sirin Tekeli, 7–40. Istanbul: Iletisim Yayinlari.

Turkish Family Structure. 1989. Ankara: State Planning Agency.

Turkish Government. 1990. *Official Gazett*, No. 20498, 20 April, pp.2–3.

Turkish Government. 1990. *Official Gazett*, No. 20679, 28 October, pp.2–3.

United Nations. 1985. *The Nairobi Forward-Looking Strategies for the Advancement of Women*. New York: The U.N. Department of Public Information.

Young, Oran. 1989. "Politics of International Regime Formation." *International Organization* 43 (3): 349–75.

10. Work Intensity and Time Use: What Do Women Do When There Aren't Enough Hours in a Day?

Maria Sagrario Floro

One of the striking effects of the economic downturn and recession which hit both developed and developing countries in the eighties is the increased and more visible role of women as significant income earners. Yet, in most instances, women continue to perform their "traditional" roles of homemakers and principle childcare providers. A significant lag persists between the labor restructuring of the economy and change in the gender division of labor within the household. The demand for women's time is heightened even more during periods of fiscal crisis and structural adjustment when governments are unable to ensure the provision of basic goods and social services. In a number of respects, the burden falls harder on women as substitute service providers and as community managers (Beneria and Feldman 1992; Moser 1992; Obbo, Chapter 11 in this volume). These factors have led women to assume a mounting share of responsibilities which compete both for their time and effort.

The increasing number of productive, reproductive and community-managing activities performed by women suggests the need to re-examine their various coping strategies in dealing with time pressure.[1] In recent years, studies conducted in various countries on women's time allocation or time allocation in households focused on answering the following questions: Do women change the balance of what gets done? Does a change in the division of labor at home compensate for any cutbacks in women's domestic contributions? Do machines or outsiders take over certain tasks? Are things done at different times of the day or week? Such studies are heterogeneous in terms of research approaches and disciplinary backgrounds. Some work, such as that of Juster and Stafford (1991), has attempted to examine trends in time allocation in various periods and across countries.

---

* I am grateful to Barbara Bergmann, Lourdes Beneria, John Willoughby, David Hirschmann, Nilufer Cagatay, and Nancy Folbre for stimulating discussions on this topic.

But one particular coping strategy which has yet to be examined extensively is the change in work intensity – defined here as the incidence of overlapping activities or the simultaneous performance of two or more tasks by the same individual. This important qualitative dimension of time use has received little attention in the literature partly as a result of the methodological limitations of existing time-use measurements. Not only is this negligence a serious omission that limits our understanding of the extent of women's work, but there are also other adverse economic implications and social consequences of work intensification which make the topic an urgent one. The options and choices available to women in coping with time pressure are economic-status and household-structure specific. They also depend on the prevailing macroeconomic and social conditions which alleviate or aggravate women's role in the reproduction and maintenance of human resources. An increase in women's work intensity may denote the very limited range of options some women face in dealing with this often ignored yet important economic activity.

This chapter attempts to fill the gap by exploring the incidence of work intensification in the day-to-day pace and organization of women's work. The first section provides an overview of the nature of work intensification and the various forms it may take. In the second section, a conceptual framework is developed to examine the main options and constraints faced by women in dealing with their multiple work burdens. It discusses the various factors that determine the incidence of work intensification as a coping strategy. The third section underscores the serious implications and consequences of the incidence of work intensification. A summary of the major points raised in this study concludes the chapter.

Incidence of women's work intensification

The debt crisis and period of economic recession has produced a resurgence of studies on the impact of macroeconomic changes on women's lives. As structural adjustment policies adopted in many developing countries began to direct the course of economic change, the importance of the sexual division of labor in determining the extent and pattern of labor reallocation became one of the critical issues in the analysis of structural adjustment. Elson (1991) highlighted the implications of withdrawal of food subsidies, devaluation and general increase in food prices for unpaid domestic labor. Household expenditure adjustments, for example, meant switching from relatively expensive to cheaper foods which tend to require more input of women's unpaid labor both in terms of preparation and shopping/marketing (the need to find the cheapest sources and to buy smaller quantities more often). Heyzer's (1986) study of a rural village in Indonesia likewise concluded that rising prices placed subsequent heavy burdens on women. Increased cost of credit, more expensive inputs, and removal of price subsidies have meant longer hours of field work for those with land, and the necessity for those without land to work more days at low wages in addition to the daily grind of household chores. Another study of an urban low-income community (Moser 1992) showed that women in Indio-Guayas, Ecuador were working between twelve and eighteen hours as drastic cuts in fiscal expenditures on public services were made. This meant an actual transfer of the costs for care of the sick, for garbage collection, and for other services from the monetized economy (the public sector) to the unpaid economy of the household and voluntary-work-based community organizations. The overall result was a longer and harder working day for most women.

The multiplicity of productive, reproductive and even community-managing roles that women perform compels them to seek ways to relieve time pressure. For some, this means reducing the time for leisure and/or sleep. But for many Third World women, the biological limit on the number of working hours has already been reached. This leaves very little room for lengthening the work day. Work hours can no longer be stretched as the recession and economic crisis persist and women search for more ways to supplement their falling real incomes. When their capacity for maneuvering their workload is limited, women tend to increase their work intensity by performing certain tasks/activities simultaneously. However, restricted data and measurement difficulties make documentation problematic.

Time-allocation surveys, for example, have provided useful data on women and their participation in various productive activities, both market and nonmarket. Despite considerable progress in the documentation of women's work and their economic contributions, however, several studies (Beneria and Feldman 1992; Robinson 1985; United Nations 1988; Floro 1992; Juster and Stafford 1985; Juster 1991) suggest that the present time-allocation survey method falls short of presenting an accurate picture. One problem is that most time-allocation surveys ignore the presence of overlapping tasks. Interviewers are often instructed to account only for one activity at a time, thereby precluding the possibility that some activities are performed simultaneously. If someone is cutting vegetables while watching over a young child, what is that person doing? This creates a response dilemma since the individual may not know whether to report the activity at a particular moment as cooking or childcare. The same is true of a woman who rocks the cradle with her foot while she mends clothes. A few studies have acknowledged directly the presence of joint activity by indicating one activity as primary and the other as secondary.

In a survey of rural women in Saltibus, St Lucia, Szebo and Cebotarev (1990) showed that 76 percent of all household activities were multi-task. For example, while the midday meal is cooking on the hearth, the mother is nursing her baby as she braids her daughter's hair. The intertwining of women's domestic activities fluctuated from a high of 92 percent to a low of 45 percent of the tasks carried out (Szebo and Cebotarev 1990: 268).[2] Primary activities often meshed with secondary activities such as cooking, childcare, carrying water, taking in laundry, and tidying the house. Combining domestic tasks is a common strategy among women income earners who have to accomplish such work within a much shorter duration.

Time-allocation studies which were conducted in the mid-1970s and the early 1980s in the United States likewise indicated that the incidence of work intensity or overlapping of two or more activities is gender-specific. By relying on two methods of recording time use – namely, time-diary keeping and the survey questionnaire form, Robinson (1985) and Hill (1985) demonstrated in their studies that certain activities are in fact done simul- taneously with other activities. Their findings show that the incidence of overlapping tasks is more prevalent among women than men, particularly in the performance of domestic chores.[3] This is not surprising since housework is "a never-ending obligation, subject to irregular and unsystematic scheduling, often interrupted and generally less tied to the time clock" (Robinson 1985: 46).

The incidence of work intensification applies not only to simultaneous domestic activities but also to the overlapping of leisure with housework. For the rural women in St Lucia, the tasks often performed simultaneously with other activities include nursing, listening to the radio, socializing with kin or friends. In another time-allocation study involving ninety-six Michigan households, the discrepancy between the results of two different time-use recordings is found to be most serious for housework activities which are combined with childcare, eating, watching television, reading and resting (Robinson 1985). The practice of combining rest/recreation/socializing with a domestic activity suggests that there is no strict demarcation between work and leisure especially in developing countries where life is not highly compartmentalized.

A third form of work intensification involves the overlapping of paid work and unpaid housework. Women intensify their time use so that they are able to perform the necessary childcare and household chores and at the same time continue to provide the necessary income for subsistence. This is contrary to the conventional wisdom that the demands of reproductive and productive roles are essentially conflicting. Consequently, women are thought to engage in a zero-sum organization of time use, that is, the more they devote themselves to one sphere, the less they have for the other. A few studies do show that women work "apparent miracles" through the overlapping of tasks so that the contradictions between dual and even triple roles are minimized. The following cases illustrate this point.

Homework or the practice of "putting-out" is a rapidly growing activity in certain industries oriented to export as well as to domestic markets both in the United States and in many developing countries (Roldan 1985; Beneria and Roldan 1987; Benton 1989; Lozano 1989; Christensen 1988).[4] The jobs done by these homeworkers, mostly female, are essentially industrial tasks being carried out in a residential context. A significant implication of this work practice is the homeworkers' ability consistently to alternate or combine paid work and domestic chores such as cleaning, cooking and childcare.[5] This is a sharp contrast to the factory job in which it is difficult for women to combine responsibility for childcare and paid employment. In fact, a study of Mexican home-based workers revealed this to be the most important reason women opted for outwork.[6] Outworking seems to provide women with the means to reconcile what could otherwise be conflicting roles. As Roldan (1985: 266) puts it: "Outworking can be started, interrupted and recommenced at will and is readily combined with other such tasks as the supervision of children and food preparation."

Informal-sector employment is another type of income-generating activity which favors incorporation of those women who are compelled to reconcile their reproductive and productive roles. The informal sector provides openings for women to market their domestic skills in a socioeconomic setting which allows them to care for their children. Two case studies illustrate this point. The first refers to beer (*buzaa*) brewing which is a prevalent activity among women in Mathare Valley, Kenya (Nelson 1979). Nelson's survey shows that, in fact, 80 percent of married women consider this to be their primary source of income. In an economic setting where the only other employment options available to women are those of domestic servant and barmaid/hostess, beer brewing is a rational choice for many, despite its illegal nature and the high risks involved. "Women brewing beer in Mathare could earn more than the minimum wage. In addition, the work is done in their homes which enables them to care for their children while they are brewing and selling" (Nelson 1979: 287). The flexible rhythm and manner of organizing work makes this informal-sector activity quite appealing.

Similar considerations hold for the street sweepers of India. While most jobs prohibit the presence of children in the workplace, the informality of street sweeping allows women to combine their paid work with childcare. The flexibility of the informal sector provides the woman income earner with an option in a social setting characterized by a lack of affordable childcare opportunities and an increased need for women to earn income. Rather than forcing the government and business to deal with this dilemma, the responsibility for resolving the conflict of roles is thrust back to women.

In a Delhi study of slum dwellers (*basti*), Karlekar (1982) points out that 30 percent of the poor women, who must generate income and whose employment takes them out of their homes, end up taking their children with them. For these women, the other alternative, which is to leave their children alone at home "in the care of God," is much less desirable.[7] This childcare arrangement is not unlike the situation of female market vendors and food sellers in Asia, Latin America and Africa (Obbo, Chapter 11 in this volume). In many cases, the children in the streets are those of the women selling cigarettes or home-made snacks in nearby stands. What do women do when their various roles as income earners, homemakers and childcare providers, and community managers/participants, increasingly demand their time and effort? Part of the answer to this question, as the preceding section has demonstrated, is to perform tasks simultaneously and to increase work intensity. While in some instances the incidence of work intensification takes the form of reducing (pure) leisure time, in other cases it intensifies the time spent on housework as well as paid work. The extent to which women are compelled to deal with their multiple roles in this manner depends on several factors. What follows is a brief discussion of the determinants of the incidence of work intensification.

Determinants of work intensification

The recent study by Juster and Stafford (1991) showed that changes are not uniform across countries in terms of either total hours worked or patterns of time allocation. The data they used were from samples of national populations, with the exception of that from the former USSR. Their findings showed that in Japan, Norway and the US, total work time (household plus market) for both men and women declined substantially between the mid 1960s and the 1980s. Moreover, the decline was generally sharper for women than for men. But the decline in total work hours for women showed varying patterns. In the former USSR, both market work and housework hours for women declined substantially; in Japan, market work hours declined substantially while housework hours hardly changed; and for the US, Norway and Denmark, housework hours declined more than market work hours increased.

There are several options available to women other than performing simultaneous tasks to relieve them of time pressure. These include strategies such as substituting capital equipment for their own labor, substituting the labor of others, whether they be husbands, paid help, or other children, and decreasing their own paid work from a full-time to a part-time basis. The choices available to women as well as the constraints they face in adopting any of these options, in turn, depend upon several factors, as follows: (i) household structure, which determines the level of assistance from other household members; (ii) life cycle of the household, which has implications for the number and ages of children; (iii) the structure of the labor market, which determines the employment options for women; (iv) household income status, which determines the capacity to substitute durable capital goods and/or outside paid labor for women's domestic contributions; (v) the prevailing social and cultural norms, which restrict women's work to selected activities; and (vi) the form and extent of discrimination that women face in the labor market.

Studies in the United States, Canada and Western Europe, for instance, have shown that as women's participation in the labor force increased following World War II, the purchase and utilization of time-saving durables and convenience items like freezers, microwaves, dishwashers, washing machines and convenience food increased as well (Strober and Weinberg 1980; Nickols and Fox 1983; Kim 1989). But the substitution of durable goods and purchased items/services (for example, laundry service) for women's own labor depends largely on the economic position of the household (factor (iv) above). Several time-use studies have demonstrated that income is a significant determinant of household durable-goods ownership, while the wife's working status seems to have no significant influence on the ownership of durables (Strober and Weinberg 1980; Nickols and Fox 1983).

For the majority of Third World women, the use of time-saving durables and convenience foods is not even an option since these market goods are either unavailable or not affordable. It is more common to substitute the labor of other household members, particularly daughters and elderly female relatives, for the mother's own labor in home production. This coping strategy depends, however, on the household structure and on the particular stage in the household life cycle (factors (i) and (ii) above). Intra-household labor substitution takes place in the extended household type and in more mature households, but not in nuclear households with very young children. It is not surprising, therefore, that a typical woman homeworker in Beneria and Roldan's (1987) study of Mexican outworkers is a married woman in the ascendant phase of the household life cycle (with young, dependent children) with little or no assistance available from older daughters.

In some cases, mothers substitute paid help or paid child services for their time in reproductive tasks. Access to this type of coping strategy depends, however, on the household income status (factor (iv) above). There is little evidence that women have been able significantly to diminish their reproductive activities by having husbands (or other male relatives) undertake a substantial share of domestic work.

Depending on the structure of the labor market (factor (iii) above), another strategy for some women is to seek part-time employment and/or income-earning activities closer to home. The criteria which guide their choices of employment are primarily related to time (and distance) limitations stemming from their domestic roles. These considerations, in fact, have pushed some women so far as to accept jobs requiring less skill and training than they aspire to or are qualified for (Hagen and Jenson 1988).

But as Karlekar's study of Delhi slum dwellers points out, the poor do not face the same choices as do middle-class women. Ramu's (1989) study of middle-class Indian women notes that most married women employees face competing goals and ultimately give low priority to their careers and attach primacy to their domestic roles. The slum dwellers in Delhi, in contrast, seldom reported role conflict or ambivalence. They were more concerned about earning adequate income so their families could survive in a hostile economic environment than with the issues of role conflict (Karlekar 1982).

The lack of alternative employment opportunities accompanied by discrimination, whether explicit or subtle, in the jobs that are available for most Third World women (factors (v) and (vi) above) have pushed some women to accept outwork or home-based work despite the disadvantages of isolation, absence of job security and very low pay (after deducting their own costs for inputs). These forces also impinge on Asian market vendors and street sweepers in Karlekar's study, who must take any type of employment even if it is away from home and means taking their young children with them. In addition, illegal activities (such as beer brewing in Mathare Valley, Kenya) have become prevalent when the only employment options available are those of domestic servant or bar hostess. Those are jobs which involve long working hours, and in many cases the wages are only half the minimum wage.

The economic necessity for women to earn income coupled with the relative shortage of employment opportunities leaves very little room for consideration of women's time constraints. Women are thus compelled to come to terms with an excessive workload by increasing their work intensity.

Implications and consequences of increased work intensity

There are negative implications of heightened work intensity which preclude any debate on whether women choose it as a positive act or whether they are forced into doing so by circumstances. Productivity loss, substantial decline in the quality of childcare, and deterioration of woman's health are some of the major consequences of the increase in women's work intensity. These outcomes ultimately affect not only the well-being of the woman and the household but also of society as a whole.

From the production standpoint, the overlapping of work and domestic activities leads to loss of concentration and poor performance. Moreover, the increased regularity of work interruptions raises the set-up time involved in shifting from one work sphere to the other. In Lozano's (1989) study of Silicon Valley homeworkers, many of her respondents admit that the only time they can really concentrate on their work is when the children are napping or asleep for the night. The loss in job productivity is officially acknowledged in the regulations and labor codes stipulated by employers of homeworkers. For example, the Southern California Association of Governments proposed terms in a telecommuter's agreement as follows: "Telecommuting is not to be viewed as a substitute for childcare. Telecommuters with preschool age children are expected to have someone else care for the children during the agreed upon work hours" (Lozano 1989: 117).

Another equally important issue arises when industrial production penetrates the spaces and relations of the household. It becomes inevitable that children will participate in the new home activity. A study of women in Bangladesh showed that in the urban informal sector, younger daughters are increasingly undertaking the work of paper-bag making, *coir fibre* or jute string production which is distributed to their mothers.[8] A chain of subcontracting occurs. A similar work pattern ensues in the case of the Alicante female homeworkers in the Spanish shoe industry (Benton 1989). In her study, Benton points out that half of the homeworkers are assisted by children who do such tasks as cutting loose threads or applying glue. The toxic fumes from glue in spaces which are inadequately ventilated have produced severe health problems for many of these child workers.

The persistence of gender norms such that women bear the primary responsibility for child-rearing pushes women into a serious dilemma, while allowing the rest of society and its government to avoid any responsibility regarding reproductive maintenance. Whether women are employed or not and whether they are able to find work close to home or not, they face the severe problem of childcare when their children are young and when there is no other female relative to assist them. The concern for their children in fact dominates the lives of women. Within the context of the Caribbean society, women of St Lucia admit their major worry about the future is the future of their children (Szebo and Cebotarev 1990). The internal dilemma posed by women's multiple roles ultimately cannot be resolved by the increase in work intensity. As shown in the case of the Delhi slum dwellers, poor women end up compromising the social needs of their children in order to meet the financial and material needs of the household (see also Obbo, Chapter 11 in this volume).

The increase in women's work intensity seems to have detrimental effects on women's health as well. Long hours of work, coupled with intermittent incidence of increased work intensity, produce considerable stress. The one resource which is stretched to bring about an improvement in the material well-being of the household is women's labor. What is therefore an advantage for the household as a whole is simply more intense work for its female members. Women's time is extended to its limits in order to accommodate the need for increased resources.

Several studies have documented the different pressures on the time use of men and women (Robinson 1985; Juster and Stafford 1985; Redclift and Mingione 1985). Findings suggest that women have "predominantly shorter resting hours, greater intensity and fragmentation of work and more frequent recourse to multiple simultaneous occupations" (Redclift and Mingione 1985: 7). The effects of such work patterns are quite disturbing. In her study of homework in Mexico, Roldan (1985) indicated that emotional and psychological disorders result not only from the physical and social isolation of the work but also from the increased intensity of their time use. Many of the women interviewed were only able to continue to combine housework and waged work through the use of tranquilizers, and if not using them now indicated that they had used them in the past (Roldan 1985). Excerpts from an interview made by Roldan illustrate the rapid pace and heavy burden of combined housework and outworking characteristic of most women in the study:

> I usually wake up between 4:00 and 5:00 in the morning. Really, I am working like mad most of the time, running here and there, up and down. While I am preparing meals, I am washing clothes or the dishes. If I am not doing that, then I am sweeping or cleaning. If I can get up at 4:00 in the morning, then I am able to finish the housework by 7:00. Then I sit down to sew ... I will carry on until about 9:00 and then give them breakfast ... (266).

Sichtermann (1988), in her study of German working women, also pointed out that increased work intensity was a major source of stress for women. She describes the situation as a "tour-de-force that represents the only way the different and often conflicting demands of the two spheres can be combined and met" (Sichtermann 1988: 277). Women are continually forced to hold together and maintain in their waking hours activities which are functionally incompatible or at least require physical and mental exertion. Women who are crushed between job and housework and who exhaust themselves in their effort to unite the two are thus subject to a triple burden.

In a time-allocation study of working mothers in the US, Wolfe and Haveman (1983) examined the determinants of women's health and the impact of time allocation on changes in health. Recognizing that changes in health over time are the result of a wide variety of exogenous characteristics and endogenous behaviors, they develop an empirically testable model to examine the impact of time allocations on women's health. Their regression results indicate that time allocation does have a significant effect on health. Market work does not, in itself, cause health problems and may in fact contribute to improvement in health. But the combination of both childcare and housework demands on women and the dual role of working and having young children appear to be associated with health deterioration (Wolfe and Haveman 1983). Although the results of this study are merely indicative, they are the only direct estimates available which attempt to disentangle the time allocation–health status nexus for women.

Increased concern about the direct relation between deterioration of women's health and work intensity is reflected in Jiggins's (1989) study of rural poor women in sub-Saharan Africa. She pointed out that even "data from official sources suggest that the stress on female labor time has become insupportable. Overall maternal mortality rates are higher than in developing countries in other parts of the world, and infant mortality rates are more than twice as high as the developing country average" (1989: 953).

For women in developing countries other than those in sub-Saharan Africa, however, the impact is less dramatic, and conventional economic and social welfare indicators are unable to capture the gradual erosion of the quality of life. But by recognizing the increasing incidence in women's work intensity and its impact on women's health, one becomes aware of the trade-off between an improvement in the material well-being of the household in the short term and the health and well-being of its female members in the medium and long term. The preceding discussion also suggests that the prevailing gender division of labor within the household, coupled with a socioeconomic environment which offers limited employment opportunities and little or no support services, are highly prejudicial and problematic for women.

Conclusions

This chapter has argued that the incidence of women's work intensification is neither an isolated phenomenon nor a trivial issue. Evidence shows that it has become an increasingly prevalent means for women to cope with their multiple roles. Through overlapping of tasks, women are able to perform the "miracle" of stretching their workday beyond the limit of the time clock.

Although it provides an important qualitative dimension of time use, the incidence of work intensification has received little attention in the literature. The majority of time-allocation studies tend to ignore the fact that certain activities are performed simultaneously. The presence of overlapping tasks strongly suggests that women's participation in certain activities and their overall economic contribution are underestimated. It also implies that the effort exerted by women may vary. As women increasingly use their time to perform two or more activities, the intensity of their work is heightened. Differences in work intensity among household members further sharpen any difference or asymmetry in the intra-household division of labor.

Work intensification does not only involve the combination of market work and household chores or of two domestic activities. At times, it may take the form of combining work and leisure. This suggests that the pace and sequencing of work and non-work activities lack what E.P. Thompson describes as the "demarcation" between "work" and "leisure." "Social intercourse and labor are intermingled – the working day lengthens or contracts according to the task and there is no great sense of conflict between labor and 'passing the time of day'" (Thompson 1967: 60)

The presence of combined work and leisure activities narrows the applicability and relevance of work–leisure trade-off models which are based on the assumption of a clear separation of work and leisure activities. Moreover, this form of work intensity indicates that there is very little discretionary leisure time for women which they can claim exclusively for themselves.

By extending the discussion of work intensity beyond the traditional workplace in a firm or business organization, this chapter has demonstrated that the concept has another, more commonplace application – the day-to-day organization and use of women's time. Although beyond the scope of this discussion, additional research on work intensification – development of indicators and direct measures – is required to refine further its observable elements. Likewise, there is a need to explore more carefully the implications of work intensification and to draw out the short-term as well as long-term consequences at the level of the individual (woman), the household, and the society as a whole. As the serious consequences mentioned in this discussion imply, this important qualitative dimension of time use deserves more attention from feminist scholars as well as from policymakers and academics.

Notes

1. Moser (1992) points out that, particularly in developing countries, women take on not two but three roles: productive, reproductive and community managing. The latter became increasingly important as a result of government cutbacks in social services. The drastic reduction in public expenditures have pressed communities to mobilize their own collective efforts to acquire infrastructural resources such as infill, water and electricity for the area. Other than in leadership roles, participation is almost entirely by women. This implies that "women take primary responsibility for the success of community level projects" as an extension of their domestic role (20).

2. The extent to which tasks overlap depends on the nature of the work, the woman's stage of life cycle, and the constraints of the day.

3. The total time spent per week by women is 180 hours based on the survey questionnaire method and 168 hours based on the diary method. For men, the discrepancy of the survey over the diary total is only 0.4 hours (Robinson 1985: 46)

4. As governments adopt a more *laissez faire* approach to labor markets and as the economic recession persists, businesses respond to these changes in the economic environment by restructuring their business strategies. The latter involves cost-cutting, shortening product cycles and increasing flexibility in the production process to better respond to unstable market conditions. This has led, among other things, to the increased practice of outworking or homeworking.

5. Lozano's (1989) study of homeworkers in Silicon Valley, California reveals the difference between male and female homeworkers. For men who are interviewed, the disadvantages of home-based work are described in terms of how work occasionally intrudes on social or life-time pursuits, e.g. reading the paper, going jogging or taking a nap, especially when the office is right next to the bedroom. The balance women must strike is a different one. It is not between work and leisure, but between productive, paid work and reproductive, unpaid work.

6. When asked why they opted for homework, 28 percent of the women in the survey emphasized the importance of childcare and another 15 percent said it is most compatible with housework. The second most important reason is the lack of alternative employment (Roldan 1985: 269)

7. Less than a third of the women in the survey conducted among Indian women sweepers of Delhi said that older relatives are prepared to help out in the caring of young children (Karleker 1982).

8. This refers to the study by Hossain (1988).

References

Beneria, Lourdes, and Martha Roldan. 1987. *The Crossroads of Class and Gender: Industrial Homework, Subcontracting and Household Dynamics in Mexico City*. London: The University of Chicago Press.

Beneria, Lourdes, and Shelly Feldman, eds. 1992. *Unequal Burden: Economic Crises, Persistent Poverty and Women's Work*, Boulder: Westview Press.

Benton, Lauren. 1989. "Homework and Industrial Development: Gender Roles and Restructuring in the Spanish Shoe Industry." *World Development* 17 (2): 255–66.

Christensen, Kathleen, ed. 1988. *The New Era of Homebased Work: Directions and Policies*. Boulder: Westview Press.

Elson, Diane. 1991. *Male-bias in the Development Process*. New York: St Martin's Press.

Floro, Maria. 1992. "Women, Work and Agricultural Commercialization in the Philippines." In *Women's Work in the World Economy*, edited by Nancy Folbre, Bina Agarwal, Barbara Bergmann, and Maria Floro, pp.3–40. London: MacMillan Press and the International Economics Association.

Hagen, Elizabeth, and Jane Jenson. 1988. "Paradoxes and Promises: Work and Politics in the Postwar Years." In *Feminization of the Labor Force" Paradoxes and Promises*, edited by Jane Jenson, Elizabeth Hagen and C. Reddy, pp.3–16. Cambridge: Polity Press.

Heyzer, Noeleen. 1986. *Working Women in Southeast Asia: Development, Subordination and Emancipation*, Philadelphia: Open University Press.

Hill, Martha S. 1985. "Patterns of Time Use." In *Time, Goods and Well-Being*, edited by F. Thomas Juster and Frank Stafford, pp.133–76. Ann Arbor: Institute for Social Research, The University of Michigan.

Hossain, Hameeda. 1988. "Industrialization and Women Workers in Bangladesh: From Home-Based Work to the Factories." In *Daughters in Industry: Work Skills and Consciousness of Women Workers in Asia*, edited by Noeleen Heyzer, pp.83–120. Kuala Lumpur: Asia Pacific Development Center.

Jenson, Jane, Elizabeth Hagen, and C. Reddy, eds. 1988. *Feminization of the Labor Force: Paradoxes and Promises*. Cambridge: Polity Press.

Jiggins, Janice. 1989. "How Poor Women Earn Income in Sub-Saharan Africa and What Works Against Them." *World Development* 17 (7): 953–63.

Juster, F. Thomas, and Frank Stafford. 1985. *Time, Goods and Well-Being*. Ann Arbor: Institute for Social Research, The University of Michigan.

Juster, F. Thomas, and Frank Stafford. 1991. "The Allocation of Time: Empirical Findings, Behavioral Models, and Problems of Measurement." *Journal of Economic Literature* 29: 471–522.

Karlekar, Malavika. 1982. *Poverty and Women's Work: A Study of Sweeper Women in Delhi*. New Delhi: Vika Publishing House.

Kim, Chankon. 1989. "Working Wives' Time Saving Tendencies: Durable Ownership, Convenience Food Consumption, and Meal Purchases." *Journal of Economic Psychology* 19 (3): 391–409.

King, Elizabeth, and Robert Evenson. 1983. "Time Allocation and Home Production in Philippine Rural Households." In *Women and Poverty in the Third World*, edited by Mayra Buvinic, Margaret A. Lycette, and William Paul McGreevey, pp.35–61. Baltimore: John Hopkins University Press.

Lozano, Beverly. 1989. *The Invisible Force: Transforming American Business with Outside and Home-Based Workers*. New York: The Free Press.

Miyazaki, H. 1984. "Work Norms and Involuntary Unemployment." *Quarterly Journal of Economics* 99: 297–311.
Moser, Caroline. 1992. "Adjustment From Below: Low Income Women, Time and the Triple Role In Guayaquil, Ecuador." In *Women and Ajustment Policies in the Third World*, edited by H. Afshar and C. Dennis, pp.87–116. London: MacMillan Press.
Nelson, Nici. 1979. "How Women and Men Get By: The Sexual Division of Labor in the Informal Sector of a Nairobi Squatter Settlement." In *Casual Work and Poverty in Third World Cities*, edited by Ray Bromley and Chris Gerry, pp.283–304. Chichester, New York: John Wiley and Sons.
Nickols, Sharon, and Karen Fox. 1983. "Buying Time and Saving Time: Strategies for Managing Household Production." *Journal of Consumer Research* 8:197–208.
Ramu, G. N. 1989. *Women, Work and Marriage in Urban India: A Study of Dual and Single-earner Couples*. New Delhi: Sage Publications.
Redclift, Nanneke, and Enzo Mingione, eds. 1985. *Beyond Employment: Household, Gender and Subsistence*. Oxford: Basil Blackwell.
Robinson, John P. 1985. "The Validity and Reliability of Diaries versus Alternative Time Use Measures." In *Time, Goods and Well-Being*, edited by F. Thomas Juster and Frank Stafford, pp.33–62. Ann Arbor: Institute for Social Research, The University of Michigan.
Roldan, Martha. 1985. "Industrial Outworking, Struggles for the Reproduction of Working Class Families and Gender Subordination." In *Beyond Employment: Household, Gender and Subsistence*, edited by Nanneke Redclift and Enzo Mingione, pp.248–85. Oxford: Basil Blackwell.
Sichtermann, Barbara. 1988. "The Conflict between Housework and Employment: Some Notes on Women's Identity." In *Feminization of the Labor Force: Paradoxes and Promises*, edited by Jane Jenson, Elizabeth Hagen, and C. Reddy, pp.276–87. Cambridge: Polity Press.
Strober, Myra, and Charles B. Weinberg. 1980. "Strategies Used by Working and Nonworking Wives to Reduce Time Pressure." *Journal of Consumer Research* 6 (4): 338–48.
Szebo, Linda, and E. A. Cebotarev. 1990. "Women's Work Patterns: A Time Allocation Study of Rural Families in St. Lucia." *Canadian Journal of Development Studies* 9 (2): 259–78.
Thompson, E. P. 1967. "Time, Work Discipline and Industrial Capitalism." *Past and Present* 38: 58–97.
United Nations. 1988. *Improving Statistics and Indicators on Women Using Household Surveys*, Studies in Methods Series F, No. 48, New York: United Nations.
Wolfe, Barbara, and Robert Haveman. 1983. "Time Allocation, Market Work and Changes in Female Health." *American Economic Review* 73 (2): 134–39.

11. Gender Stratification and Vulnerability in Uganda

Christine Obbo

This chapter elaborates the connection between gender stratification and women's socioeconomic vulnerability in Uganda; it shows how gender differentiation constructs the differing bases from which women and men approach the exchange relationships affecting the distribution of power between them. In Uganda, the limited nature of women's rights to resources makes them dependent upon men, particularly as husbands. Women are marginalized in the modern economy and often work in the informal economy of self-employment and low income. So-called entitlements elude women, keeping them poorly educated and impoverished.

Many of Ugandan women's actions since the 1950s can be seen as strategies to keep encroaching poverty at bay. Between the 1950s and 1960s, women campaigned for the registration of all marriages and divorces. Wives fought to protect the inheritance of their children against their husbands' other children born to women not legally married. But their attempt at legal reform largely failed; widows and orphans are still dispossessed by outside children and greedy relatives. In the 1960s, women from the popular sectors adopted two strategies – either abandoning marriage and/or migrating to the cities to work – aimed at achieving independence, self-respect and changing their individual social and economic situations. Then, the economic and political crises of the 1970s and 1980s drastically reduced women's economic status. Women's low educational attainment and their marginalization from other entitlements, such as health-care services, made their situation worse still. The initiation of official strategies to change the situation of women is promising, and grassroots organizations are also actively working to enhance women's well-being.

However, much remains to be done, particularly to meet the needs of the majority of women who are poor. Women still have little reason to believe that powerful male businessmen, bankers, lawyers and officials will do more than pay lip service to their needs and hopes. Moreover, women remain enmeshed in a system of kinship and gender relations which operates to their social and economic disadvantage.

Kinship and the gender system

Kinship groups recruit members through marriage and birth; the price of membership in kinship groups is the acceptance of social definitions, duties, and obligations. Social identity, the division of labor, and property transfers are anchored in kin relationships which are maintained, in part, through systems of gender stratification – that is, the gender system. Much ideology surrounding kinship (and other) relations between men and women defines them according to whether they are social males or social females and specifies the norms for each gender. The beliefs and values associated with each gender in turn force men and women to behave according to this gender differentiation. Biological differences are elaborated into social differences as well as power inequalities; men and women have unequal access to scarce and valued resources of society. This arrangement typifies the gender system in most parts of Ugandan society.

Like women everywhere, Ugandan women bear and care for children; they perform housework, including getting and preparing food; they provide a preponderance of the health care;[1] and they are responsible for maintaining exchange relationships between relatives and neighbors through such acts as gifts of food and visits. (See Lomnitz, Chapter 3 in this volume for analysis of women's key role in the maintenance of exchange networks among kin, friends and neighbors in Latin America.) In other words, the gender division of labor requires women to be the main providers of domestic labor, affection, and moral and psychological support, all seen as an integral part of kinship. Under the same specifications, men monopolize extra-domestic labor and the control and distribution of rights in resources. Elder men, as guardians and fathers, decide what and how much members of the kin group should get. This distribution depends upon the ideological constructs that distinguish between (male) elders and minors (sons and daughters) within groups and the essential outsiders (wives) upon whom the groups depend.

Although erosion of gender inequality can occur through intentional and unintentional changes which enhance women's opportunities in the system, social forces strongly favor the maintenance of the system of gender inequality. When kin relations become integrated into the market economy of cash-crop production and wage labor, for example, women typically are relegated to the reserve pool of unpaid labor. Thus, in such market economies, as in subsistence economies, women continue to work for men without changes in the ideology determining their legal rights or their share in resources. In Uganda's market-economy system, women's subordinate position stems from both the lack of paid-job opportunities, due largely to women's high illiteracy rate, and the lack of access to institutional banking credit, due to the fact that they do not control vital resources, such as land and livestock. And both derive directly from the gender system. Women are maintained in a dependent position because lack of skills and resource control means they are deprived of the social power to secure, in their own right, the use of labor in and outside the market system. Thus, this system of gender stratification puts women at a serious disadvantage.

In general, the unequal control of resources between African couples is unsuited to the current unequal division of parental duties. In many societies, including Uganda, mothers bear the brunt of daily household costs, and fathers contribute from time to time for specific expenditures. The market economy involving cash-crop sales and wage labor provides men with individual incomes over which their wives have no control. In a market economy, relative access to money (a generalized resource) is a key indicator of the degree of gender stratification (Chafetz 1990). Women who do not control societal resources or the money resulting from their own labor have limited negotiating power in society generally or with their husbands. Moreover, Ugandan wives who assert themselves may lose effective support from their husbands; at the same time, mistresses may secure effective economic support. This issue is one long-standing element of the gender system which operates to impoverish women and which women have struggled to change.

Women's strategies to ward off poverty

Ugandan women's experiences since the colonial encounter can be characterized by strategies to ward off encroaching poverty. These strategies have included campaigns for legal reforms carried out by educated women, as well as the rejection of marriage by rural women in the popular sectors which, in many cases, also involved migration to urban areas. These strategies have had both positive and negative impacts on women. Often the disadvantages were unintended consequences but, at other times, they were perceived by the women as necessary hazards. The following section deals with elite women's efforts to reduce the vulnerability of women in relation to laws of property which define marriage and inheritance.

The campaign for reform of the marriage, divorce and inheritance laws: the 1950s and 1960s

The state of gender inequality based on unequal access to and control over resources was reinforced by the colonial legal system. The colonial laws of marriage, divorce, and inheritance created new hurdles for women. In the 1950s, the daughters of the chiefs in the colonial system, who had been groomed in Western education, decided to organize in order to bring about legal reforms. The women declared they would use women's education to fight injustices in society through legal means. That it was educated and relatively privileged women who took the lead in challenging discrimination in Uganda reflects a pattern found in other countries (Kardam, Chapter 9 in this volume). The various groups of elite women who campaigned for legislative reform of the 1904 Marriage, Divorce and Inheritance Laws were brought together around the issue: "All marriages and divorces should be registered and their validity should depend on their registration."

The campaigns explicitly focused on "Christian Marriages," although civil and customary marriages were also implicated. The most active group to convene a national conference on the issue was the Uganda Council of Women (UCW), which was predominantly Christian. Other groups involved included the Widows' League, Namirembe Young Wives (consecutively chaired in one period by a mother and her daughter), Mothers Union, and the Forward Society Anglican and Catholic Associations of "Ring Wives" which defended the rights and status of women married in church. The Mothers Union provided pamphlets and engaged in discussion on "the meaning of wedding rings." In 1953, Christian Baroga women from Eastern Province complained that while their husbands were not taking other women as wives, they were giving them rings, which they felt usurped their own status as church wives (Uganda Government Report 1965). In 1955, Kigezi "Ring Wives" complained that their husbands often try to get rid of them by making their lives impossible after they have brought second wives into the home.

The 1904 Marriage and Divorce Ordinance had actually prohibited bigamy, in terms of: (i) contracting another marriage while married under the Ordinance; (ii) contracting a marriage under native and customary law while a registered marriage is still in existence; (iii) contracting a marriage registered under the Marriage Ordinance while still married under native custom (Brown 1988: 59; Morris 1960). A five-year prison sentence was the maximum penalty for each offense. However, while a husband could divorce his wife on the grounds of adultery alone, a wife could not so divorce her husband. To grant a wife a divorce from her husband his adultery must be accompanied by further offenses, such as incest, bigamy, or cruelty. Consequently, desertion rather than divorce became the most common method of separation for women married under Church, civil and customary law. The Ring Wives thus faced a difficult dilemma as they felt it wrong to leave their marriages, however undesirable they were (Brown 1988).

These sentiments were echoed in 1956 by Acholi women in a memorandum they presented to the governor, Sir Andrew Cohen, when he was on a tour of the district: "Women in villages are not at all happy with this question of marriage because when a man has married a women he does not take any thought in the least to give her *comfort, happiness, and freedom*" (Brown 1988: 6, emphasis added). Their statement also complained about forced remarriage and the difficulty and shamefulness of divorce. In addition, the women complained that women lose control not only over property left to them by their husbands but also over their own personal possessions.

Since the 1950s, recognizing that widows are often too overwhelmed with sorrow and funeral arrangements to defend their property, some wealthy men have instructed their wives that, in the event of the husband's predecease, they were to lock up all the belongings in one room before the relatives arrive for the funeral. The act of dispossessing widows is the result of general poverty, which promotes redistribution of wealth by grabbing it from the vulnerable. In 1958, women raised the issue of the widow's inheritance and of whether a man's legitimate heir was his son or his nearest relative. In the same year, the Widows' League issued a memorandum appealing to the Church Leader and Ganda King *(Kabaka)* to open up the discussion with the clan leaders and presumably take action because:

> As things stand, all married women would prefer predeceasing their husbands for fear of the hardship and suffering if they were to survive their husbands. Such fears are already [spreading the inclination] among some young women against committing holy matrimony for fear of the experiences their mothers have taught them, of what they are likely to go through in the event of their surviving their husbands (Brown 1988:18).

Women fear being widowed or divorced because those life-cycle changes render them propertyless. If, however, women acquire a material base, then the end of a marriage is less fearful. Because some communities in Uganda regard the return of bride price as divorce, a woman with her own resources could even manage some control of her fate. The following response from the prime minister of Toro to the bishop who had sought clarification on a complicated divorce case involving a Church and customary marriage illustrates this option:

> In our tradition, a court cannot force anyone to live with anybody if they no longer wish to do so, because it might lead to some calamity. ... When a wife refuses to stay with her husband, or when a man refuses to have his wife back, the court assists the wife's relations to return the bride price. Sometimes when a woman decides to leave her husband, she brings the bride price to a native court and thus she is released from her marriage. (Brown 1988: 11)

In the campaign for reform described above, women became very skilled at producing, and getting to the right people, their memoranda on "man's inhumanity to man." The Church of Uganda and the Catholic Church were both compelled to enter the campaign. In 1963, the Church of Uganda issued a statement in support of the revision of marriage laws (Church of Uganda 1963). The campaign and the conference organized by the Uganda Council of Women resulted in a 1964/5 Commission on Marriage Laws (1965). The Commission recommended that the High Court should appoint a committee of "Men of Wisdom and Experience" (Commission on Marriage Laws 1965) to hear divorce cases. In 1972, Succession (Amendment) Decree 22 was passed to protect women and children from being disinherited by clan leaders. The Decree gave a woman legal claim on her house and part of her husband's property in cases where a husband left a will in which the wife was not included (Decree 22 1972). In 1973, the Customary Marriage Decree provided for the registration of customary marriage. The Decree made polygamy legal, but to contract a customary marriage while married under the Ordinance requiring monogamy was deemed a criminal offence (Decree 16 1973).

These changes looked good on paper, but ultimately they did not address the needs of women, the majority of whom could not afford to employ lawyers. A decade passed before a decree allowed the registration of marriages and permitted widows to claim what was rightly theirs. The liberal legal reformist approach had hitherto been characterized by the use of education to change the law through memoranda campaigns, holding conferences and, if possible, getting women elected to the legislative body. For reforms to be beneficial, however, women need to be educated about the law for their empowerment.

The Uganda Association of Women Lawyers (FIDA) has, through a grant from OXFAM (UK), produced and translated into local languages pamphlets on inheritance, marriage and divorce and on the legal jurisdiction of Resistance Councils. This project is based on the assumption that if women learn about their rights under the law, they can fight to defend themselves. FIDA members visit districts to explain the laws to the women, an admirable practice that should be promoted and supported with more resources. However, the methodology of teaching rural women needs to be revised. The "advocates" must be willing to stay in the villages with women for longer periods of time, instead of making quick visits during which they reside in township lodges. A pedagogical approach involving small focused groups would empower women to discuss the law, associated problems, and effective courses for action.

Popular change strategies: abandoning marriage and migrating to urban areas

Abandoning marriage

The women's reform campaign reached a dead end in the early 1960s, but prosperity then marked the economic climate. Individual women began either to abandon their marriages and work to support themselves or, for those who stayed married, to find creative ways to share in the wealth they were producing. Women who abandoned marriage usually did so to settle on a piece of land acquired in the rural areas or to run a trade or entertainment business in the urban areas. These women were asserting that they were "tired of working for men and bearing children for them." This was a radical critique of the production and reproduction requirements of the social system in which women were ideologically expected to be hard-working wives and mothers. Other women expressed unease at being married to poor men who insisted on controlling their labor. Women referred to this as being "the slave of a slave."

This period was the decade of optimism; people believed that hard work was everyone's salvation. Rural women could grow fruit, sell it to travellers or sell some of the cash crop and in return buy the clothing, china or jewelry from hawkers who visited their homes or sold their wares at the weekly markets. Men bought bicycles, dresses for their wives at Easter and Christmas, radios and clocks; and, in addition, affluent rural homes had record players and automobiles. People were not aware that cash-crop production depended upon the world market; they would learn this lesson in the 1970s and 1980s.

Meanwhile, economic prosperity was eroding gender inequality: women were able to work for themselves. They were paying particular attention to educating their daughters so they would not have to depend on marriage for survival. Whenever possible, women invested in resources such as land, cattle, and material goods. Money was also invested in business ventures, some of which were of petty commodity proportion. There was an increase in the number of economically and otherwise viable households headed by women. Desertion became the preferred method of separation for women in the popular sectors (although elite Christian women stayed in marriages with varying degrees of satisfaction).

However, there was also a backlash against women's improved situation. In the newspapers, men were voicing the concerns of men in general; these were the same newsmen who had gleefully reported that the predominantly male parliament had earlier dismissed women's campaigns for legal reform. Public sentiment derided urban women for trying to destroy the family; single women were collectively branded "loose" and characterized as "prostitutes." Kardam (Chapter 9 in this volume) discusses other forms this reaction takes. Some unmarried women were indeed prostitutes or mistresses of influential men, but these women's lifestyles were largely a response to the economic clout enjoyed by men relative to women. If men used money, jobs, and resources to control women sexually, women felt they could share in men's wealth under such controls. Nonetheless, by accumulating their own resources, women had been able to challenge the disadvantageous arrangements of production and reproduction determined by the gender system (see Obbo 1980).

Migrating to cities

In the late 1950s, women started migrating from the rural to the urban areas to escape rural drudgery (in favor of a lifestyle that offered more leisure), the controlling power of men sanctioned by marriage as well as unsatisfactory and unworkable marriages, filiation and inheritance laws, and the sometimes stultifying social sanctions regulating women's sexuality. By the late 1960s, escape from rural poverty also emerged as a motive for women to migrate to the urban areas. Some women migrated alone, some with their husbands; most were young, but there were also a few older women. The majority of women lacked education and the skills needed to secure jobs in the government or private companies. Therefore their economic activities became concentrated in the self-employment sector where they worked as hairdressers and dressmakers or prepared and sold food, beer and local gin (*Waragi*). Lomnitz's discussion (Chapter 3 in this volume) of the informal economy provides a useful context for understanding the economic activities of Ugandan women in urban areas. These activities, although visible, were sometimes illicit, and therefore not included in official figures. Some self-employed people were so successful that they attracted the attention of civil servants, who saw extracting bribes from them as a way of getting rich quickly while at the same time maintaining respectable pensionable jobs. On the whole, both men and women viewed urban life as better than rural life despite the extra hard work needed for survival and the fact that housing, water, fuel and food were commodified.

By the 1970s, in Uganda, as in other African countries, the rapid migration of peasants to the cities overloaded the urban infrastructure and overcrowded the self-employment sector of petty commodity production and services; there was intense competition between men and women. At about the same time, the International Labour Organization (ILO) was persuading local planners and governments that self-employment (at that time termed the "informal *sector*") was the solution to the urban unemployment problem.

In 1972, Asian traders and industrialists were expelled by a military government decree, and their properties and businesses were acquired and plundered by a new class of businessmen consisting of civilians and soldiers. This process of acquiring money, jobs and prosperity one had not worked for was generally known in Uganda as "falling into things." These new captains of the economy became known as *Mafutamingi,* which is Swahili for "a lot of fat," as they literally grew fat and indulged in conspicuous public consumption activity. Women – wives, girlfriends, sisters, daughters – became the medium through which to display new wealth.

By 1975, the Ugandan formal economy had collapsed and had been replaced by the underground economy characterized by speculation and black-market activities. State violence and anarchy in the rural areas created a reign of terror which forced many people to seek safety in urban centers. Without the international business connections and know-how for international trade, people resorted to selling smuggled coffee in return for consumer goods from neighboring countries. Some women participated in this trade which became known as *Magendo* or pilgrimage of greed. People risked their lives and money to make the goods available; customers reluctantly accepted that the exorbitant prices demanded were necessitated by shortages of goods. Self-employment in service activities flourished at the truck stops, townships and fishing ports as their populations increased. Purveying sex became much more widespread in various places as inflation drove prices ever higher. By the late 1970s, the most visible actors in the urban areas were prostitutes, traders, truck drivers and soldiers. The soldiers extracted a "road toll" *(amagendo)* of goods from both men and women traders; women had to make further payment in sex (see Obbo 1980).

Vulnerability in the economic climate of the 1980s created several trends. The situation drove many people to return to the rural areas to rehabilitate the homes they had abandoned in the 1970s. But the task was too daunting for many young people who returned again to the urban areas to live. In both urban and rural households, husbands continued to pay school fees, but the wives had to find money for uniforms and other school requirements. Women and children are particularly vulnerable to poverty, and this development forced women to assume increasing burdens for the daily survival of their children, by producing food and engaging in petty trade and craft production. The mass of Ugandans struggled for a "living wage" to ward off poverty, but the economic situation had differing impacts upon different classes. Growing differentiation between the upper class and the rest of the population based on unequal economic and political power exacerbated existing regional, ethnic and gender differences (Obbo 1986).

Structural adjustment: impacts and responses

The Ugandan economy has not recovered from the collapse of the 1970s, although since 1980 there have been numerous programs to rehabilitate it. This failure can be attributed to poor accountability, policy discontinuity, and preoccupation with short-term crisis management of the debt burden. In discussion and analysis of the economic/debt crisis as well as the application of the supposed cure, the Structural Adjustment Programs (SAPs), women and children remain shadowy figures. Yet all available evidence suggests they bear the brunt of SAP.

At the seminar held in 1989 to assess Uganda's economy since 1986, one writer on the credit crisis, which was characterized by inflationary interest rates, poignantly stated the problem:

> The overall overriding problem is the catastrophic poverty whose iron grip on our nation is evident everywhere. The poverty is in the pockets of hundreds of thousands who cannot find jobs; those families with relatives suffering from

catastrophic illness and unable to find medical care; the young and old who are hungry and malnourished; the university students for whom the nation can no longer afford textbook allowances; the civil servants whose monthly wages cannot suffice to feed their families even for one week. (Suruma 1989: 2)

Many speakers echoed these views, insisting that the poverty resulting from the economic crisis and the measures to correct it was killing people. The Ministry of Planning's Permanent Secretary caused consternation when he countered that "No one was dying of poverty." This assertion prompted one speaker to ask whether the official had noticed the poorest hawkers, many of whom were women with babies, stationed in front of his Ministry building.[2]

The 1980s were characterized as the decade when many families in Uganda lacked the economic wherewithal to meet their basic needs. There were widows and other displaced people, orphans of war and of AIDS, and vast numbers of unemployed people in both the rural and urban areas. There was a blurring of formal and informal activities; commercial and domestic space; public and private concerns. The changes which had begun in the 1970s were threatening the living wages of the majority of Ugandans.[3]

The elites in public-sector positions could not maintain themselves on their salaries, but they stayed in their jobs because of the prestige associated with working in the public sector and because the fringe benefits of houses and sometimes transportation made survival possible. However, elites not employed in banking or development agencies often had two jobs to keep their families' standard of living at the level they expected. The wives of all elites, except the ministers, also had two or more jobs. Many depended upon less-educated relatives to engage in petty trading in the right locations and at the right time. Young men and women not lucky enough to be employed by elites were either unemployed or self-employed as street hawkers.

The serious decline in employment opportunities for poor women meant that in urban areas women figured far more prominently in informal or petty commodity activities than in the formal sector. Even the increased employment opportunities for educated women in urban technical and professional jobs did not offset the marginalization of women in the labor market. Young girls and women who sell newspapers and small quantities of such items as peanuts, candy, pencils and pens emerged as the most visible group of hawkers. Some young women hawkers would sit all day in the sun with their infants and toddlers.

When, in March 1990, the government announced reforms in the health services, requiring patients to pay a user fee (*The New Vision* 1990), there were mixed reactions. On the one hand, people felt there would be little change in the system as health workers had already been extracting fees from patients. On the other, they expressed disappointment at the failure of the government to reform the health system and protect poor people who are often victimized by the system. This latter concern was framed with reference to what was seen as a typical story which gained wide circulation at about the time of the March announcement:

> When a woman in labor was rushed to a hospital clinic, a male health official demanded 1,000 shillings as a fee to have a bed assigned to her. She had no money but assured the official that her husband would bring the money. The official ordered the patient to be dragged out of the clinic. A few meters away from the hospital clinic, the woman delivered with the help of a good Samaritan midwife. (*The New Vision* 1990)

This is but one illustration of the desperate need for improvement in women's situation. A recent Save the Children Fund study (Obbo 1992) found that women's educational and financial status affect their access to health care, and thus their ability to care for their own health as well as their ability to be effective health care providers for their families. Women often postpone their own treatment and fail to initiate hospital treatment for their children because they are financially dependent on their husbands. Women's inability to obtain institutional credit, and their lack of control over the resources of land, cattle and the labor of kin are factors that reflect in their lack of access to health services, because the main criterion is the ability to pay. The division of labor in which men control cash, and women are food producers and home managers, affects the immunization of children because women may lack either the money to travel to hospital or someone to care for other children for the day. Thus, the fact that most immunization services are financed by foreign, non-governmental organizations (NGOs) does not entirely resolve the access problem.

Finally, the crisis in health care has been exacerbated by the AIDS scourge. Most AIDS patients are cared for at home by women because the health services have limited resources. In order to cope with the great need for medicinal treatment, women have revived herbal gardens. Other women have worked to relieve suffering in AIDS-ravaged as well as war-torn areas by organizing viable community-development projects. In Rakai District, where nearly every household is afflicted or affected by AIDS, women, as food producers, care-providers and parents, have been instrumental in transforming traditional practices. For example, women individually initiated the reduction in the traditional mourning period, from three days to one or even half a day, during agricultural work. Women extended the practice of "a friend in need" (*Munno Mukabbi*), which traditionally provided a neighborhood support system for bereavement and for funerals, to encompass a community-development support system for widows with children as well as for orphans. Such grassroots efforts are often supported financially and technically by foreign NGOs, some of which serve as catalysts for local and even national efforts.

NGOs have also initiated community-based efforts to help with income-generating activities to enable families to survive. In Teso District, an individual woman initiated Vision Terudo (Teso Rural Development Organization) to help the war victims. This project has been so successful that some non-government organizations, like the British Action Aid, have offered financial and technical support. Vision Terudo promotes small-scale community cooperatives and trains members for self-reliance through the acquisition of empowering skills such as management, book-keeping, marketing and saving.

In addition to these grassroots efforts, recent responses to women's plight have included attempts by banks to reach poor women with credit, as well as some official government attention to women's affairs. For the last decade, women in development (WID) researchers have asserted the necessity of women's access to institutional banking if they are to improve their economic situation and reduce their vulnerability. In 1987, the Uganda Commercial Bank decided to use some of its profits to start a Rural Farmers' Scheme (Uganda Commercial Bank 1987). The aim is to make available monitored loans to the poor granted on the basis of character assessment. These "character" loans seemed like a bonus to women who were traditionally denied bank loans because they lacked tangible resources to offer as collateral. However, poor women report that the loans go predominately to men and rich women. Many women, after wasted trips to the bank, decide to stop seeking loans. Moreover, some bank officials still expect women to kneel in bank offices and to speak only when spoken to. Thus, the scheme has been disappointing to poor women. There is also the Women's Trust Fund, a Ugandan branch of a New York-based bank, which was hailed as women's salvation in that it was committed to granting them access to loans. Poor women, however, see it as yet another instrument to serve elite women. While paying lip service to the principle of lending money to the poor is becoming common practice among banking institutions, there is considerable distance to cover before attitudes towards the credit needs of poor women change.

Official government responses reveal some of the same limitations when it comes to the situation of poor women. Uganda has thirty-eight women parliamentarians, elected under the National Resistance Council political system which requires there be women representatives in village, parish and district-level elected governing bodies. At the national level, women parliamentarians who speak out on women's issues, such as rape, access to resources, reforms in marriage and inheritance laws are ridiculed by their colleagues and the press. At the other levels, some women are very active and vocal, but at most meetings they sit separately and quietly at the back of the meeting room.

Uganda has followed the trend, started in the 1970s in other African countries, of establishing women's bureaus. The Ministry of Women in Development, Youth and Culture has, with Danish foreign-aid money and advisers, developed a program to inform women about their predicament and thus involve them in changing the situation. But as far as poor women are concerned, the women's development decade passed them by, and the Ministry of Women in Development is one more effort by elite women to speak to and for poor women, in the English language. "No one listens to the poor," insisted one woman. The Ministry must tackle directly the issues of class divisions and gender-neutral development, both of which work to the disadvantage of the majority of Uganda's poor women (Obbo 1986).

Conclusions

This chapter has explored the issues of gender stratification and the vulnerability of women in Uganda. Societal ideologies accord to men privileges which give them relatively greater access to resources such as land and cattle, the labor of their wives, and the wealth they produce. Women's entitlement to societal resources is heavily dependent on men, particularly husbands. This context is important in understanding women's public efforts in the last thirty years to deconstruct marriage and inheritance laws, as well as their private actions to improve their conditions by deserting their marriages and/or migrating to the urban areas. Moreover, the economic crises of the 1970s and 1980s resulted in many families existing below a living wage, burdening women further and driving more of them to eke out a living in the informal economy.

Because gender differentiation determines the differing realities men and women bring to the exchange relationship, it affects the distribution of power between them. The most vulnerable women are those married to poor men, single women with children, widows, and divorcees. Poor women especially are left to shape their own strategies to achieve independence, mobility, security, and self-respect. The consequences of women's dependence on men for entitlement to societal resources is clearly demonstrated by their position with regard to health care. Men control cash; women take care of the sick. Health services require financial expenditures, but women as health-care providers are dependent on men for money. Thus, children are less likely to be immunized or properly treated when ill because the initiating of medical care requires the assumption of financial responsibility. Women often postpone their own treatment until their condition is serious. The health-care crisis has been exacerbated by the AIDS scourge which has affected and afflicted increasing numbers of households in Uganda.

While internal conflicts and the AIDS scourge have worked to worsen women's situation, political policies which have encouraged women to participate at all levels of elective politics, along with the establishment of the Ministry of Women and Development, Youth and Sports, are promising steps toward improving their conditions. Yet, development policies applied in a gender-neutral way have had a negative impact on women. Women are subordinate in the gender stratification system, and poor women bear the brunt of development policies. Thus, women and children are bearing the cost of the efforts, through the International Monetary Fund's Structural Adjustment Programs, to improve the economy, pay off foreign debts, and institute government fiscal responsibility. The resultant low wages, low prices for crops, and reduced government expenditure on services have accentuated women's poverty and vulnerability. There is a further need to address effectively the impact on women of gender-neutral development activities with corrective policies that are mindful of the class interests involved.

At the same time, in the face of meager societal resources, women's own agency and actions generate a new kind of resource. They are reshaping kinship and the meaning of community in Uganda. And even as poverty remains a grinding experience for most women and their children, women's self-reliance strategies, especially during Uganda's postwar aftermath, may reconstruct the bases from which women and men approach gendered exchange relationships.

Notes

1. Until 1986, Ugandans lived through a reign of terror. Development became secondary to personal safety. Poor women, as the food producers and health-care providers, paid a high price to ward off constantly approaching poverty.
2. This reportedly occurred on 16 December at the seminar on Uganda's economy.
3. The Salaries Review Commission (1982: section 441) defined "a living wage" as one which does not grossly compromise the standard of living of the employee in keeping with social status.

References

Brown, W. 1988. "Marriage, Divorce and Inheritance." *Cambridge African Monographs*, 10.
Chafetz, Janet S. 1990. *Gender Equity: An Integrated Theory of Stability and Change*. Beverley Hills: Sage.
"Commission on Marriage Laws, 1964–5." 1965. Entebbe: Uganda Government.
Church of Uganda. 1963. "Statement on the Revision of Marriage Laws." Namirembe: Church of Uganda.
Decree 22 (Succession [Amendment] Decree). 1972. "Protection of Widows," Resolutions G and H.
Decree 16. 1973. "Customary Marriage Registration Decree," Resolution 13.
Morris, H.F. 1960. "Outline of Central Government Law on Family Matters," unpublished manuscript.
The New Vision. 1990. 26 March.
Obbo, Christine. 1980. *African Women: Their Struggle for Economic Independence*. London: Zed.
Obbo, Christine. 1986. "Stratification and the Lives of Women in Uganda." In *Women and Class in Africa*, edited by C. Robertson and I. Berger, pp. 178–94. New York and London: Holmes and Meier.
Obbo, Christine. 1992. *Demands, Needs and Resources in Relation to Primary Health Care in Kampala City*. Kampala: Save the Children Fund.

"The Salaries Review Commission." 1982. Kampala: Uganda Government.
Suruma, E. 1989. "Credit Policy in Uganda, 1987–1989", paper presented at the Seminar on Uganda's Economy, 12–16, December, Kampala.
"Uganda Commercial Bank Rural Farmers' Scheme." 1987. Kampala: Uganda Commercial Bank.
"Uganda Government Report of the Commission on Marriage, Divorce and the Status of Women." 1965. Entebbe: Government Printer.

Part IV

Challenges to White Western Middle Class Gender Analysis and Agendas

Kathryn B. Ward is Associate Professor of Sociology, Southern Illinois University at Carbondale. She is the author of *Women in the World-System* and editor of *Women Workers and Global Restructuring*.

Vidyamali Samarasinghe is Associate Professor in the School of International Service at the American University, Washington DC. She is co-editor of *Women at the Crossroads: A Sri Lankan Perspective*.

Elizabeth Fox-Genovese is Eleonore Raoul Professor of the Humanities at Emory University, Atlanta, Georgia. She is the author of several books, including the highly acclaimed *Within the Plantation Household: Black and White Women of the Old South*. Her latest book is *Feminism without Illusions: A Critique of Individualism*.

12. "Lifting as We Climb:" How Scholarship by and about Women of Color Has Shaped My Life as a White Feminist

Kathryn B. Ward

> So be careful when you talk with me;
> remind me not of my slavery;
> I know it well.
> But rather tell me of your own.
> (Beah Richards [1950] in Washington (1986: 39))

One change in direction that would be real cool would be the production of a discourse on race that interrogates whiteness. It would be just so interesting for all those white folks who are giving blacks their take on blackness to let them know what's going on with whiteness. ... Only a persistent, rigorous, and informed critique of whiteness could really determine what forces of denial, fear, and competition are responsible for creating fundamental gaps between professed political commitment to eradicating racism and the participation in the construction of a discourse on race that perpetuates racial domination. Many scholars, critics, and writers preface their work by stating that they are white, as though mere acknowledgement of this fact were sufficient, as though it conveyed all we need to know of standpoint, motivation, direction. I think back to my graduate years when many of the feminist professors fiercely resisted the insistence that it was important to examine race and racism. Now many of these same women are producing scholarship focusing on race and gender. *What process enabled their perspectives to shift? Understanding that process is important for the development of solidarity; it can enhance awareness of the epistemological shifts that enable all of us to move in new and oppositional directions. Yet none of these women write articles reflecting on their critical process, showing how their attitudes have changed.* (hooks 1991: 54, emphasis added)

Over time, I have undergone my own version of intellectual, political, and curriculum integration in regard to race and gender. As I describe my journey, I will highlight how scholarship by and about women of color has changed my life as a White Western feminist. Instead of writing a traditional "scholarly" paper on gender, women of color have encouraged me to tell my story/narrative (Beah Richards [1950] 1986).

Two contrasting experiences in the summer of 1990 strengthened my resolve to write about my journey. First, in May I was on the staff of the curriculum integration workshop run by the Center for Research on Women at Memphis State University.[1] Second, in June I attended the annual meeting of the National Women's Studies Association (NWSA), where many women of color walked out over issues of racism and the firing of Ruby Sales, an African American NWSA employee. I walked out with them.[2] On the one hand, the Memphis State curriculum workshop gave me the opportunity to work with many dynamic scholars of color who put race, class, and gender at the center of the program. This energizing experience was juxtaposed, on the other hand, with struggles over racism at the NWSA meetings. Although many people pay lip service to race, class, and gender, these issues and women of color have not been at the core of NWSA and its administration[3] (or many Women's Studies programs) but rather are merely tacked on. In times of perceived crisis, many White women retreat to racist behavior, rules, and privilege. I even overheard, in halls and the cafeteria at NWSA, some White women engaged in paranoid speculation about women of color taking over the organization. We would be furious if White men in control of our institutions did similar sexist things to us, such as firing a woman after she complained of sexism.

These experiences stimulated my thinking about my relationships and behavior as a White feminist committed to an inclusive vision of feminism. Over time, I had incorporated many ideas from African American women's groups into my teaching, research, and activism – for example, the notion of "lifting as we climb" (Giddings 1985) or the commitment to bring other people with us as we rise. Further, this research and ideology insists on putting women of color at the center of our activities and theories (Baca Zinn et al. 1986; Aptheker 1989; Collins 1990). These ideas have transformed my teaching, because I have integrated research by and about women of color in all of my classes. I have also brought this perspective to the Women's Studies program at Southern Illinois University and to my feminist groups. And, finally, I have transformed my research by putting women of color explicitly at the center. This has moved me from using quantitative methods for analyzing secondary data to the qualitative analysis of interviews, which at this point offer the most appropriate source of information for my research concerns.

---

* An earlier version of this paper was brought out as Working Paper No.13, Center for Research on Women, Memphis State University. I thank Elizabeth Higginbotham, Gay Young, Jane Adams, Melanie Baise, Christina Brinkley, Linda Grant, Beth Hartung, Shirlene Holmes, Mary O'Hara, and Rachel Rosenfeld and the participants of the conference "Experiences of Gender: Color, Class, and Country" for their comments. Betty Wiley provided valuable assistance in the preparation of an early version of this paper. Of course, I am responsible for the contents.

At the same time, these activities have brought into focus my White or Euro-American identity and how this identity shapes my place in the world. An inclusive vision requires conscious and purposeful identity with my location at the intersection of race, class, and gender. Acknowledging White privilege means being aware of my identity and the consequences of my identity. With this consciousness comes recognition of the different levels or intensity of identity, that is, that racial or gender identity is not dichotomous, but arrayed along a continuum (Helms 1985). However, I also experience the accompanying feelings and behavior of fear, denial, and competition which occur to many White people as we grapple with the implications of gender, race, and class identities.

This chapter describes my experiences with race and gender as I was growing up, in undergraduate and graduate school, and at Southern Illinois University – Carbondale. In particular, it explores how interactions with women of color profoundly changed my personal and intellectual life as I increasingly recognized my race and gender identities. It closes with a discussion of the implications for other White feminists and our organizations.

Early learning

I was born in Lafayette, Louisiana in 1955. We later lived in Oklahoma City, Oklahoma and in Tyler, Texas before settling in Russell, Kansas in 1963. My father came from a working-class background, while my mother was raised middle class. My paternal grandmother, Lula Ward, was part Cherokee, and her husband was Danish. My mother's family came from Germany and England; her great-grandmother had graduated from Oberlin College. Both of my parents had college degrees: my father was a petroleum engineer and my mother taught science and English in a middle school. My parents moved into the middle class owing to my father's work in the oil industry and my mother's teaching.

As a child, racial and gender differences puzzled me, and I asked many questions about race and gender when I was growing up. My earliest memories of race are of fishing alongside Black people in Pauls Valley, Oklahoma. If we caught any carp we gave the carp to them. I vaguely remember my mother saying that Black people lived across the river. I also remember receiving a letter from one of my Pauls Valley, Oklahoma classmates after we moved to Russell, Kansas (a very White town in Western Kansas). She wrote, "They came to school this year," meaning that Black students were being integrated into my former school. This was about 1965, and in Russell I had a few Black classmates from a large extended family.

My first memory of gender differences is from a really hot summer day in Kansas when I wanted to take off my shirt like my little brother. My mother declared that I was too old to do that. I was aged probably 4 or 5.

Growing up in Russell during the 1960s and 1970s, I was fascinated by the civil-rights movement, the counter-culture, and peace activism. In seventh grade, I was kicked out of my church for organizing an alternative Sunday school against the war. I read everything that I could find about these three social movements. In particular, I read about Black peoples' struggles, including Eldridge Cleaver's *Soul on Ice* and his descriptions of activism and of violence against women. I remember getting into an argument in junior high with a young White woman classmate when I confronted her about calling a Black man on the opposing basketball team a racist name. From the safe distance of television I watched Black ghettos burn. When I visited my mother's parents in Washington, D.C. in 1967, I saw the ghettos. And I heard my grandfather's stories about going to the 1963 March on Washington, which was one of the proudest moments of his life. At the same time, I remember Gertie Jackson who did domestic work for my grandmother. I did not acknowledge this contradiction in my grandparents' lives until college.

In high school in the early 1970s, I had more contact with the local Black extended family than most of my classmates because the youngest daughter, Teresa Murphy, was on the debate squad along with her cousin, Gwen Washington. Teresa was my debate partner, and Gwen lived nearby; we hung out together. Close proximity was a real eye-opener on race and gender. It was one thing to read about Black people and another thing to interact. At Gwen's house, I smelled my first batch of chitlings cooking.

At one point, Teresa told the debate class that when the revolution came she was going to shoot all Whites (my own debate partner!), while Gwen said that she would spare the debate class. Yet Gwen, Teresa and the rest of the debate squad were very scared as we walked up the sidewalk to Topeka High School (Brown vs. Topeka Board of Education), which was still segregated and predominantly Black. At another time, I went to the local African Methodist Episcopal church with Teresa and met her male minister friend. I remember the tension between Teresa and me when her friend began to direct his attentions my way and call me long distance. I was not interested in a relationship with him, and the calls soon stopped. Only much later did I understand the racial-gender politics in this possible triangle. However, at this time, my experiences with Black men ranged from the anger of Elridge Cleaver to the attentions of the minister. I was less conscious of the history of lynching of Black men for interacting with White women and how White women have exercised their privilege to associate with Black men to the detriment of some Black women. Although at times interactions were uncomfortable, I treasured my friendships.

Specifically regarding gender, in debate I learned that women debaters were supposed to be nice and sweet, especially during cross-examination. And beginning in junior high school, I learned more about gender differences through music activities. By high school, I had learned that men conductors considered men french horn players superior to women hornists. Even so, I did not identity as a feminist. But I did have a strong sense of outrage over social injustice and Republicans, in particular Richard Nixon. My experiences with my friends, debate, and music only added to my puzzlement over race and gender differences during these years of early learning.

My schooling

As I started to write about my undergraduate and graduate years, I had an image of time spent almost totally with White people of Volga German ethnicity in Western Kansas and the corn farmers of Iowa. Then memories started flooding in, and I realized that learning about race was an important, though not necessarily conscious, part of my undergraduate and graduate education. My emerging awareness of my gender identity occupied much of my time.

I entered Fort Hays State University in the fall of 1974. Hays, Kansas was a town with an informal sundown law. This law was instituted after a fight many years ago between Black and White soldiers at old Fort Hays. Until the 1960s, African American and African students lived in rooms at the football stadium instead of in the dorms. The faculty was 100 percent White and predominantly male. The staff at the university were also White and composed mostly of working-class women and men displaced from family farms. My classes were almost totally White with only a few African American, African, and other international students. I recall two African American women from St Louis who lived on my dorm floor. They were very lonely and ran up enormous phone bills calling home. The White women on our floor did not involve them in our activities, including my new feminist group. They didn't return after the first year.

I acquired a very active feminist consciousness during my first year at the Fort and delved into whatever women's courses I could take. Of course, they were about White Western women's history and sociology. Comparisons and contrasts were made between the position of women and that of minorities; for example, we discussed (White sociologist) Helen Hacker's (1951) classic article 'Women as a Minority Group'. In these discussions, women of color were invisible. At this time I went into Sociology under the tutelage of Rose Arnhold, a White woman faculty member.

In my second year at the Fort, I organized an International Women's Year conference. Flo Kennedy was the guest speaker and caused quite a stir with her very radical Black feminist analysis. I loved it. I got in trouble with the Dean of Women because of the swearwords that Flo used liberally in her talk. The Dean cooled off after a while, but I naively did not realize the larger impact of bringing a Black feminist activist to this very racist campus. The feminist conferences in Kansas and Colorado which I attended were predominantly White, but I was not conscious of the absence of women of color. However, in Colorado, my friend Juanita Ramirez showed me the Denver barrio. From her I heard about Chicanas and La Raza for the first time.

A year later, in Lawrence, Kansas, I saw Flo Kennedy confront a group of White women from Iowa City who were heckling her during a speech after she noted that no White women had shed blood for the women's movement as had Black women and men for the civil-rights movement. This episode gave me a first glimmering of understanding about some of the differences between Black and White women, especially in the intensity of our commitments, and about the denial of White women who refuse to listen when a Black woman is speaking. I was disturbed by the young White feminists trying to shout down the disconcerting words of a Black feminist – a situation which I have unfortunately seen repeated too many times since then.[4]

Gloria Steinem, a White feminist activist, came to Fort Hays State and talked on her version of women and caste. I began to learn about international women's issues from Shirley Nuss, a White working-class sociologist, at a Women's Institute at the University of Colorado. And once again, from a distance, I read about struggles over race – now in feminist newspapers. Gender remained foremost in my analyses despite my earlier experiences, and I had little consciousness of my identity or standpoint as a White woman.

I went to graduate school at University of Iowa in 1977 and plunged into the feminist vortex of a women's community which was emerging from some violent struggles over class and sexuality. The White feminists had not begun to address race, as witnessed by the Iowa City women's behavior towards Flo Kennedy. A Black male graduate student in Sociology, Eugene Kennedy, observed that there were more Asians than African Americans in Iowa City. I knew only two African American women and one Chicana in the community.[5] The Women's Studies program was oriented toward White Western women's thought, and my Sociology program was generic White male fare. This changed somewhat with the arrival of Jane Weiss, a White sociologist, who had a global perspective and a strong consciousness about gender and class. From Jane I developed my interests in the world system and women in development. However, race did not enter our analyses.

I was like many White feminists. I would say I "understood" because I was a woman, but gender always seemed more salient to me than did race or class. However, this was just a way of denying how my White middle-class privilege mediated my position as a woman and my role in perpetuating racism. This perspective let me avoid the hard work of learning more about racism and people of color because I only had to refer to "parallel" analogies with sexism. In this way, too, White women often have failed to acknowledge the important role the civil-rights movement played in the emergence of the women's movement.

Research on women in development was probably easy for me to do because I was working at a distance and on secondary data rather than conducting fieldwork. At the same time, I began to understand the importance of expressing my standpoint as a Western woman and examining how I benefitted from my position in the United States. I was unconsciously beginning to put Third World women at the center of my analyses and to build my theories and models around their experiences. In my research on the Igbo women's war in Nigeria, I started constructing a model of what happened as women interacted with the global economy. This model underlies much of the work I do today. In essence, Igbo women lived in a dual sex system and had a great deal of power which they used vis-à-vis men. If a man violated the women's rules, they would literally "sit on a man" – a ritual I propose should be brought back to use with recalcitrant men. The arrival of British colonial officials meant the imposition of patriarchy on these women and the loss of economic resources – a classic case of what happens to women during economic development (Van Allen 1976; Ward 1988). In this context, I also started looking at the effects of transnational corporations on women workers in developing countries and the accompanying exportation of Western values of femininity (Ward 1984).

When I taught a gender course for the first time in 1981, I tried occasionally to mention women of color. I felt inadequately prepared in front of an African American woman who sat in class. What I did not understand at this time was that I should teach about how both women of color and White women experience race and gender. My discontent with my teaching about race motivated me to attend the first conference on racism at the University of Iowa in the spring of 1982. Here I made my first fumbling attempts consciously to deal with my racism and to articulate the connections among race, class, and gender. I felt awkward and scared. I lacked a vocabulary to describe the intersection of race, class, and gender because my sociological and feminist experiences had done little to prepare me to work with this interaction. Instead, in Sociology I had learned to treat race and class as categories that were tacked on to my gender analyses. This conference showed me what a long way I had to go in dealing with these issues.

Teaching and learning in tandem

In 1982, I went to Southern Illinois University at Carbondale (SIUC) for my first job. This environment was another eye-opener for me. First, Carbondale was small, southern, and 20 percent Black. Second, SIUC had 11 percent Black students, many of them from the south side of Chicago or East St Louis. Third, I had more Black students in my gender classes than at Iowa. So, I did like many White women faculty: I assigned a few more articles or chapters on Black women – for example, (White sociologist) Elizabeth Almquist's piece from the Jo Freeman reader and research on race/gender in the elementary classroom by my frequent collaborator, Linda Grant, a White sociologist/ethnographer.

My colleague Linda Grant taught me about being sensitive to the interaction of race and gender and introduced me to the growing literature on this topic. The few articles about women of color I assigned were placed in the labor-force section of the course and very few were by women of color themselves. As a demographer and labor-force researcher, I preferred discussing numbers of gender/race differences in occupations and earnings. I would remind my class that the gender gap was greater than the race gap, thereby rendering invisible the disparate occupation opportunities and distributions of women and men of color relative to Whites.

A White student in one of my classes, Bobbie Bennett, was a single parent. Bobbie had been in an interracial marriage and was an organizer around poor women's issues. She taught me that the aggregate categories race, class, and gender could not be used in a neat, additive way. From her, I learned about the survival strategies of poor women and the difficulties of racial-gender identity for her racially mixed kids. Partly at her instigation, I started tracing how processes of the global economy linked back to US women's economic crises and how the interaction of race and class increased women's impoverishment (Ward 1987b). This research was important for my integration process because I began to make the connections between the treatment of women from currently developing countries and the situation of women of color and poor women in the United States.

To make up for my lack of knowledge on race, I occasionally invited African American or Native American women to speak in my classes. But this was typically with little preparation for their visits and/or when I was going out of town and would not attend class. My students would ask: "Is this going to be on the test?" Only later – on receiving similar treatment when I gave guest lectures on gender issues – did I realize what kinds of messages I was giving my classes and my guest lecturers.

The final stimuli to my emerging consciousness on race came from teaching the subject. This happened when the lower division gender class was removed from the general education curriculum. Then, I was assigned to teach the course on comparative race and ethnic relations – because I did international research and not because I knew about race! My students for the first few semesters were very understanding, and I realized how little I knew about people of color, particularly in the United States. This was a very humbling experience. What I did know exemplified the stereotypical teaching by White faculty. I talked about exceptional people of color or the few commonly mentioned in history classes, Harriet Tubman or Sojourner Truth. I taught about race as a social problem by citing negative stereotypes rather than images of strength and resistance. I knew many people from other nations, but few native-born women or men of color on campus. Moreover, people of color meant African Americans, and I paid less attention to Latinos, Asian and Native Americans. The textbook did not even contain a chapter on Native or Asian Americans!

I realized that I needed help, and in 1986 I went to my first Memphis State curriculum integration workshop. The workshop was designed to help faculty view gender inclusively and to integrate both race and gender into their teaching. Here I learned that the fundamentals of curriculum integration involved: (i) increases in personal knowledge; (ii) changes in classroom dynamics; and (iii) changes in course content. I was also in a situation where women of color were in the positions of authority – in my small group, and on my dorm floor. This was very different for me because I had rarely been around women of color with more authority than myself (and who had what I perceived as important things to teach me). In essence, I was constantly around women of color. I became very aware of my White identity rather then drifting along in a race-blind mode in my daily interactions.

Moreover, I saw women of color and White women collaborating with one another. For example, Bonnie Thornton Dill, Elizabeth Higginbotham, and Lynn Weber worked together in their teaching, research, and the operation of a research center (The Memphis State Center for Reseach on Women). I was challenged on my confrontational teaching style and learned about Lynn Weber's course ground rules (Cannon 1990). I learned about different learning styles and the types of class structuring needed to accommodate these styles. Fortified by the Memphis State bibliographies and mortified by the quantities of reading and work I had to do, I returned to Carbondale and starting reworking my classes.

Of course, I was eager to share the new information I had learned that summer so I put it all at the beginning of the gender course. My goal was to give the students an overview of race so that they could critique materials throughout the rest of the course. I incorporated Lynn Weber's ground rules to change classroom dynamics. I thought my classes would be quickly transformed and my colleagues overjoyed to learn these new techniques.

The White students were overwhelmed in the gender class by the information, and they could not wait until we moved into the White-oriented theories and other topics of the course. Students of color who responded eagerly to this material had to deal with their disconcerted White classmates. However, I was not happy with the gender class because although White students seemed happier (a palpable sign of relief) after we got through the big section on race, very little analysis of race appeared in the rest of the course. I was continuing to treat race as a supplement in my courses instead of integrating it throughout.

In the race and ethnic relations course, I added gender material. The introduction of the ground rules profoundly changed the course. Classroom participation by Black students increased and, over time, enrollments grew. Some of the classes were 40–50 percent Black as word spread on the campus about the class, which was the only course on race in the General Education curriculum. I still felt only semi-connected with the Black students in the race course and experienced some of their anger, which I could not understand given the structuring of the course.

In my graduate seminar in social change, students who were used to an additive survey of race, gender or class issues (or no consideration at all) found the new readings on race, class, and gender difficult because their previous education had left them unprepared for integration. They needed to learn how to see the world in different ways. I did not resolve this tension until a few years later when I changed the ordering of topics in the course. Instead of starting with the traditional White European theories on social change, I started with the new scholarship on race, class, and gender. Only after midterms did I begin discussion of the older theories. The students were amazed at how little these theories explained!

I knew that I was having an impact on my department when some of my colleagues started sputtering that knowing about experiences of people of color and women was unimportant for understanding sociological theory. My students received little external reinforcement for this knowledge and classroom style. However, course ground rules had made a definite difference in the classroom dynamics and the teaching evaluations in all of my classes. The students started demanding this new race, class, and gender scholarship in their other classes.

Meanwhile, I came across Janet Helms' (1985) research on racial identity. Her work built on Bill Cross's ideas of levels of racial identity for both Blacks and Whites and how this can affect Black–White interaction in professional/counseling situations (see, for example, Cross 1991). Some of my Black students did not want to be identified as Black people, some were into Black consciousness, and others were openly hostile to me and Whites in the class. Still others were involved in a process of reflection with regard to race. Similar things were happening for my White students but in different ways. They exhibited various levels of identification with their Whiteness. For example, some of my White students enjoyed hanging out with Black classmates and talking in Black English without understanding that they were playing at being Black. A handful of White students were patronizing toward Blacks. A few students were openly hostile to Black people in general, while others were seeking some intellectual and personal understanding of their interactions with their Black classmates and roommates in the dorms. My job as teacher was to coordinate these different levels of racial (class and gender) identity into the classroom content and discussions, for example, of interracial dating.

I also became much more aware of my own racial identity as a White woman and how in different situations I might display differing levels of identity. Helms'

(1985) research provided an important framework to understand my own life and experiences with race. For example, in my early interactions with my Black friends in debate, I thought it was neat to hang out, but I did not realize how past history affected our friendships. Later I was matronizing toward Black students by the way I was teaching negative stereotypes and then angry at students who did not seem to appreciate my efforts to bring at least some material on people of color into the classes.

The response from most of my White male colleagues to my integration process was indifference and hostility. They questioned everything from the ground rules to the content of my courses. For example, many questioned whether Sociology should include the experiences of diverse groups. In the face of discouragement, I openly did anti-racist work. Thus, I discovered the consequences for White women who take such a stance: other Whites start to accentuate and draw racial boundaries. For example, White administrators made racist remarks in my presence. When I did a workshop on racism with a Black man, my feminist friends noted that I spoke for fewer minutes than he, rather than listening to the messages and collaboration that we sought to convey. Nonetheless, I insisted on inclusiveness in the Women's Caucus programming with programs on apartheid, African American women's poetry, and anti-racism. I supported the Black American Studies program which the administration was dismantling through tenure denials. I reached out to Black faculty, spoke up at their tenure hearings, and insisted that the administration provide a strong commitment to the program. I also dealt with the anger of some Black women who thought I was not doing enough in my feminist activities. I tried to demonstrate through my behavior and programming that my commitment was more than lip service or trying to be "cool." Throughout these experiences I stayed in contact with the Memphis State women who dispensed advice and wisdom and, most importantly, encouraged the cultivation of an inclusive vision of race, class, and gender in guiding behavior and programs (Cannon 1990b).

I spent my sabbatical in the spring of 1989 reading feminist theory by and about women of color. I began to acquire the intellectual background to articulate my emerging vision on research and curriculum organized around the intersection of race, class, and gender. Before I became coordinator of Women's Studies in the fall of 1989, I proposed a curriculum integration project. There was strong support from Women's Studies faculty and students for this goal. I went to Memphis State in May 1989 with the purpose of designing a program and rethinking my courses. This time the Memphis State staff members were unequivocal – you include race, class, and gender in your courses. Patricia Hill Collins, who led my small discipline group, was very insistent on this matter. They also talked about decentering White upper-middle-class women and men from curriculum and research and putting women of color at the center of research and teaching. Hill Collins gave a very powerful talk (1989) which anticipated her book in progress, *Black Feminist Thought* (1990). Her presentations and work have continued to challenge me at every turn, especially her work on Black feminist epistemology. However, my small discipline group was pessimistic about my prospects for doing a curriculum project without much administrative and grant support.

Fortunately, things came together very rapidly for several of my goals as coordinator of Women's Studies. Right before the Memphis State workshop, Southern Illinois University at Carbondale hired a new Black American Studies coordinator, Christina Brinkley, a sociologist/demographer/feminist. I asked her to teach a Women's Studies seminar on Black women and to participate in our curriculum project. I also explained that I wanted to have a collaborative relationship and no "divide and conquer" dynamics between our two programs. I also offered to help in any way possible with her efforts to revive a dead program. I soon learned about the meaning of collaboration. Fortunately, Christina was fairly patient with me. In the fall, we had three colloquia on curriculum integration: overview, classroom dynamics, and course content. From my White feminist perspective, I thought if White faculty learn to call on their women and minority students and use the course ground rules, then much of the problem would be solved. Christina disagreed and maintained that course content was more important. She was right. Changes in class dynamics do not help much if you are teaching the same old stereotypes. She labelled our work curriculum integration, and I called it curriculum transformation. She viewed the latter perspective as adding minorities/women and stirring or tacking on. I now call it curriculum integration. Finally, I began to notice that I always seemed to "know" what would or would not work when we were talking about projects and ideas. I thought many of Christina's ideas wouldn't work, but they always did. As a consequence, I started working on my "White is always right" streak and started to shut up and listen more.

But our collaboration occurred within a racist context. When Christina received racist treatment at a local post office where I was always treated fairly and with courtesy I was forced to see the community differently. When one White male colleague brought refuting articles and complaints to me after he and Christina disagreed, I recognized and challenged these blatant appeals to race solidarity. We coordinated our demands and took turns with the university administrators. Over time, more White people who were affiliated with Women's Studies came to Black American Studies events. We were able to serve as bridges into one another's worlds. Unfortunately, after a year and a half, Christina moved on to another school and is now a professor of Sociology and Women's Studies at Bates College.

Meanwhile, the curriculum integration project has grown. The Women's Studies newsletter has become a women/multicultural resource on campus. The curriculum integration project so far has involved over sixteen colloquia, several speakers, and one syllabus workshop. We have also conducted teaching-assistant-training workshops for the Graduate School and for individual departments. We have a core group of forty faculty who are actively engaged in curriculum integration. Working with others, I have conducted curriculum workshops at universities in Illinois and at professional meetings. For my part, I have given special emphasis to the importance of White people getting involved in curriculum integration. From these activities, I am writing a workbook on curriculum integration which will make these ideas accessible to White faculty members in particular, who are the majority of professors and teachers. At the same time, I vigorously work on the recruitment and retention of faculty of color.

Integrating my research, intellectual, and teaching life

Among the many new ideas I acquired in this process was the idea of "lifting as we climb". As discussed in Paula Giddings's (1985) book, *When and Where I Enter*, this is an underlying principle of Black women's groups and sharply contrasts with the exclusionary racism of White women's groups. This notion also motivated the refocusing of my courses to put women of color at the center because their explanations often shed light on the lives of men of color as well as White women and men. The reverse was often not true.

From Bonnie Thornton Dill's (1988) work, I discovered the notion of survival as resistance and saw new ways of defining women's resistance. For example, where I once defined as sexist the situation in which Reconstruction-era Black men encouraged Black women to stay home instead of working outside, I now saw as a sign of resistance Black women's claiming the right to stay home as did many White women. Each article and book I read by and about women of color gave me new insights and challenged my past frameworks and lecture notes. Aptheker's (1989) work as a White feminist historian who had cast off White-centered theories provided much inspiration for this process.

These changes spilled over into my research on women and work, particularly the editing of my book, *Women Workers and Global Restructuring* (1990a). By looking at work from the standpoint of women of color, I began to question past definitions and conceptualizations of resistance and work. I began to define resistance in new ways other than joining large groups such as the National Organization for Women (NOW) or unions. Where I had depicted women from currently developing countries as passive recipients of underdevelopment, I now saw sources of strength and daily resistance. And I noted how women of color have always worked and thus were more interested in putting their feet up and resting than in getting excited about White women's demands to work outside the home. I learned about this very dramatically during December 1987 when I sat up nights with Meneal Walker, an African American woman attending my grandmother Searle who was dying at home. Meneal was a 65-year-old home nurse aide. During those long nights, as we waited to turn or change my grandmother, she told me about her life and how tired she was. She had raised twelve children and put them through high school by working the night shift at hospitals, nursing homes, and now for a nursing service. However, she could not retire because she had no pension or money put away for retirement.

In my latest research, I have redefined work to include a vast array of women's economic activity: formal, informal, and household labor, or what Karen Hossfeld (1988) calls the triple shift (Ward 1990b and 1993; Ward and Pyle forthcoming). This redefinition challenges our traditional understanding of the labor force to include a model of how women simultaneously may work in some combination of formal, informal, and household labor. This complexity of tasks is missed if we look at only women's formal employment. Choosing to work outside the home was a new idea for White middle-class women, while women of color and working-class women have been working outside the home for years. In fact, their labor as domestics and childcare providers enabled White middle- and upper-class women to do volunteer work and take paid employment outside the home.

Further, I used the scholarship by and about women of color to make connections in my research on international women, especially how issues of race, class, and gender are internationally related, in particular how women of color in the US are displaced from factory work when assembly plants go overseas or when women who have worked in factories in other countries then immigrate to the US (Ward 1990a, 1990b; Ward ,Grant and Pyle forthcoming). By making these connections I was able to break down the intellectual ghettoization of women in development research from the new race, class, and gender scholarship (see Samarasinghe, Chapter 13 in this volume). More recently, I have explored how race, gender, and occupations intersect in Brazil (Fiola and Ward 1991). I also contemplated how many White US women researchers might feel more at ease studying women in other countries rather than dealing with the racism at home, and how without some consciousness of our geographic location, we fall into the trap of imposing our Western values upon these women's lives (Mohanty 1988).

Reading Patricia Hill Collins (1990) on epistemologies and Bettina Aptheker (1989) on women's daily survival strategies, the conditions for research and women's standpoints were also central to my intellectual transformation. I began to immerse myself in narratives and case studies by women researchers with some of these sensibilities since I now questioned my use of quantitative cross-national statistics. I have also begun the critique of my past use of world-system theory – a perspective which has neither race nor gender at the core – although I tried every way to make them fit (Ward 1993).

This critique has led me to new areas and methods of inquiry. Although Linda Grant and I had done some quantitative research on gender, research and publishing in sociology (Ward and Grant 1985; Grant et al. 1987; Ward and Grant 1991; Grant and Ward 1991), we also were interested in how scholars frame and conduct research – how knowledge is generated. We have extended this inquiry to the role of gender *and* race in mentoring, collaboration, and the production of research. Finally, for the first time since graduate school, I am not just crunching numbers in my research. Instead, I am out interviewing people in their labs, seeing how they are doing science, and noting how this may vary according to race, gender, and class.

These research interests transformed my classes, too. I have become interested in narratives and photos and have found a long history of stories and poems belonging to women of color. An African American student and solo performance artist, Dr Shirlene Holmes, gave me Beah Richard's ([1950] 1986) poem, "A Black Woman Speaks," when I found I could not successfully articulate White women's racist complicity with White men against Black women and men. This poem showed me how my slavery as a White woman was connected to Black women's slavery. I have distributed this poem in my classes, and students have read segments aloud.

Shirlene Holmes also shared with me photography books about women of color. I now use the photos from the Schlesinger Library Black women's oral history project, *Women of Courage*, and Brian Lanker's (1989) book, *I Dream a World*, in my classes. Other Black students, whom I have mentored, have shared with me clippings and *Essence* magazine articles. In effect, we have been jointly teaching one another.

I have strongly supported women students of color as they have attempted to weave this vibrant research on race, class, and gender into their theses and dissertations. In my graduate and undergraduate classes and among White graduate student advisees I insist on the inclusion of these same perspectives. This means no more papers or theses on only White women!

I discovered that women of color did not mean only African American women. My eyes were opened to Asian women (Japanese, Chinese, Korean, Vietnamese, Hmong, Laotian, Filipina, Hawaiian, Cambodian); Native American women; Latinas (Mexicanas, Chicanas, Puertoriqueñas, Cubanas). I began to study Spanish and learned new insights in Gloria Anzaldúa's (1987, 1990) books and from other works which included Spanish. Mary Romero (who is a contributor to this volume) reminded me to look at the multiple dimensions of Chicana sexuality via an issue of *Third Woman* (Alarcón et al. 1990) on Chicana sexuality. I discovered the matriarchal orientation of Cherokees from Marilou Awiatka (1989) and gained some insights into my grandmother, Lula Ward. Meanwhile, the stacks of books and articles which I need to read on all these women continues to grow.

Finally, I have begun to question my feminist organizational strategies. I have looked at the issues in which I am involved and asked why more women of color are not involved locally or in my professional organizations. I have begun to reach out to women of color rather than waiting for them to come to me.

What this means for white feminists

Being inclusive now means much more than merely acknowledging that I am White. I become exhausted throughout February and March since I attend and speak at many events. Sometimes I get tired of all the anti- racist/anti-sexist work, but then I remember that my woman friends of color can never stop such work. Also my White identity and privilege will never stop until we eradicate the oppressive structures of race, class, and gender. Furthermore, I cannot go back to my old exclusive theoretical perspectives. I know too much about the costs of exclusion, and I am continuing to see the world in new and interesting ways that I previously missed. At the same time, I realize how little I know and how much I have to learn from scholarship on race, class, and gender.

I am energized in my teaching as my students respond to the gorgeous mosaic of people and voices they have in their classes. As Shirlene Holmes has taught me, I have provided them with a mirror. However, I have four sets of lecture notes I need to consolidate as I work on my integration efforts. With the new scholarship on race, class, and gender, my teaching materials and notes are in a constant state of change.

I appreciate my friends, what I have learned, and the world we can share. Meanwhile, I have the excitement of watching and participating as we reconstruct the world from a multitude of perspectives, with women of color creating themselves as subjects at the core. This means examining and reconstructing daily lives as affected by the intersection of race, class, and gender. I am learning to live with the ambiguity of the new scholarship rather than working with deterministic grand theories. I am trying out new research strategies, forms of data collection, and consulting with new communities of experts around the world (Collins 1990; Minnich 1990).

I have concluded that many White women need to be silent for a spell, while they read, study, and listen to women of color. Then we can take an honest look at our own standpoints, motivations, behavior, work, and theories relative to race, class, and gender. If these perspectives are missing, then we need to be accountable for their omission and move to incorporate them as they intersect in social life. Or, if necessary, we must be brave enough to move beyond theories which do not have race, class, and gender at the core. We need to insist on this stance for our students, our journals, and our textbooks. At the same time, we must be careful not merely to appropriate the work of women of color and relegate them to footnotes within our own theories (Childers and hooks 1990).

For our organizations, we need to place women of color at the core and learn new organizational strategies which stress survival and empowerment. The increasing presence of women and men of color in our organizations should not be a signal for competition but a spur to our efforts so that all of us are lifted as we climb. I have discovered the power of a strong and inclusive vision of feminism which rejects zero-sum approaches and moves beyond the barriers posed by administrators and others. Personally and organizationally, my life has taught me how to deal with the discomfort and fears of struggling with my racism – rather than withdrawing – and the benefits of staying with the struggle. As a result of all of our struggles, some day soon I hope to see more White feminists truly demonstrating a vision of an inclusive world and a feminism where all of us can climb together.

Notes

1. The Center for Research on Women conducts workshops on curriculum integration, maintains and updates computerized and hardcopy bibliographies on women of color and southern women, and publishes two series of working papers on curriculum integration and southern women. Staff members have ongoing research projects on the intersection of race, class, and gender. For more information, contact: Center for Research on Women, Memphis State University, Memphis, TN 38152, USA, or call: 901-678-2770 or FAX: 901-678-4365.

2. For the best account of what happened at the meeting, see the articles in August/September 1990 *off our backs*. For more information about an organization of women of color that formed after this meeting, contact: Dr Barbara Scott, Department of Sociology, Northeastern Illinois University, Chicago, IL 60625.

3. In the summer of 1991, however, I attended a Women's Studies Coordinator conference of the NWSA. This organization has gone through big changes since the 1990 national conference. An African American woman, Deborah Louis, is director, and the organization is restructuring the way the various constituent groups participate in its operation.

4. I have seen this kind of interrupting and talking behavior at numerous conferences and speaking events. However, the best response to this situation I have seen was at the 1985 Michigan Women's Music Festival when a Black woman MC, who was having problems quietening the crowd for announcements, intoned: "New rule: when Black women speak, White women listen." I find this statement quietens restive White students and audiences.

5. In the spring of 1991, I went to a feminist reunion and talked with one of these African American women, Vanessa Lowe, and noticed that more women of color are in Iowa City these days. I also told her about my memory of a night in 1981 when she stood up to Mary Daly, a White feminist philosopher, and challenged her on her focus on sexism instead of the intersection of racism and sexism.

References

Alarcón, Norma, Ana Castillo, and Cherríe Moraga, eds. 1990. *Third Woman*. Special Issue on the sexuality of Latinas. Berkeley: Third Woman Press.

Almquist, Elizabeth. 1985. "Race and Ethnicity in the Lives of Minority Women." In *Women: A Feminist Perspective*, 3d Edition, edited by J. Freeman, pp.423–53. Palo Alto, Calif.: Mayfield Publishing Co.

Anzaldua, Gloria. 1987. *Borderlands: The New Mestiza – La Frontera*. San Francisco: Spinsters/Aunt Lute Foundation Books.

Anzaldua, Gloria. 1987. *Making Face, Making Soul – Hacienda Caras: Creative and Critical Perspectives by Women of Color*. San Francisco: Aunt Lute Foundation Books.

Aptheker, Bettina. 1989. *Tapestries of Life*. Amherst: University of Massachusetts Press.

Awiakta, Marilu. 1989. "Amazons in Appalachia." *Women of Power* 13: 70–72.

Baca Zinn, Maxine, Lynn Weber Cannon, and Elizabeth Higginbotham. 1986. "The Costs of Exclusionary Practices in Women's Studies." *Signs: Journal of Women in Culture and Society*, 11: 290–303.

Cannon, Lynn Weber. 1990a. "Fostering Positive Race, Class, and Gender Dynamics in the Classroom." *Women's Studies Quarterly* 18: 126–34.

Cannon, Lynn Weber. 1990b. "Curriculum Transformation: Personal and Political." The Research Clearinghouse and Curriculum Integration Project Publication. Center for Research on Women, Memphis State University.

Childers, Mary, and bell hooks. 1990. "A Conversation About Race and Class." In *Conflicts in Feminism*, edited by M. Hirsch and E. Fox Keller, pp.60–81. New York: Routledge.

Collins, Patricia Hill. 1989. "Toward a New Vision: Race, Class, and Gender as Categories of Analysis and Connection." The Research Clearinghouse and Curriculum Integration Project Publication. Center for Research on Women, Memphis State University.

Collins, Patricia Hill. 1990. *Black Feminist Thought*. Boston: Routledge.

Cross, William E., Jr. 1991. *Shades of Black: Diversity and African-American Identity*. Philadelphia: Temple University Press.

Dill, Bonnie Thornton. 1988. "Our Mothers' Grief: Racial Ethnic Women and the Maintenance of Family." *Journal of Family History* 13: 415–31.

Fiola, Jan, and Kathryn Ward. 1991. "Gender and Race Occupational Inequality in Brazil." Paper presented at the Meetings of the Midwest Sociological Society, Des Moines, April.

Giddings, Paula. 1985. *When and Where I Enter: The Impact of Black Women on Race and Sex in America*. New York: Bantam.

Grant, Linda, Kathryn B. Ward, and Xue Lan Rong. 1987. "Is There an Association Between Gender and Methods in Sociological Research?" *American Sociological Review* 52: 856–62.

Grant, Linda, and Kathryn Ward. 1991. "Gender and Publication." *Gender & Society* 5(2): 207-23.

Hacker, Helen. 1951. "Women as a Minority Group." *Social Forces* 30: 60–69.

Higginbotham, Elizabeth. 1990. "Designing an Inclusive Curriculum: Bringing All Women into the Core." *Women's Studies Quarterly* 18: 7–23.

Helms, Janet. 1985. "Toward a Theoretical Explanation of the Effects of Race on Counseling." *Counseling Psychology* 12 (4): 153–65.

hooks, bell. 1991. *Yearning*. Boston: South End Press.

Hossfeld, Karen. 1988. "Divisions of Labor, Divisions of Lives: Immigrant Women Workers in Silicon Valley." Unpublished dissertation. University of California at Santa Cruz.

Hossfeld, Karen. 1990. "'Their Logic Against Them': Contradictions in Sex, Race, and Class in Silicon Valley." In *Women Workers and Global Restructuring*, edited by Kathryn B. Ward, pp.149–78. Ithaca, NY: ILR Press.

Lanker, Brian. 1989. *I Dream a World*. New York: Stewart, Tabori and Chang.

Minnich, Elizabeth. 1990. *Transforming Knowledge*. Philadelphia: Temple.

Mohanty, Chandra. 1988. "Under Western Eyes: Feminist Scholarship and Colonial Discourses." *Feminist Review* 30: 61–88.

Richards, Beah. 1950/1986. "A Black Woman Speaks." In *Nine Plays by Black Women*, edited by Mary Helen Washington, pp.29–40. New York: New American Library.

Van Allen, Judith. 1976. "'Aba Riots' or 'Igbo Women's War'?" In N. Hafkin and E. Bay, eds. *Women in Africa*, pp.59–86. Stanford, Calif.: Stanford University Press.

Ward, Kathryn. 1984. *Women in the World-System: Its Impact on Status and Fertility*. New York: Praeger.

Ward, Kathryn. 1987. "The Impoverishment of US Women and the Decline of U.S. Hegemony." In *America's Changing Role in the World System*, edited by T. Boswell and A. Bergesen, pp.275–90. New York: Praeger.

Ward, Kathryn. 1988a. "Women in the Global Economy." In *Women and Work*. No. 3, edited by B. Gutek, L. Larwood, and A. Stromberg, pp.17–48. Beverly Hills: Sage.

Ward, Kathryn. 1988b. "Female Resistance to Marginalization." In *Racism and Sexism in the World-System*, edited by J. Smith, J. Collins, T. Hopkins and A. Muhammad, pp.12–36. Westport, Conn.: Greenwood.

Ward, Kathryn ed. 1990a. *Women Workers and Global Restructuring*. Ithaca, NY: ILR Press.

Ward, Kathryn. 1990b. "Introduction and Overview." In *Women Workers and Global Restructuring*, edited by Kathryn B. Ward, pp.1–24. Ithaca, NY: ILR Press.

Ward, Kathryn. 1993. "Reconceptualizing World-System Theory to Include Women." In *Theory on Gender/Feminism on Theory*, edited by Paula England, pp.43–68. Hawthorne, NY: Aldine.

Ward, Kathryn and Linda Grant. 1985. "The Feminist Critique and a Decade of Research in Sociology Journals." *The Sociological Quarterly* 26: 139–57.

Ward, Kathryn, and Linda Grant. 1991. "On a Wavelength of Their Own? Gender and the Production of Sociological Theory." *Current Perspectives in Social Theory* 11: 117–40.

Ward, Kathryn, Linda Grant, and Jean Pyle. Forthcoming. "Gender, Work, and Development." In *Women in Development in the Third World*, edited by Christine Bose and Edna Acosta-Belen. Philadephia: Temple.

13. The Place of the WID Discourse in Global Feminist Analysis: The Potential for a "Reverse Flow"

Vidyamali Samarasinghe

> Alright, let's talk about the two of us. But if you'll let me, I'll begin. Señora, I've known you for a week. Every morning you showed up in a different outfit and on the other hand, I don't. Everyday you showed up all made up and combed like someone who has time to spend in an elegant beauty parlor and who can spend money on that, and yet I don't. I see that each day you have a car waiting at the door of this place to take you home, and yet I don't. And in order to show up here like you do, I'm sure you live in a really elegant home, in an elegant neighborhood, no? And yet we miners' wives only have a small house on loan to us, and when our husbands die or get sick or are fired from the company, we have ninety days to leave the house and then we are in the street.
>
> Now, señora, tell me: is your situation at all mine? Is my situation at all similar to you...?
>
> (Domitila Barrios De Chungara, 1978: 202)

Domitila's famous words, uttered in 1975 at the Mexico City conference on women, were her response to the request by the head of the Mexican delegation to join her to "talk about us ... about you and me ... well, about women" (1978: 202). This exchange reveals a sharp difference between two women, both of whom were from the Third World. It represents the same uneasiness and even anger which bell hooks (1984 and 1991) as well as other African American feminist scholars (Dickerson, Chapter 6 in this volume; Dill 1987; Hood 1984) feel in the face of the domination of white middle-class women in shaping feminist analysis in ways which take little account of African Americans whose gender, class, and race experiences differ from those of the dominant group. Both examples remind us that differences and commonalities among women cut across regionally articulated divisions of the "developed" West and the "underdeveloped" Third World and must be part of any global feminist analysis.

---

*I acknowledge with thanks Gay Young's comments on earlier drafts of this chapter.

The need for a "reverse flow"

In this chapter, I argue that collapsing the study of Third World women's issues into a collectively designated, geographically oriented Women in Development (WID) discourse, as separate from Western feminist studies, highlights the differences and obscures the commonalities of global gender inequality. Separating Third World women into WID has also contributed to a stereotyped woman of the Third World as distinct from the Western woman. Such rigid compartmentalization of discourses tends to highlight inter-group differences, to imply the existence of within-group homogeneity, and oftentimes to ignore inter-group commonalities. In what follows, I first briefly review the genesis of WID in an effort to understand its continued preoccupation with "development." My main concern, then, is that the emphasis on development, with its Third World-specific agenda focused mainly, if not exclusively, on poverty eradication, has inhibited a "reverse flow" of knowledge on women's issues from the Third World to the Western feminist agenda. This inhibition has been particularly strong in terms of both the adoption of methodological approaches to, and the identifying of tools for, analysis of women's subordination.

Women's Studies in the West, emerging in the wake of the second wave of feminism, undoubtedly laid the basis for the analysis of global gender inequality and paved the way for the Women in Development discourse.[1] The efforts of WID scholars/practitioners were both timely and necessary. WID emerged in the context of evidence that conscious efforts were essential in order to draw Third World women into the development strategies being planned for poor countries. Stimulating economic growth in Third World societies was the key issue of the planners. "Integrating" women into the process as effectively as possible was the main concern of early WID efforts. Initially, the primary goal of WID activities was to make certain the Northern funding agencies and policy-makers made provisions for the incorporation of women of the South when funding development projects. Influenced by Ester Boserup's critical analysis in *Women's Role in Economic Development* (1970), the focus was primarily on economic development (Tinker 1990). The way to women's emancipation was through their economic empowerment.

The defining paradigm used for achieving Third World women's equality had as its base the experience of women in the West: the model was Western, and the Third World was the recipient. Hence, there was no impetus to look beyond the Western model for understanding global gender inequality. Any channels available for a reverse flow of knowledge from the highly diverse set of women's issues in the Third World to the West were inhibited by the very purpose of WID strategies. Thus, this early "single track" concern of the WID discourse, focused narrowly on economic development issues, was implicitly responsible for the compartmentalization of the analysis of women's situation in the South into this one WID box.

The context in which this occurred was one in which the majority of women in the West – although perceived as better off than most women in the Third World – themselves had not succeeded in "integrating" into the economic (or social or political) system on a par with men. In 1991, more than forty years after the formation of the United Nations Commission on Women and following four decades of constant pressure and advocacy in the area of women's rights, the UN conceded that, although women's inequality issues have reached the global agenda, continuing gaps between women and men in their access to and use of critical resources persist (United Nations 1991). The Human Development Index (HDI), created and calculated for the United Nations Development Program (UNDP), clearly reflects the world-wide disparity between women and men in terms of their well-being and access to the resources needed for a decent living (UNDP 1992). Indeed, the analysis by Fort et al. (Chapter 8 in this volume) reaffirms the assertion by Seager and Olson that "[L]ooking at the world through women's eyes raises the question about the validity of conventional distinctions between 'developed' and 'underdeveloped' countries" (1986: 10).

First and foremost, there is a need to understand the meaning of global gender inequality in all its dimensions and how it operates with all its ramifications. As Mohanty (1991) has argued, attempts to analyze such a universal phenomenon using a methodology based on a model built from Western experience alone cannot achieve the explanatory power needed to understand and interpret the diverse socioeconomic and political experiences of non-Western women. Equally problematic is the tendency to legitimize a one-way flow of feminist scholarship, that is, from the West to the Third World, for the result is the "hegemony of Western scholarship." This has had a profound influence in the stereotyping of the "Third World woman" (read: poor, oppressed, unable to overcome her fate without external/Western help), as against the "Western woman" (read: affluent, liberated and mistress of her own fate). The emergence of the WID discourse in the West as the study of "other" women has led to an overgeneralization of what are identified as characteristics of Third World women. As Amos and Parmar (1984) have noted, it has also led to a paternalistic attitude by Euro-American feminists in the definition of priorities for "other" women.

Thus, while Third World women account for more than three quarters of the total number of women in the world, the study and analysis of their reality is relegated to a peripheral segment, an "area study" if you will, under the rubric of Third World development. An examination of the course listings for Women's Studies in any college or university catalog makes clear the larger space occupied by Western feminist studies compared to the WID discourse. One finds courses from "Women and Art" to "Women and Work" with dozens of listings in between – *one* of which will very likely be "Women and International Development." The large volume of current literature on women of the Third World demonstrates that the so-called WID agenda encompasses all areas which bear on Third World women's lives, not only economic development issues. Hence, as Asoka Bandarage (1984) suggested a few years ago, it is time to move Third World women's studies from the periphery it now occupies to the center alongside the Western feminist discourse.

However, this is not to say that WID activists, practitioners and scholars from the North have been unaware of the absence of a "reverse flow" from the South or of the need to stimulate a dialogue about women's issues between the economically developed West and economically underdeveloped Third World. For instance, in 1991 the year-long theme for the activities of the WID working group of the Society for International Development (SID) Washington Chapter, the very organization which initiated the WID discourse in the 1970s, was "Making the Connections: Women Here and Abroad." There was a conscious attempt to forge interaction between women from the North and the South. Moreover, the 1991 Fifth Forum of the Association of Women in Development (AWID) held in Washington D.C. also illustrates this concern. The theme of the conference was "Learning Together/Working Together: A South–North Dialogue." AWID President Jane Jaquette's message in the Forum program made the aim explicit: "[T]he Board chose the theme in response to requests from many of you for a *more deliberate sharing of the lessons gained from women in development initiatives in the South for efforts to improve the lives in the North* " (emphasis added). Both efforts are laudable. However, the compartmentalization of WID into a Third World-specific area of analysis limited the participants in SID/WID activities and the AWID meeting to those working on Third World women's issues, and thus there was no significant cross-fertilization with scholars, advocates or policy-makers who deal with women's issues in the West – because they were not present.

Rethinking global feminist analysis

How does one proceed to bring about an effective dialogue between two areas of discourse which have developed side by side with very little two-way interaction? This challenging task requires a rethinking and restructuring of the frameworks of Women's Studies globally to incorporate common concerns which transcend political, regional or economic lines and, at the same time, to leave space for effective articulation of important diversities. First, we need to revisit the basic rationale that underlies feminist studies. Second, in doing that we need to assess which methodologies will help us reduce the tendency to categorize and stereotype women based on their place of birth and residence. Third, we must now take stock of the vast body of knowledge amassed from the research on Third World women in order to expand and enrich the analytical tools available for scholarly debate in feminist discourse.

The rationale for the existence of a field of inquiry is based on the acknowledgment of certain fundamental tenets of its discourse which clearly separate it from all other discourses. The nerve center of any discourse lies in its body of theory, the substance of which is formulated and fed by diverse experiences. In the social sciences and humanities the human actor is at the center of the discourse, while the differentiations in scope and content in the disciplines are a product of the methodologies adopted. In feminist studies, women are the focus of the discourse and the basis for theory building. The rationale for its separateness from all other discourses is based on the premise that distinct methodologies are required to analyze and explain the systems which determine the power relationships in society and result in the persistent subordination of women.

As used here, methodology includes a theoretical approach to the way in which research should be undertaken in order to establish the "truth" of an explanation. As Harding (1987: 2) notes, "[d]iscussions of *method* (techniques for gathering data) [and] *methodology* (a theory and analysis of how research should proceed) have been intertwined with each other ... in both the traditional and feminist discourses" (emphasis added). An initial theoretical framework is necessary for the identification of methods of analysis for empirically testing the applicability of a theory to a situation. Moreover, the evidence generated is often useful in changing or expanding the propositions of the initial explanation itself. In the next sections, I explore a few areas in the WID discourse where data emerging from particular methods of analysis have resulted in refinements of earlier ideas in order to illustrate the usefulness of a "reverse flow" in effecting a fuller feminist discourse.

Identifying themes for a reverse flow

Gender differentiation is not the only type of human differentiation that leads to the domination of one group over another. Race and ethnicity, social class, the place of a nation in the world economic system, or any of many other socially constructed markers are perceived to differentiate between groups of people. While each on its own forms the basis for hierarchial divisions in society, each intersects with others leading to complex patterns of domination and subordination. The focus here is on gender as the major category of differentiation. However, as in the case illustrated by Domitilla and the head of the Mexican delegation, or in the experience of African American women in the United States, or in the situation of Asian women on the verge of independence from colonial rule (Jayawardena 1986), the immediate struggle in which both women and men participate may be against class, race, or colonial oppression, and the issue of gender subordination often lies in the background.

One of the characteristics of gender subordination is that it seems to trigger a "push back" mechanism. That is, no sooner is a particular type of oppression – against which both women and men have been struggling – eliminated or reduced than women are pushed back into an oppressed position based on gender. Shabaan (1988) reports an example related by a female combatant in North Africa: "It did not matter who did what: we were all the servants of the revolution which was going to liberate and restore our identity" (187), but after the revolution the trend reversed and gender subordination re-established itself in post-revolutionary society. Where class cleavages are supposed to have diminished, as in the case of the former "Soviet bloc" or in Cuba, women's oppression has not disappeared. And where nationalist revolutions triumphed over colonialism and political oppression, as in the case of India or Mozambique, gender subordination persisted.

Gender subordination seems to form the bottom layer over which are layer upon layer of other forms of human oppression. Peeling away these other layers has not eliminated men's domination of women, and nor should we expect it to do so. In other words, gender differentiation leading to women's subordination is a generalized, worldwide phenomenon. It is the nature and degree of gender oppression which differ over time and space. The intersection of gender with other hierarchies of domination leads to a diversity of analytical approaches for understanding the many meanings of gender subordination.

In this sphere the reverse flow of women's experiences from the Third World can contribute to the enrichment of the feminist discourse. As Sen and Grown argue, "feminism cannot be monolithic in its issues, goals, and strategies, since it constitutes the political expression of the concerns and interests of women from different regions, classes, nationalities and ethnic backgrounds" (1987: 8). However, the major areas of feminist discourse, that is, liberal, Marxist, radical, socialist, psychoanalytic, postmodernist, separate spheres, or eco-feminism, have emerged mainly through Western feminist experiences and observations (Harding 1987; Jagger and Rothenburg 1984; Tong 1989).

In studying "development" issues WID scholars extracted what they deemed as the most appropriate analytical approaches implicitly contained in the various theoretical frameworks indicated above. However, the refined methodologies and tools of analysis which have resulted from the selective application of explanatory perspectives to Third World situations are hardly ever transferred back in order to investigate and analyze issues among women in the West. The strength of WID is in the rich accumulation of field-based empirical knowledge of women generated over the past two decades. Lessons learned from this research could be adopted and adapted to enrich the Western feminist discourse and to expand the methodologies and tools available to probe gender subordination in general. Some examples suggest the potential of reverse flow.

Gender and class

One area in WID scholarship in which significant refinements of methodology have been achieved is empirical research on the intersection of gender and social class. Class relations affect women in many ways. First, the essence of a class structure is the economic (in the broadest sense) domination of one group over another, and men's domination over women in terms of their access to and control of critical resources has been a primary factor in the gender-based subordination of women. Second, as Sen and Grown have shown with many examples, Third World "women's experiences with processes of economic growth, commercialization, and market expansion are determined by both gender and class" (1987: 21). Sen and Grown's particular emphasis is on the economically poorest class of women who, due to the impact of complex gender-based socioeconomic and political factors, occupy the lower stratum even within that class.

Beneria and Roldan (1987) go a step further, which leads to the third point. They not only analyze the home-based work of women of the lower class but also document women's individual work histories to illustrate the changing dynamics of class, a process of recomposition between the pre-marriage and post-marriage periods. They note that in "the same historical period, proletarianization tends to absorb the young, single and better qualified women, while the wives/mothers and older women make up the subproletariat rendering reproductive support to the proletarianized male gender" (102).[2] The individual work histories, which Beneria and Roldan compiled from their sample of women, show that, while the father's class, level of schooling, and job experience and skills were decisive in a woman's entry into the proletariat, in the post-marriage stage gender has a significant influence on women's entry into the lowest paid sectors of the urban subproletariat.

Feminist literature in the West abounds with studies of women's work-related subordination (Bergmann 1974 and 1976; Blau and Ferber 1986). Western feminists have also brought into focus such themes as the "feminization of poverty," which revealed how, among the poor, women have the least access to critical resources and thereby form the lowest class. And scholars such as Hartmann (1987) have used class analysis to explain gender dynamics in housework. Studies of Third World women by Beneria and Roldan and others (Mies 1982) bring an additional dimension to the understanding of the intersection of gender and class in the subordination of women. They use a methodology in their work which provides understanding not only of the dynamics of women's work among the poorer segments of women, but also of how women's social position and marital status affect their work trajectories and remunerations. Such insights are clearly applicable beyond the Third world, especially in understanding the effects of marriage and withdrawal from marriage on the class affiliation of women.

Household observation and time allocation as tools of analysis

The established norms of gender-based subordination are such that women's struggle in the US has been described as an exercise in "moving the mountain" (Davis 1991). To move mountains, women worldwide are in a constant quest for the emergence of potential "gaps" within the male-dominated social, economic and political systems. This search for a wedge is clear in the sphere of productive activity. Compared to men, women have been able to emerge only in the lower strata of the formal wage economy. And when such opportunities are not to be found, Third World women, in particular, have sought economic refuge in the informal economy. By finding some type of remunerative work in the informal sector, poor women in Third World societies "straddle" the income-generating productive sphere and the child-centered reproductive sphere – where women alone shoulder virtually all the responsibilities.

Methods of analysis which have been developed in the WID discourse are useful in understanding how women straddle the two spheres. One such method is found in the use of the household as a unit of observation, and another in time-allocation studies. The household has been used increasingly by WID scholars as a basic unit of observation primarily in order to "locate" women and then to measure and analyze their contribution to the well-being of the family. Analysis at this level has been successful in measuring the total economic contribution of women to the maintenance of life on a daily basis in many Third World societies.

The household as a unit of analysis has become one of the central themes in the analysis of labor and income-allocation studies in economics. Becker's (1981) work, which gave the initial impetus to the line of analysis embodied in the New Home Economics, conceived of the household as a basic unit where both production and consumption take place; he proceeded to analyze the interactive input of members of the household in maximizing their utility for home-produced goods. The most contentious issue in the New Home Economics model is its argument that household-level behavior is guided by "altruism" and "voluntarism." Critics of the Household Bargaining model dispute the validity of the altruism/voluntarism norm in household behavior patterns and argue that individuals in a household will, in fact, have differential bargaining positions depending on their access to economic resources. Bringing an explicit gender dimension into the Household Bargaining model, Sen (1990) contends that the "perception" of women and of their interests and contributions is likely to give them a less than equal bargaining position within the household. He argues that the dimension of perception should be taken seriously in the identification of variables which make up a Household Bargaining model.

Katz (1991) criticizes the "harmony of intent" which the Household Bargaining model implies exists between women and men in the allocation of household labor. She presents an alternative model of the household in relation to production and consumption. While retaining the household as a fundamental unit of analysis, Katz argues that a "[f]eminist model of the household must specify the actual mechanisms whereby household members are mobilized to work in various productive and reproductive activities" (46). She offers what she calls "the beginnings of a feminist economic model of the household in which *gender is the central mediating phenomenon of all household economic activity"* (54).

The models proposed by Sen and Katz both represent very specific attempts to analyze household behavior in relation to economic activity, and they focus on, and are thus most useful in explaining, household behavior in the rural subsistence sector of the Third World. However, these models accomplish three important tasks: they highlight the importance for the decision-making process of the household as a basic unit of observation; they acknowledge implicitly or state explicitly both the gender dimension in household utility functions and the inherent reciprocity of productive and reproductive functions in maintaining the level of economic welfare of the household members; and they bring into focus the importance of the time dimension in disaggregating human activity at the household level, which is discussed further below.

In many instances, Third World feminist scholars have no alternative but to use the household as a basic unit of observation for data generation because reliable, well-documented data – that is, "official statistics" – are simply not available. However, the positive side of this lack of statistical data is the ability of household level observation to provide a window on the behavioral dimension of gender relationships and women's management of production and reproduction, which are inextricably linked. The more rigid physical separation of productive and reproductive spheres in the industrialized West and the relatively greater visibility of the productive sphere tend to mask the linkages between the two, which are equally essential in maintaining and sustaining households. Nonetheless, the masking of the linkages means the importance of productive activities in sustaining the reproductive sector is emphasized, while the significance of the reciprocal reproductive activities in supporting the productive sector is diminished. And being devoid of monetary value, these activities are further undervalued socially with the label of "unproductive labor."

Yet, Sen's (1991: 128) observation, made in relation to Third World agricultural societies, that 'so-called 'productive' activities may be parasitic on other work being done, such as housework and food preparation, the care of children" seems to be valid for any society. Downplaying the significance of reproductive activities not only ignores reciprocal linkages between production and reproduction, but also, and perhaps more importantly, leaves uncounted the contributions women make in the reproductive sphere where they are the main actors. The household-level analysis undertaken in the WID discourse to "locate" women in the so-called invisible rural subsistence sector and then to analyze how they straddle the reproductive and productive spheres of activity provides valuable insights into the importance of the reciprocity of human activity between the two spheres and women's contribution to household economic welfare. Analyzing activities which produce well-being through the prism of the household brings the significance of activities in the reproductive sphere, where women predominate, from the less recognized margins to the center of human activity alongside productive activities. Hence, one of the major ways household-level analysis from WID enriches the feminist discourse is through revealing the gender dimension of the essential reciprocity between the productive and the reproductive in economic life.

Using the household as the unit of analysis also brings into focus the necessity of looking more closely at the time dimension in gendered human activity. Studies of time allocation have been pursued in the WID discourse mainly in an effort to clarify and separate women's work trajectories, which often mix with reproductive activities carried out within the same physical space. But in the process of this analysis, several important issues have emerged that are crucial in understanding women's total contribution to the sustenance of societies anywhere on the globe.

The conventional wisdom regarding labor productivity neatly compartmentalizes human activity into the visible public sphere of monetized production, on the one hand, and virtually all household production into the non-monetized private sphere, on the other. The popular practice has been to view the productive/public sphere as the realm of male activities and the reproductive/private sphere as the realm of female activities. Focusing on the time dimension forces transcendence of the "two spheres" notion as well as recognition that goods and services are created in a *production process* and all participants in any given process count (Samarasinghe 1993). A study by Dixon-Mueller (1985) demonstrates very clearly how the use of time-allocation analysis captures women's productive work patterns effectively in many Third World societies. More recent studies using time-allocation analysis dispel the myth of women's so-called nonproductivity and expose the problematic fact of their invisibility in production processes (Momsen and Kinnaird 1993).[3]

Most time-allocation studies have focused on Third World agricultural societies and have attempted to probe the actual levels of direct economic productivity of women in such societies. But time allocation as a tool of analysis serves as a basis for deconstructing human activity more broadly. This has importance for the global feminist discourse in two ways. First, the emphasis on time does not allow the invisibility of female components of human activity to stand simply because they are carried out primarily in the non-monetized reproductive sphere. Second, time as the denominator of human activities demonstrates the vital importance of female activity in the domestic sphere in sustaining the social and economic structure of society.

This understanding of women's contribution to the socioeconomic survival of society reveals another significant concept, namely, "multiple uses of a unit of time" (see Floro, Chapter 10 in this volume). For example, in a Colombian case study of a newly colonized settlement, Meertens (1993: 264) notes that "peasant women carry out a diversity of tasks during the day, some more visible than the other, all of them frequently interrupted by another activity. One working day is not 'just one job' for women but a permanent combination of tasks and allotment of attention and energy." And in Else Skjonsberg's (1989) study based in an African village, one of the researchers, Agnes Bande, observed that she could not record all activities of a village woman named "Tisalare" because she was busy doing so many things.

The intensity of women's work has come to light mainly as a result of the relentless efforts by WID researchers to document and analyze Third World women's varied productive activities, many of which were hitherto hidden within the reproductive sector. Indeed, no matter where their productive work is located women are expected to be able to "straddle" the public and the private spheres. Two examples from the West are illustrative. Hochschild's (1989) study of working couples in California gives valuable insights into how women cope with the demands of production and reproduction as well as conflicts and changes occurring in the relationships of oppression within the households of two-earner couples. Hartmann's (1987) analysis of the impact of demands of housework on the full-time formal productive work of US women as well as women of several European countries shows how women are called upon to cope, adjust, and make choices as they straddle the spheres of production and reproduction. Hochschild's study also demonstrates that, in their efforts to straddle the two spheres, wives' time-allocation patterns are distinctly longer than those of their husbands. Both studies underscore the importance of focusing on the time dimension in order to gain a better understanding of the gendered division of labor between the productive and reproductive spheres.

Finally, current US statistics indicate that nearly 60 percent of mothers with young children are engaged in full-time work and that increasing numbers of women, especially African Americans, are seeking multiple jobs (Ries and Stone 1992). Hence, developing methods to document and explain the work intensity of women within and particularly beyond the traditional workplace would add an important direction for feminist studies. It will undoubtedly be a useful tool in analyzing gender differentiation in activity trajectories as well. Thus, time-allocation and work-intensity studies can form a critical basis for developing new strategies for measuring the value of work activities by taking into account on an equitable basis the time-based total contribution of men and women in all areas of productive and reproductive activity.

Conclusions

While women across the globe are victims of gender subordination, the form and nature of subordination varies over time and space. This chapter contends that the separation of Third World women's concerns into WID, although convenient at the outset, has contributed to an artificial duality in feminist discourse between the West and the Third World. It also argues that the rich accumulation of data on Third World women's issues during the past few decades should be used to stimulate a "reverse flow" of knowledge from the WID discourse to the Western feminist discourse and thereby set the stage for adding new dimensions to the global feminist analysis. In Western feminist discourse, especially in the area of economics, the availability of relatively reliable and well-documented statistics may inhibit researchers from probing fully the household gender mechanisms that influence labor allocations and other decision-making processes. The methods used in WID scholarship to give a "face" to the hidden form of women has brought in its wake new ways of probing women's position in society at the micro-level of analysis. Household observations and time-allocation studies are particularly important foci for feminist discourse since they show new directions in analyzing the reciprocity of human productive and reproductive activities essential for survival. They call for deconstruction of the value system embedded in identifying activities separately in public and private spheres and for careful consideration of the use of time as a more just way of measuring the importance of gendered activities. And these examples illustrate the potential of Third World women's studies to enrich the scholarly debate in feminist discourse and to expand the methodologies and tools available to probe gender subordination in general. This reverse flow will result in moving the discourse on Women in Development from the periphery it now occupies to the center alongside Western feminist discourse.

Notes

1. In this essay I use the acronym WID to identify the study of women's issues in the Global South since it is the most commonly used term to define the women's studies discourse in the Global South. It should be noted that other acronyms such as WAD (Women and Development) and GAD (Gender and Development) are also used, sometimes interchangeably, in the analysis of women in the South. However, there are distinct theoretical differences between the three frameworks of analysis (see Rathgeber 1990).

2. Beneria and Roldan explain that the proletariat and the subproletariat are similar in their lack of economic ownership and possession of the means of production. They differ, however, in the way they are remunerated. Those who are in the proletariat have permanent jobs and earn legal minimum wages; those in the subproletariat receive casual wages and lack job security.

3. In the Momsen and Kinnaird volume, see especially: Ardayfo-Schandorf, "Household Energy Supply and Women's Work in Ghana," pp.15–29; Mwake, "Agricultural Production and Women's Time Budgets in Uganda," pp.46–52; Barret and Browne, "The Impact of Labor-

Saving Devices on the Lives of Rural African Women: Grain Mills in Gambia," pp.52-61; Raghuram, "Invisible Female Agricultural Labor in India," pp. 93-108; and Wikramasinghe, "Women's Role in Rural Sri Lanka," pp.159-75.

References

Amos, Valerie, and Pratibha Parmar. 1984. "Challenging Imperial Feminism."*Feminist Review* 17: 3-19.
Bandarage, Asoka. 1984. "Women in Development: Liberals, Marxists and Marxist Feminists." *Development and Change* 15 (4): 495-515.
Barrios De Chungara, Domitilla, with Moemma Viezzer (Elizabeth Ortis, trans.). 1978. *Let Me Speak: Testimony of Domitilla, A Woman of the Peruvian Mines*. New York: Monthly Review Press.
Becker, Gary S. 1981. *A Treatise on the Family*. Cambridge: Harvard University Press.
Bergmann, Barbara D. 1974. "Occupational Segregation, Wages and Profits When Employers Discriminate by Race and Sex." *Eastern Economic Journal* 1 (1-2): 103-10.
Bergmann, Barbara D. 1976. "Reducing the Pervasiveness of Discrimination." In *Jobs for Americans*, edited by E. Ginsberg, pp. 120-41. Englewood Cliffs, New Jersey: Prentice Hall.
Beneria, Lourdes, and Martha Roldan. 1987. *The Crossroads of Class and Gender: Industrial Homework, Subcontracting, and Household Dynamics in Mexico City*. Chicago: Chicago University Press.
Blau, Francine D., and Marianne A. Ferber. 1986. *The Economics of Women, Men, and Work*. Englewood Cliffs, New Jersey: Prentice Hall.
Boserup, Ester. 1970. *Women's Role in Economic Development*. London: Allen and Unwin.
Davis, Flora. 1991. *Moving the Mountain: The Women's Movement in America Since 1960*. New York: Simon and Schuster.
Dill, Bonnie Thornton. 1987." The Dialectics of Black Womanhood." In *Feminism and Methodology*, edited by S. Harding, pp.97-109. Bloomington: Indiana University Press.
Dixon-Mueller, Ruth. 1985. *Women's Work in Third World Agriculture: Concepts and Indicators*. Women, Work, and Development Series, No. 9. Geneva: ILO.
Hartmann, Heidi. 1987. "The Family as the Locus of Gender, Class and Political Struggle: The Example of Housework." In *Feminism and Methodology*, edited by S. Harding, pp.109-34. Bloomington: Indiana University Press.
Harding, Sandra, ed. 1987. *Feminism and Methodology*. Bloomington: Indiana University Press.
Hochschild, Arlie. 1989. *The Second Shift: Working Parents and the Revolution at Home*. New York: Viking.
Hood, Elizabeth M. 1984. "Black Women, White Women: Separate Paths to Liberation." In *Feminist Frameworks: Alternative Theoretical Accounts of the Relations Between Women and Men*, 2d Edition, edited by A. M. Jagger and P. S. Rothenberg, pp.189-202. New York: MacGraw Hill.
hooks, bell. 1984. "Black Women: Shaping Feminist Theory." In *Feminist Theory: From Margin to Center*, pp.1-15. Boston: South End Press.
hooks, bell. 1991. *Yearning: Race, Gender, and Cultural Politics*. Boston: South End Press.
Jagger, Allison M., and Paula S. Rothenberg, eds. 1984. *Feminist Frameworks: Alternative Theoretical Accounts of the Relations Between Women and Men*. New York: MacGraw Hill.
Jayawardena, Kumari. 1986.*Feminism and Nationalism in the Third World*. London: Zed Books.
Katz, Elizabeth. 1991. "Breaking the Myth of Harmony: Theoretical and Methodological Guidelines to the Study of Rural Third World Households." *Review of Radical Economics* 23 (3/4): 37-55.
Meertens, Donny. 1993. "Women's Roles in Colonisation in the Colombian Rainforest." In *Different Places, Different Voices: Gender and Development in Africa, Asia and Latin America*, edited by J. H. Momsen and V. Kinnaird, pp.236-69. London and New York: Routledge.
Mies, Maria. 1982. *Lacemakers of Narsapur: Indian Housewives Produce for the World Market*. London: Zed Books.
Mohanty, Chandra Talpade. 1991. "Under Western Eyes." In *Third World Women and the Politics of Feminism*, edited by C. T. Mohanty, A. Russo, and L. Torres, pp.51-80. Bloomington: Indiana University Press.

Momsen, Janet Henshall, and Vivian Kinnaird, eds. 1993. *Different Places, Different Voices: Gender and Development in Africa, Asia and Latin America*. London and New York: Routledge.
Rathgeber, Eva M. 1990. "WID, WAD, GAD: Trends in Research and Practice". *The Journal of Developing Areas* 24 (July): 489–502.
Ries, Paula, and Anne E. Stone, eds. 1992. *The American Woman, 1992–1993. A Status Report*. Women's Research and Education Institute. New York: W.W.Morton.
Samarasinghe, Vidyamali. 1993. "How Do You Count and Whom Do You Ask? Use of Statistical Data in Gender Research." Paper presented at the Fifth International Interdisciplinary Congress on Women, San Jose, Costa Rica, 22–26 February.
Shabaan, Bouthaina. 1988. *Both Right and Left Handed: Arab Women Talk About Their Lives*. Indianapolis and Bloomington: Indiana University Press.
Seager, Joni, and Ann Olson. 1986. *Women in the World: An International Atlas*. New York: Simon and Schuster.
Sen, Amartya K. 1990. "Gender and Cooperative Conflicts." In *Persistent Inequalities: Women and World Development*, edited by I. Tinker, pp.123–49. New York: Oxford University Press.
Sen, Gita, and Caren Grown. 1987. *Development, Crises, and Alternative Visions: Third World Women's Perspectives*. New York: Monthly Review Press.
Skjonsberg, Elsa. 1989. *Changes in an African Village: KefaSpeaks*. Hartford, Connecticut: Kumarian Press.
Tinker, Irene. 1990. "Making of a Field." In *Persistent Inequalities: Women and World Development*, edited by I. Tinker, pp.27–33. New York: Oxford University Press.
Tong, Rosemarie. 1989. *Feminist Thought: A Comprehensive Introduction*. Boulder: Westview Press.
United Nations. 1991. *World's Women: The Trends and Statistics, 1970–1990*. New York: United Nations.
United Nations Development Program (UNDP). 1992. *Human Development Report*. New York: Oxford University Press.

14. Difference, Diversity, and Divisions in an Agenda for the Women's Movement

Elizabeth Fox-Genovese

Today, as in the past, the women's movement in the United States primarily reflects the experience and aspirations of white, middle-class women. The growing rhetorical attention to the differences among women of different classes, races, and ethnicities has changed little of substance. Of course much depends upon the way in which we define the "women's movement." If the term is taken to include the myriad of national, local, and neighborhood organizations which act in the name of women, it implies considerable diversity, openness, and internal conflict. Women display extraordinary courage and ingenuity in acting in defense of their and their families' interests. But if the women's movement is broadly taken as more or less synonymous with "feminism," it must be recognized as considerably more homogeneous, exclusive, and unrepresentative of the majority of American women, including those who care most deeply and immediately about "women's issues." Feminism *has* generated its own complexities and divergent tendencies but mostly within the academy.

Historically, the women's movement has always divided into the two broad tendencies of "women's rights" and what Naomi Black calls "social feminism" (Black 1989). The first tendency focused on the struggle for women's rights in an attempt to promote women's equality with men and culminated in the long campaign to secure the ERA. The goals of this movement have been fundamentally white and middle-class and have rested on the assumption that what was good for one woman would be good for all women. Social feminism, in contrast to equal-rights feminism, has grown from an acceptance of women's differences from men and a determination to work for women's specific interests as the social feminists defined them. Like equal-rights feminists, social feminists demonstrated their share of class and racial bias and exclusivity, occasionally even supporting reactionary political movements (Blee 1991).

The women's movement is now at a crossroads. During the past decade, difference has replaced equality as a central concern of feminist theory. In part, this shift reflects a growing awareness that the early easy assumptions of similarities among women and their needs masked the variations of women's experience by race and class (as well as nationality). In part, it reflects an uncomfortable recognition that equality with men has continued to elude women or failed to satisfy their needs. Although these two sets of attitudes towards difference intertwine, they do not necessarily reinforce each other, much less yield a clearly unified women's movement. At the most basic level, women of different classes and races do not necessarily agree about the measure of equality between women and men the women's movement should struggle for. And women assuredly do not agree about the significance of differences among women themselves. Thus, a white, middle-class, career woman may easily say that she does not believe in discrimination among women according to race and class and, nonetheless, assume that superior education should help to determine the selection of leaders. Or she may just as easily oppose social policies to benefit poor women which would significantly increase her own tax burden.

The problem of difference

Academic theorists who stress difference are trying to work their way through the complex overlapping of different kinds of difference, mainly by arguing for a "decentering" which abolishes the implicit norm that makes others different. Does not the very idea of woman as "different" presuppose an idea of man as the norm? Martha Minow, in particular, has convincingly argued that difference presents us with a dilemma (Minow 1990). To recognize difference is effectively to stigmatize those who are labeled as different. To emphasize the difference between women and men is implicitly to accept men as the norm and to accept the male view of women as differing from that norm. In Minow's view this perspective inevitably results in the drawing of boundaries which disadvantage those perceived as different. We cannot, she insists, escape the dilemma unless we recognize difference as a relationship which implicates both parties. How, she asks, "can historical discrimination on the basis of race and gender be overcome if the remedies themselves use the forbidden categories of race and gender? Yet without such remedies, how can historical discrimination and its legacies of segregation and exclusion be transcended?" (Minow 1990: 47). To complicate matters further, the dilemma of difference between women and men has tended to universalize a model of woman which obscures differences by race and class among women themselves.

This project, which directly challenges any notion of hierarchy, has been extended to differences among women (and men) by race and class. If white, middle-class women are no more normative than poor black women, then the significance of difference understood as departure from the norm collapses.

We are all different from one another. Furthermore, we all belong to different categories of difference. Some of us are women, but also black and rich. Where, in this case, does our primary allegiance lie? With our gender, our race, or our class? This line of thought logically leads to the conclusion that all categorizations are invidious, especially if they lead to judgments about the allocation of social resources.

The academic attack on that notion of difference which implies a stable norm primarily concerns questions of personal respect. Who are you to treat me as in some way lesser simply because I am different – that is, not you? The argument and sensibility are, at their core, radically individualistic: each of us deserves the same respect as any and every other; there are no legitimate grounds to discriminate among any of us, least of all because of attributes such as gender, race, or class. But if such arguments have opened interesting philosophical questions, their practical implications for political and social movements have as yet received little sustained attention. Iris Young's (1990) work embodies the main attempt to engage the practical implications of these questions. In practice, political and policy agendas are normally cast with respect to individuals or groups. Either each individual should receive the same treatment, regardless of personal attributes, or some individuals should receive different treatment because of personal attributes which identify them as members of a group. And, in this thinking, some attributes are taken to outweigh or erase others. Thus, our affirmative-action policies do not exclude some African Americans because their income exceeds a certain arbitrary line. It is possible to have attended elite schools throughout one's life and still benefit from opportunities that were initially designed to assist those who, presumably because of the color of their skin, had been barred from specific educational or employment opportunities.

The very idea of a woman's movement implicitly assumes that at least some differences between all women and all men have greater significance than the differences among women, or at least sufficient significance to justify the design and implementation of policies for all women. Women may need and deserve to be men's equals as citizens (voters) and, nonetheless, need and deserve some special status because they are women. Yet even feminists would not necessarily agree upon the reason women merit special consideration. Some would argue that women are different from men in ways which matter, normally ways which pertain to biology or sex. Others would argue that women are in no essential way different from men but have suffered from a history of oppression which makes them (at least for the moment) different in their command of a variety of salient resources. These two groups may forge a tactical alliance to defend, for example, affirmative-action programs for women, but they will continue to disagree theoretically on the justification for such programs. They will, accordingly, disagree about the ultimate role of equality and difference in the long-term agenda of a woman's movement.

As a general rule, the entire effort of the women's movement has been to redress the disadvantages women have historically suffered, and continue to suffer, as a result of their being women. The underlying argument nonetheless persists: were women disadvantaged because they were different, or because they were (brutally) excluded from equality? Recent debates over specific issues have clearly demonstrated that the mere recognition of difference does not guarantee justice or security for women and may even be invoked to deny them opportunities (Williams 1982). The case brought by the Equal Employment Opportunity Commission against Sears Roebuck chastened feminists by revealing the ways in which arguments for women's differences from men could be used to bar women from the most prestigious and best-paying jobs.

In the Sears case, the salient issues concerned women's purported preferences for some kinds of work over others and can, accordingly, be seen as broadly historical and cultural. In the soul-searching which followed in the wake of the Sears case, many feminists began to question the wisdom of invoking difference in matters of policy. In effect they reasoned that Sears had won the case by virtue of the argument that women, for a variety of reasons including risk and schedules, preferred not to work in commission sales. The Sears argument depended heavily on statistical reasoning: most women who had been given the opportunity to enter commission sales had chosen not to. But the decision which purportedly reflected most women's choices also reinforced the norms that excluded statistically atypical women from pursuing new opportunities (Scott 1988; Haskell and Levinson 1988, 1989; Fox-Genovese 1991). Such policy questions as these depend upon some ability to generalize and impose choices. They thereby challenge the women's movement to reflect upon its agenda.

At the time, most feminists agreed in opposing Sears' policies and joined in excoriating Rosalind Rosenberg, who served as expert witness for Sears. But, in the aftermath, it has become clear that the issues will not go away. The most complex and hotly contested issues concern the desirable consequences of women's reproductive capacities and "traditional" childcare responsibilities. Where can we draw the line between biological difference and social equality? Should pregnancy be treated like a disability, thus entitling women equal access to benefits available to all other workers? Does the defense of "maternity leave" benefit women or further imprison them in traditional roles, which they may not have wanted in the first place? Do parental or family-leave policies help to free women from stereotypical roles, or perhaps further disadvantage women who do not have husbands with whom to share the responsibilities?

The debate over women's participation in the military underscores the complexities with a vengeance. During the war in the Persian Gulf we were inundated with images of bereft children whose mothers had been called to active duty overseas. Some women in the Gulf were pregnant. Do we really want to separate mothers from their small children? Do we really want pregnant soldiers in a battle zone? And what of women's roles in the military? Should they, for example, have the right to participate equally with men in combat – and to receive equal pay for doing so? Many still recoil at the idea of any woman's participation in armed combat. Others insist that, in the case of a volunteer army, women, including mothers, are very likely to depend upon the incomes they receive from the military or want to develop their careers. As individuals, they should be allowed to make their own choices, to enter into contractual relations with which society has no right to interfere.

It should be obvious that women's roles in combat still have an overdetermined symbolic significance. Even without direct participation in combat, women increasingly serve in dangerous and exposed military roles, notably in supplying troops at the front. The risk of death is arguably no (or not significantly) greater in the one case than in the other. Some would even argue that the support services bear the greater risk because they are not armed to defend themselves against attack. Yet there has been little public outcry against the risks women incur in serving at or just behind the front in non-combat roles. Clearly, there remains a deep tendency in the culture which rejects the image of women as soldiers – a role that has traditionally been viewed as quintessentially male. And since we know that the public, however uneasily, tolerates the separation of incarcerated mothers from their children and does not even notice the separation of some working women, notably immigrants, from their children, it is reasonable to argue that, in the case of the military, the emphasis ultimately falls on excluding women from equality rather than on protecting their difference.

And yet it remains possible that the case of the military dramatizes the role of the mother as much as it dramatizes that of the male warrior. It remains possible, in other words, that the instinct to exclude mothers of young children from combat, even when we tolerate high risk to other mothers of young children, embodies noble as well as self-serving tendencies. Or, to put it differently, do we best serve women's interests by defending the right of mothers to serve in combat or by insisting that no mothers should be separated from their children? It is hard to say. But this much we know: the successful defense of the right of mothers to serve in combat will do nothing to restore incarcerated women or migrant women workers to their children and is very likely to make their separation from those children more generally acceptable.

Similar questions arise in the recent case (Johnson Controls) of women's right to chose to work at high-paying jobs which endanger a foetus they may be carrying. That case, like the question of *maternal* leave, has sharply divided feminists. Many find the question of children troubling, although if we think of women only as individuals we have no grounds to interfere. We can argue that men can and should share equally in the responsibilities of child-rearing, but they cannot share equally in child-bearing. Yet we have, as a rule, failed to develop policies which protect women as child-bearers (as different from men) which do not also penalize them as individuals (as similar to men). As individuals, women should not be excluded from the most prestigious and remunerative work. But then, they should not be entitled to special privileges either. The question remains: do we collectively choose to view pregnant women, or even the mothers of infants, only as individuals among other individuals? That question should be separable from women's equal opportunity and obligation to serve, in some capacity, in the armed forces. But it is only separable if we, as a society, have policies which defend mothers' economic condition and professional prospects. Those are matters of public policy. And in the absence of appropriate policies we can only leave individual women to wrestle with conflicting claims alone.

Thinking differently about difference

Minow's work, like that of other feminist legal theorists, challenges us to think differently about difference in order to avoid certain traps in the continuing struggle for equality. Her thought, in this respect, has much in common with those who insist upon the importance of appreciating divers- ity. Women, who have suffered the burdens of difference, should be especially sensitive to the burdens it inflicts on others. Culturally, this position enjoins us to respect the individuality and traditions of others. Politically, it poses more difficult problems.

The continued existence of a women's movement in our time depends upon the agreement that women do share some characteristics which differentiate them from men. If not, women's interests would, as Marxists long argued, collapse into general social and political struggles. The vitality of a women's movement in our time depends upon the recognition that women are also divided by class and race. If women do not believe that they share some important interests with other women, there is no reason for them to organize as women, no reason for them not to define their primary struggle as one of class or race. But to deny the divisions among women by class and race is willfully to ignore the real challenge of feminist politics in our time, which cannot completely escape the legacy of the dream of equality.

Strictly speaking, equality evokes a mathematical relation – the two sides of an equation – and hence quantity rather than quality. Seen in this light, equality appears abstract and unrealistic. We do not expect women to be strictly equal to men in the sense of completely interchangeable with them. But then we do not expect men to be strictly equal to each other. Knowing that human attributes cannot be measured with mathematical precision, we expect all individuals to display a certain variability. But if we can accept variations in culture and personality, what about resources and, beyond resources, power?

Recent experience suggests that if women do need the protection of legal equality, they need more than that. Legal equality can help to guarantee women equality of opportunity but, since it does not create a "level playing field," it cannot guarantee them equality of results. Child-bearing, sexual harassment, and acquaintance rape all suggest, as many feminists are coming to recognize, that sexual or biological asymmetry cannot simply be legislated away. Our inherited (male) model of autonomous individualism is proving incapable of meeting women's needs. Indeed, the pursuit of autonomous individualism for women is increasingly exposing the limitations of the model for society as a whole.

Originally, equality was implicitly and explicitly taken to mean equality of opportunity. Today, disillusion with equality of opportunity runs so deeply that many people have come to mistrust a wide variety of purportedly objective standards, such as standardized intelligence or aptitude tests, which were taken to guarantee equality of opportunity to people of different classes and races. Manifestly they did not. Yet even those who most sharply criticize the model of equality of opportunity have been loathe openly to criticize the individualistic principles on which it rests.

In *Feminism Without Illusions* I have argued that to escape the dilemma of equality versus difference women need a conception of equity which rests on the notion of individual right as grounded in society rather than as prior to it. The argument is not, as some have taken it to be, an attack on individualism, which does anchor our conceptions of individual rights and responsibilities. Rather, the argument rests on the assumption that we enjoy those rights and bear those responsibilities not because of innate attributes but because we are social beings: society, not nature, has endowed us with rights and is entitled to hold us accountable for meeting the attendant responsibilities (Fox-Genovese 1991, 1992a, 1992b).

Specifically, women's most pressing problems are social and economic in the broad sense and can never be adequately addressed on the basis of innate or presocial individual right. From this perspective, the differences among women of different classes and races emerge as especially important and potentially devastating. Although few of us like to discuss it openly, the grim possibility remains that the needs of middle-class (especially but not necessarily exclusively white) women could be met at the expense of poor women. For, notwithstanding the debilitating effects of abiding racism and the growing threat of ethnic tribalism, the most pressing issues remain economic. As our troubled economy makes abundantly clear, secure jobs which include the essential benefits of health care have emerged as the basic, and increasingly elusive, condition of a decent life – the functional equivalent of industrial workers' "family wage" or, before it, independent property in a farm or workshop which could support a family (May 1982).

Easy access to abortion, which many women passionately defend and which has virtually become the litmus test of feminism, can solve a woman's immediate problem of pregnancy, but cannot diminish most of the miseries that led her to become pregnant in the first place. At best, access to abortion will permit a poor woman to re-engage the dreary struggle for a more promising future without the encumbrance of a child, but it will not necessarily improve her education or her job prospects, provide her with medical insurance, or increase the likelihood that she will marry. And access to abortion does nothing for the poor woman who chooses to keep her child. Yet feminists, who claim to speak in the name of the women's movement and emphasize society's responsibility to accommodate women's lives and values, continue to defend abortion on the grounds of absolute individual right. The rhetoric in which the debate over abortion has been cast merits attention, for in discussing that which is most peculiarly personal and female (the ability to bear a child), it has drawn primarily on the public language of rights – that is, the language of (male) citizenship (Fox-Genovese 1992a, 1992b). Although some feminist scholars (Vogel 1990; Young 1987) argue in favor of this treatment of equality and difference.

In effect, that rhetoric casts the reality of difference in the language of equality, thereby collapsing the one into the other. Something similar is occurring with respect to sexual harassment and acquaintance rape. In each of these cases, the argument seems to be that women have a right to be free of the consequences of their sexuality – their difference. Yet normally the political and policy discussions do not emphasize the theoretical complications; they focus on concrete objectives. Women must have access to abortion; women must be free of all forcefully imposed sexual attentions. In the measure that these issues have taken pride of place in the most visible agenda of the women's movement, they have tended to influence the discussions of other issues as well.

The radical individualism which informs so much feminist theory and thought has, willy-nilly, led middle-class spokeswomen for the women's movement to emphasize the issues which divide women from men, at the expense of the issues which divide women against one another. Poor women, indeed, have as much experience of male bullying and even brutality as middle-class women. The relations between women and men in the African American and Hispanic American communities are, if we can credit the reports, conflicted and strained. But even after all allowances have been made and caveats filed, it is safe to say that most poor women, both white and women of color, are more concerned with social and economic problems than they are with the "war between the sexes." We have no reason to doubt that many of them remain committed to establishing and sustaining marriages and families as one of the strongest bulwarks against economic insecurity. They may even remain attached to some aspects of "traditional" women's roles, if only because they know they will never be able to afford the kind of care for their children which can substitute for their own attention.

Ruth Sidel (1990) has argued that large numbers of young women of different classes and races have recently come to share a particularly female vision of the classic American dream. These young women have grasped the idea of themselves as future career women (presumably in the manner of *LA Law*) and in classic individualistic fashion are embracing the vision of financial equality. Other young women, Sidel reminds us, tend to cling to a more conservative vision of themselves as primarily future wives and mothers. Still others perceive themselves as "outsiders" – as fundamentally alienated from both the dream of professional success and vision of traditional domesticity. Although there is some tendency for these attitudes to cluster by class, the correlation is far from absolute, and examples of each can be found in every class.

These divisions among young women mirror the complex divisions among women in American society at large. Normally, the women's movement does not much attend to the neo-traditionalist group, frequently viewing them as enemies of women's needs and progress. For the neo-traditionalists, women's best protection still lies in their assumption of inherited female roles and their dependence upon men. Nor has the women's movement seriously attended to the outsiders whose attitudes, in extreme cases, border on despair or nihilism. Ironically, the women's movement may not even fully encompass the complicated attitudes of the aspiring new professionals, many of whom are reconsidering the relations between career and family, frequently in order to emphasize the latter. In my judgment, for the women's movement to coalesce and succeed in its goals, it must attempt to engage the imaginations of all these young women – or at least to engage what they see as their most acute problems.

These different groups of women differ in their aspirations for their lives or even in whether they hope for anything at all. Within the groups, women differ according to temperament, talent, and family background. They nonetheless all share some general problems, notably how to provide for themselves, and possibly their children, in a world in which men cannot necessarily be obliged or even enticed to support them. The neo-traditionalists may be least likely to recognize their situation, but even as they affirm their commitment to "traditional" values and roles, they know, on some level, they are at risk. To reach such women, the women's movement needs to respect their values and desire to hold men accountable for wives and families. Frequently, neo-traditional women do work, are active in political movements, do engage in a variety of activities outside the home. They simply refuse to define themselves by their independence. If the women's movement could begin by listening respectfully – even if not in agreement – to the neo-traditionalists who oppose abortion, we would have made a beginning.

A different agenda

Conversations with poor African American and Hispanic American women, who would not dream of calling themselves feminists, have convinced me that they understand and are deeply committed to women's issues, beginning with women's need for "independence."[1] But they do not recognize feminism, or even a more diffuse women's movement, as having any relevance to their lives. Most do not even associate feminism with the social programs and services they, as women, most desperately need.

The lives of these women, and others across class and racial lines, nonetheless confirm that the women's movement potentially constitutes the cutting edge of a thorough reconsideration of the very notion of public policy and national priorities. In a society in which women must overwhelmingly rely upon their own earning power, they still earn 63 cents for every dollar earned by a man. And, in the measure that this figure represents an improvement over the 59 cents to every male dollar which women earned a few years ago, it represents growing equality between women and men in the worst-paying least secure jobs of the service sector – MacDonalds or the supermarket check-out counter – and, in lesser measure, in the more prestigious middle-class professions.

Attempts to redress this inequality have led members of the women's movement variously to support affirmative action and comparable worth. Both policies have registered some successes, both have left something to be desired. Affirmative action, which originated in the individualistic conception of equality of opportunity, has probably been most effective for women at the upper end of the income scale, although even there it has not successfully cracked what is known as the "glass ceiling." Comparable worth has primarily benefitted female public-sector employees from clerical workers to civil servants. A broad extension of the principles of comparable worth could potentially lead to a vast increase in economic security for women, but would certainly constitute a massive challenge to the principles of the free market. Moreover, the unlimited extension of comparable worth on the existing basis of re-evaluating forms of work traditionally ascribed to women would inescapably perpetuate traditional stereotypes of women's roles, risking the kind of stigmatization that Minow warns against.

In ways which both are and are not similar, the feminist campaigns against sexual harassment and acquaintance rape uneasily combine the goals of ensuring women's equality with men and protecting their difference from men. But, above all, both campaigns draw the battle lines squarely between women and men and thus, perhaps unintentionally, reinforce the individualist tendencies of middle-class feminism. Tellingly, both campaigns have drawn heavily upon the language of rights to make their claims: "Women have a right to be free of ...", in contrast to "Society has an obligation to protect women against ..." Both reinforce the impression that feminism seeks to free women from the consequences of their sex in order to make them truly equal competitors with men. But competition between women and men may be precisely what women disadvantaged by race and class can least afford – and perhaps even what they least want.

The experience of disadvantaged women suggests that if the women's movement is to avoid the pitfalls of the dilemma of equality versus difference, it must recast women's issues as social issues in contradistinction to individual or even sexual issues. In this perspective, the agenda for the women's movement should emphasize health care, daycare, education, and benefits for part-time workers. Surely none of us needs reminding that the burdens of health care fall disproportionately upon women, who still assume primary responsibility for the care of the young and the elderly. And even if we believe that, ultimately, men should share that responsibility equally with women, it is unlikely that the best way to encourage them to do so is to cast them as competitors, much less as enemies. Does it not make more sense to provide the kind of social supports women so desperately need on the assumption that support and respect for the work women have traditionally done might encourage men to share in it?

Above all, the women's movement should acknowledge that it is presumptuous to fight battles about women's and men's "roles" in the name of women whose own preferences in the matter have not been consulted. Arlie Hochschild has argued that, with respect to household responsibilities, working-class men are, if anything, more likely than middle-class men to pitch in and help with whatever needs doing with no regard to "traditional" gender roles (1989). For such people gender roles are not the issue, although they may well adhere to conventional representations of those roles. As men's and women's activities within families change, and especially as men spend more time in caring for children, the representations of the roles may also change. Certainly severely disadvantaged women who, more often than not, have no resident men to share their burdens, need assistance in bearing their burdens more than they need debates about men's and women's roles.

Traditional assumptions about gender do play an important and debilitating role in the allocation of medical resources, however. The women's movement has pioneered in criticizing the inherent sexism of much medical thinking and care. As Carol Tavris has recently argued in some detail, most medical research and treatment remain fixated on the seventy-kilogram man, with such shocking results as the exclusion of mammography from most health-insurance coverage, low funding for breast cancer research, and an alarming tendency among male physicians to advise hysterectomies with wanton abandon (1992). In addition, as Tavris convincingly maintains, too many women's understandable responses to the circumstances of their lives, notably economic dependence, are reconstructed by mental-health professionals as

Difference, Diversity, and Divisions in the Women's Movement 243

illness or disorders which require protracted care. Men's problems must be dealt with, whereas women's illness must be stabilized through endless hours of group therapy which make the woman feel better about herself while leaving her circumstances unchanged. In Tavris's view the process amounts to little more than trapping a potential adult in a state of perpetual adolescence.

At this point a feminist campaign for national health policies would have to include close attention to the national allocation of medical resources. One might, for example, imagine a national system of health-care delivery which included the equivalent of a five-year national service for all prospect- ive doctors. Such a system would help to ensure adequate medical care in impoverished rural areas and in inner-city emergency rooms. It could also ensure an adequate supply of obstetricians/gynecologists. A national policy might also include some rationing of health services, especially the more expensive and least effective, as the state of Oregon has done. A national health policy might even include the perpetuation of private insurance plans, perhaps in conjunction with some national insurance. It is, in other words, possible to imagine a variety of plans, no one of which need be biased according to gender no matter how much it might be biased according to income.

Health care in particular raises the question of benefits in general. It is common knowledge that the United States lags behind all other developed countries in its provision of support to its citizens. Countries like France and Canada provide family allowances to ease the burdens of raising children. Many countries provide guaranteed maternity leave and comprehensive daycare systems (Kamerman and Kahn 1978). In many instances, for example France and Israel, the various supports for child-rearing originated as populationist incentives. Traditionally, such pronatalism has reflected a concern for quantity of population, with a special eye to military security. It has also regularly figured as a favorite target of feminists, who tend to view pronatalism as a sinister plan to keep women barefoot and pregnant. There is, however, no reason not to adopt a pronatalism which promotes quality, in terms of health, education and well-being, rather than quantity, just as there is no reason to assume the bearing of children must always oppress, or disadvantage, women.

The question of quality of population leads directly to the question of childcare. The women's movement should promote a comprehensive, national policy of childcare, including parental leave, on the grounds that only such a policy can adequately recognize children as a social rather than a private responsibility. The defense of a national childcare system implies nothing about the form such a system could take and does not even imply that an effective system need be either uniform throughout the country or run by the federal government and staffed by federal employees. There is no reason why the women's movement cannot lead the way in considering a variety of forms of childcare and, in so doing, help to generate new support for childcare workers.

Good childcare services are expensive. In Atlanta, in the fall of 1992, several daycare centers were closing because the cost of meeting federal standards was forcing them to charge more than many parents could afford. As the costs presumably continue to rise, more centers will raise their rates or close, leaving the poorest working women unable to pay for the daycare they need in order to go to work. At the same time, childcare workers, who themselves are normally poor women who lack specialized skills, need to make a decent wage. The more childcare is professionalized, the more expensive it will become. The women's movement should be responsible both to the needs of working mothers and to the needs of childcare workers, who are very likely to be women and who are also working mothers. In a negative regard, the lessons of health care are instructive. The United States spends a larger proportion of its GNP on health care than other developed nations, provides those who are insured – or can pay – with as good or better health care than any other nation in the world, and still has a larger proportion of its population without adequate health care than any other developed nation.

As with the care of young children, so with education. None of us needs reminding of the deplorable state of most of our system of public education. Education, in a variety of ways, brings to the surface class and race differences among women themselves. There is no use pretending the solutions will be easy, but if the women's movement does not confront the problems directly, women of all classes and races will live with the consequences. Here again, the primary responsibility of the women's movement may well lie in encouraging the discussion of policies among feminists, rather than assuming there could be no difference of opinions and priorities. Can there or should there be a "feminist" position on multiculturalism, bilingual education, special education, local control, the teaching of math and science to girls, and all the rest? Not until the women's movement begins to recognize these issues as questions for discussion will we begin to develop coherent policies on women's position in society.

As the question of education confirms, the issues which most seriously affect women also affect men, however differently. As a number of feminist theorists have argued, all women and men exist and define themselves in specific historical situations and as members of specific social groups (Spelman 1988; Fox-Genovese 1988). In any given instance, group membership, notably by race and class, may more powerfully affect women's needs than their sex – at least in relation to the larger society. In our society, education constitutes the gateway to future economic prospects. Most dramatically, those with a college degree earn on average $16,000 more a year than those without one.

This perspective should help us to recognize the singular importance of a comprehensive policy of benefits for all workers. Many women who cling to traditional roles are, at least in part, clinging to the tangible, if precarious, security of their husbands' incomes, but especially their benefits. Women still comprise the majority of part-time workers who, notoriously, receive no benefits at all. Thus, espousing a policy of full benefits for all part-time workers should rank high on the economic agenda of the women's movement.

Conclusion

Any inclusive agenda for the women's movement must begin with comprehensive economic and social policies. In emphasizing economic issues I am not for a moment underestimating the pervasive aspects of sexism, which many feminists regard as primary. Without doubt, reproductive issues in particular and sexual issues in general will rank high on most women's agenda for the next decade and beyond. With no intention of trivializing the importance of these issues, I do believe that the economic issues take priority, if only because enforced economic dependence and lack of social support for the bearing and rearing of children decisively color the way in which the issues are perceived.

Women invariably understand reproductive and sexual experiences within a complex cultural and social matrix. Even the decision of whether to carry a pregnancy to term depends at least in part upon the network of support available, as well as upon religious and cultural values. The extreme tendency to argue for women's absolute reproductive rights as individuals cannot be divorced from the context which confronts most women with the necessity of dealing as individuals with a free market. Were women guaranteed a panoply of social and economic rights simply by virtue of their membership in society, they might be more willing to see child-bearing and child-rearing as social rather than individual activities.

As things now stand, women are more often than not penalized for being female individuals. The main tendency in the women's movement has, understandably, been to attempt to strengthen women's position as individuals. However understandable, that strategy has inevitably encouraged the heightened consciousness of differences – and even divisions – among women. Without doubt, some of the emphasis on difference derives from a commitment to value the traditions of one's own people and community. But some of it also comes from a frightening awareness of competition for scarce resources. In this respect, the theoretical writings about difference have failed to engage the depressing specter of possibly serious divisions among different groups, including different groups of women. If equality of opportunity has not benefitted all women relative to men, it assuredly has not benefitted all women relative to each other. Indeed, equality of opportunity, whatever its limitations, has probably benefitted some women not merely at the expense of other women, but also at the expense of the men upon whom other women in some measure depend.

Iris Young has argued that "where social group differences exist and some groups are privileged while others are oppressed, social justice requires explicitly acknowledging and attending to those group differences in order to undermine oppression" (1990: 3). But how are we to establish the salience of membership in more than one group. Are we to identify African American women primarily by gender, race, or class? Many African American feminists, like Beverly Guy-Sheftall, insist that the distinct character of African American feminism derives from attention to all three (1989). Normally, however, the attempt to establish policy priorities requires a decision about which war to fight first and about whom to take as allies. And, as Bette Dickerson's analysis (Chapter 6 in this volume) conveys, this issue of alliances has been particularly problematic for leaders of African American women's organizations.

A greater measure of economic justice will not automatically eradicate differences of gender, race, or class. It assuredly will not guarantee economic equality among women, although it may well promote a greater measure of economic equality between women and men within specific social groups. But then, it has never been clear that the majority of middle-class feminists have ever seriously wanted genuine economic equality among women. The point of a modicum of economic justice is not to level all economic distinctions, but to provide some combination of supports and incentives which will permit women some prospect of decent survival (Jencks 1992). This much at least is certain: if society fails to provide all women with a reasonable opportunity to help themselves, alone or with their families, we are likely to find ourselves increasingly divided.

In proposing an agenda of social and economic policies, I have tried, as a white, middle-class feminist, to take account of the needs of women of other classes and races. But I know full well that whatever my efforts, I cannot experience their situation from the inside; I can, however, be purposefully conscious of my own location at the intersection of gender, race, and class (see Ward, Chapter 12 in this volume). The white, middle-class women's movement has a long and ambiguous history of trying to act well towards women of different classes and races. Sadly, it has all too frequently fallen into the mode of lady bountiful. The assumptions of universalism and essentialism have permitted elite women to speak and act in the name of all women as if their success would unambiguously benefit others. We cannot be sure that it will. We cannot even be sure that some women's victory against gender discrimination will not result in the intensification of other women's experience of discrimination by gender, race, or class. In this perspective, it seems abundantly clear that if we are to have even the semblance of a comprehensive or inclusive women's movement, the leadership of that movement must reflect women's different backgrounds and goals.

Women's issues have emerged as central to the health and vitality of

American society, yet their very centrality confronts any women's movement with unprecedented challenges. The vast majority of American women share needs for health care, daycare, education, and benefits for part-time work which transcend their differences of race and ethnicity and, in some measure, their differences of class. But the challenge of implementing and financing policies of this kind and on this scale reveals not merely the differences, but the divisions among American women. The most pressing agenda of the women's movement is to understand the magnitude of this challenge and to engage it in ways which might possibly negotiate the deep cultural, ideological, and economic divisions among the millions of women whose future prospects are at stake.

Notes

1. These conclusions come from interviews I have conducted for my book-in-progress, *What Do We Want for our Daughters (And Our Sons)?*

References

Black, Naomi. 1989. *Social Feminism*. Ithaca, N.Y.: Cornell University Press.
Blee, Kathleen M. 1991. *Women of the Klan: Racism and Gender in the 1920s*. Berkeley: University of California Press.
Fox-Genovese, Elizabeth. 1988. *Within the Plantation Household: Black and White Women of the Old South*. Chapel Hill: University of North Carolina Press.
Fox-Genovese, Elizabeth. 1991. *Feminism Without Illusions: A Critique of Individualism*. Chapel Hill: University of North Carolina Press.
Fox-Genovese, Elizabeth. 1992a. "Feminism and the Rhetoric of Individual Rights, I & II," *Common Knowledge* 1, (1 & 2).
Fox-Genovese, Elizabeth. 1992b. "Feminist Rights, Individualist Wrongs." *Tikkun* 7(3): 29–34.
Guy-Sheftall, Beverly. February 1989. "Women's Education and Black Women's Studies." Paper presented at the annual meeting of the Southeastern Women's Studies Association, Emory University, Atlanta, Georgia. February.
Haskell, Thomas, and Sanford Levinson. 1988. "Academic Freedom and Expert Witnessing: Historians and the Sears Case." *Texas Law Review* 66: 1629–59.
Haskell, Thomas, and Sanford Levinson. 1989. "On Academic Freedom and Hypothetical Pools: A Reply to Alice Kessler-Harris." *Texas Law Review* 67: 1591–1604.
Hochschild, Arlie, with Anne Machung. 1989. *The Second Shift*. New York: Viking Penguin.
Jencks, Christopher. 1992. *Rethinking Social Policy: Race, Poverty, and the Underclass*. Cambridge, Mass.: Harvard University Press.
Kamerman, Sheila B., and Alfred J. Kahn, eds. 1978. *Family Policy: Government and Families in Fourteen Countries*. New York: Columbia University Press.
May, Martha. 1982. "The Historical Problem of the Family Wage: The Ford Motor Company and the Five Dollar Day." *Feminist Studies* 8: 399–424.
Minow, Martha (1990). *Making All the Difference: Inclusion, Exclusion, and American Law*. Ithaca, N.Y.: Cornell University Press.
Scott, Joan Wallach. 1988. "Deconstructing Equality-Versus-Difference: Or, the Uses of Poststructuralist Theory for Feminism." *Feminist Studies* 14: 33–50.
Sidel, Ruth. 1990. *On Her Own: Growing Up in the Shadow of The American Dream*. New York: Viking.

Spelman, Elizabeth. 1988. *Inessential Woman: Problems of Exclusion in Feminist Thought.* Boston: Beacon Press.
Tavris, Carol. 1992. *The Mismeasure of Woman.* New York: Simon and Schuster.
Vogel, Lise. 1990. "Debating Difference: Feminism, Pregnancy, and the Work Place." *Feminist Studies* 16: 9–32.
Williams, Wendy. 1982. "The Equality Crisis: Some Reflections on Culture, Courts, and Feminism." *Women's Rights Law Reporter* 7: 175–200.
Young, Iris Marion. 1987. "Difference and Policy: Some Reflections in the Context of New Social Movements." *University of Cincinnati Law Review* 56: 535–50.
Young, Iris Marion. 1990. *Justice and the Politics of Difference.* Princeton: Princeton University Press.

Index

abortion, 238, 239, 240
African American Women's Associations, 97-114; Leadership Project, 100
African Americans: labour participation of, 119; marginalization of, 115
agriculture, women in, 20, 21, 22, 142, 143, 145
AIDS, 191, 192, 194
Almquist, Elizabeth, 206
Anzaldúa, Gloria, 213
Aptheker, Bettina, 212
Arnhold, Rose, 203
aspirations of women, 17-35; downscaling of, 18
Association for Discrimination Against Women (Turkey), 158
Association of Women in Development (AWID) (USA), 221
Ataturk, Mustafa Kemal, 154, 155, 156, 157, 161, 164, 165
Awiatka, Marilou, 213
Aykut, Imren, 160, 165

Baktir, Gultekin, 162
Bande, Agnes, 228
battering of women, 158, 165
beer brewing, 172, 175
Bennett, Bobbie, 206
Black History Month, 106
Boserup, Ester, 219
Brinkley, Christina, 210

Canada, 84-96, 144, 145, 174, 243
Catholicism, 142, 144, 146
Chicanas, 73, 75, 81, 204; in white collar work, 36-52
childbearing, 23, 132, 137, 138, 143, 144, 146, 188, 238, 239
childcare, 32, 39, 40, 46, 73, 105, 123, 137, 145, 146, 168, 170, 171, 175, 176, 177, 183, 212, 228, 236, 243, 244, 247
Chile, 58-61

China, 140, 141, 142, 146, 147
Cicek, Cemil, 160, 162, 163, 165
Clark, Bonita, 85-96
Cleaver, Eldridge, 202
Cohen, Andrew, 185
Collins, Patricia Hill, 209-10, 212
compadrazgo, 62
confianza, 53, 55, 57, 59, 62, 66, 68
conservative agenda: on family policy, 117; on growth, 121
contraception, 136, 138, 141, 142, 145, 146
Cornish, Mary, 88
credit, access to, 170, 183, 192, 193
Cross, Bill, 208

daughters: education of, 188; labor of, 174, 176
daycare centres, closure of, 244
De Chungara, Domitila Barrios, 218
deindustrialization, 117, 119, 124
Delhi, slum dwellers in, 175, 176
democracy, 126, 157, 159; economic, 124
difference, 232-48
Dill, Bonnie Thornton, 207, 211
Directorate for Women's Status and Problems (Turkey), 154, 160-4
discrimination, 43-6
diversity, 232-48
division of labor, 30, 37, 38, 47, 119, 132, 144, 153, 168, 177, 228
divorce, 155, 185, 194; fear of, 186; laws, 184-7
domestic labour *see* housework
domestic work, 20, 24, 26, 65, 72-83, 212; as bridging occupation, 73; racial organization of, 23; restructuring of, 72-83

education, 19, 40, 61, 136, 138, 140, 141, 143, 145, 182, 184, 188, 192, 247; college, 25, 26, 27; futility of, 22; girls in, 141; secondary, 29, 59; segregated, 20; university, 59

Egypt, 138, 139, 146
emotional labor, 80
empowerment of women, 101, 102, 103, 111, 133, 139
equality, 93, 237; economic, 246; legal, 238; measure of, 233; of opportunity, 245; versus difference, 242
ethnic identity, 97-114
ethnicity, 105-7

factory work, 21, 33
family: as unpaid workers, 146; Black, 116, 117, 118, 119, 123, 124; cooperation, 62; disintegration of, 160; enterprise, 64; extended, 159 (economy of, 65); formation, 116; importance of, 54, 55; in Italy, 144; maintenance of, 57; networks, 61, 63; nuclear, 117; political shaping of, 123; poor, 98; racial typing of, 124; Turkish, 163, 165
family policy, 116; restructuring of, 123-6
Family Policy Act (USA), 117
Family Security Act, 125
favores, 58, 59, 60
female headed households, 115, 116, 117, 122, 125, 188
femininity, conceptualization of, 39, 41
feminism, 40, 122, 154, 218-31, 232, 241, 244; African American, 246; and ethnic identity, 97-114; Black, 108-10, 210; concept of, 111; definition of, 107; equal-rights, 232; Kemalist, 157, 159, 160, 164, 165; liberal, 161; radical, 158; social, 232; socialist, 157, 158; White, 199-217
fertility of women, 136, 139, 141, 142, 144, 146
food: preparation of, 183; production of, 137, 138
food subsidies, withdrawal of, 169, 170
Forward-looking Strategies, 153, 165, 166
Freeman, Jo, 206
full employment, 124-5

gender: and class, 224; intersection with race, 37, 40
gender courses, teaching of, 205
gender difference, 201, 202, 223
gender inequality, 131-51
gender policy, in Turkey, 152-67
gender stratification, in Uganda, 182-96
Ghana, 133, 138, 146
Giddings, Paula, 211
Grant, Linda, 213

Hacker, Helen, 203

hawkers, women as, 191
health and safety hazards, 87, 88
health care, 138, 175, 191, 192, 194, 242; in USA, 243, 244; of women, 177, 178, 182, 243, 247
health insurance, 243, 244
Helms, Janet, 208
Higginbotham, Elizabeth, 207
Hispanic Workers Advocacy Group, 46
Holmes, Shirlene, 213, 214
Hossfeld, Karen, 212
household: as unit of analysis, 227; as unit of production, 66, 141; model of, 226
household observation, 225-8
housework, 39, 46, 47, 122, 145, 158, 168, 169, 171, 177; multi-task nature of, 170
housing, 61, 65, 189
Human Development Index (HDI), 220

Igbo women, 205
illiteracy *see* literacy
immigrants, women as, 74, 145, 212
immunization, 192, 194
industrialization, 142, 159, 160
industry, women in, 139, 143, 145
informal economy, 53-69, 82, 189, 194, 225; employment in, 172
inheritance: laws of, 184-7, 193, 194; of widows, 186
integration: of Black students, 201; of curricula, 207
intensity of women's work, 168-81, 228
Islam, 140, 146, 156, 160, 162, 163; and women, 138
Italy, 144, 146

Jackson, Gertie, 202
Japan, 140, 141, 142, 146, 173
Jaquette, Jane, 221
Johnson Controls case, 236
judges, women as, 27, 31

Kececiler, Mehmet, 162
Kennedy, Eugene, 204
Kennedy, Flo, 203
Kenya, 133, 138, 172, 175
Keynesianism, 120
King, Martin Luther, 106
kinship, and gender system, 183-4
Kwanzaa, 106

La Raza, 204
labor market: mechanisms of, 41; segmentation of, 119
labor process, control over, 76-9
Lanker, Brian, 213
lawyers, women as, 31

leadership development, 99, 101, 103-5
leisure time of women, 179
"lifting as we climb", 199-217
literacy, 136, 140, 143, 183
live-in work, in domestic labour, 76

maids, 77, 78
majorette, aspiration to be, 31
male chauvinism, 93
Mali, 133, 138
mammography, 242
marriage, 20, 28, 40, 56, 119, 136, 139, 140, 141, 143, 146, 156, 224, 239; abandonment of, 187-90; Christian, 185; laws, 184-7, 193, 194; registration of, 182, 187; rights within, 144
maternity leave, 235, 243
Mexico, 55, 62-7, 142, 143, 146, 172, 174
migration, 142, 182; labor, 137, 139; to urban areas, 187-90
military, women and, 236
Minow, Martha, 233, 237
mobility, 18, 29-33; constrained, 46; of Black women, 22
mortality: infant, 136, 145, 178; maternal, 178
mothering, multiple, 109
Mozambique, 223
Murphy, Teresa, 202

Nairobi conference, 153, 154, 160
National Committee of Household Employment (NCHE), 81
National Leadership Forum (US), 101
National Organization for Women (NOW) (US), 211
National Pan-Hellenic Council (US), 101
National Women's Studies Association (NWSA) (US), 200
networks: informal sector, 62-7; social, middle-class, 58-61; social, upper-class, 55-8
New Home Economics, 225
non-governmental organizations (NGOs), 192, 193
nuns, women as, 20, 30
nurses, women as, 21, 22, 30, 33, 119, 143
Nuss, Shirley, 204

Occupational Health and Safety Act (US), 87
outworking, 171-2, 174, 175

part-time working, 245, 247
patriarchy, 38, 46, 108
pay of women, 44, 73, 74, 81, 172, 175; disparities of, 145

Personal Status Laws, 139
pink collar work, 29
polygamy, 155, 156, 187
pornography, 94; men's use of, 88
poverty, 54, 98, 115, 116, 119, 138, 143, 182, 186, 191; feminization of, 145, 224; of women, 184-7, 190, 195; regulation of, 117
power: women excluded from, 143; women in positions of, 138, 147
pregnancy, 20, 235, 237, 239; teenage, 117
productive and unproductive labor, 226, 227
promotion, 41, 43
prostitution, 158, 162, 188, 190

race, intersection with gender, 37, 40
race-ethnicity, construction of, 36-52
racism, 98, 99, 104, 109, 111, 118, 119, 142, 204, 205, 209, 210, 211, 212
Ramirez, Juanita, 204
rape, 158, 193, 238, 239, 241
reproductive rights, 245
research on women, 161, 162, 163
resistance of domestic workers, 74, 75, 79, 81
restructuring, 122, 126, 168
reverse flow of analysis, 218-31
Richard, Beah, 213
Rosenberg, Rosalind, 235
Rural Farmers' Scheme (Uganda), 193

Sales, Ruby, 200
Sears Roebuck case, 235
secretaries, women as, 21, 25, 26, 30, 33
segregation, 20, 23, 24, 144
self-employment, 189, 190
service work, 119, 123
sexism, 92, 94, 98, 99, 104, 107, 108, 109, 111, 204, 214, 245; and class experience, 90-2
sexual harassment, 84-96, 238, 239, 241; as health and safety hazard, 89, 92, 93; in collective context, 89; policy against, 95
sexuality: Chicana, 213; of women, control of, 139, 142, 189
shoe industry, in Spain, 176
Silicon Valley, 175
simultaneity of women's work, 170, 171, 212, 228
single mothers, 116, 194
smuggling, of coffee, 189
social wage, 117, 120, 121, 122
Society for International Development (SID), 221
St Lucia, 171, 176

state: legitimization of, 121; relations with society, 155-7; role of, 120
statistics on women, 132; lack of, 226
Steel Company of Canada, 85-96
Steinmen, Gloria, 204
stereotypes: of Black women, 31; of women, 219, 220
street sweepers, women as, 172
structural adjustment, 168, 190-4, 195
Sweden, 144, 147

teachers, women as, 17, 133, 136, 138, 140, 141, 143, 205-11
technology, and reproductive labour, 80
telecommuting, 176
Third World women, stereotyping of, 219, 220
time allocation, 225-8; studies, 171, 228
tranquillizers, use of, 177
triple shift, 212
Truth, Sojourner, 206
Tubman, Harriet, 206
Turkey, 152-67

Uganda, 137, 182-96
Uganda Association of Women Lawyers (FIDA), 187
Uganda Council of Women (UCW), 185
UN Convention on the Elimination of All Forms of Discrimination Against Women (CEDAW), 131, 133, 152, 158
UN Development Program (UNDP), 220
UN Women's Indicators and Statistics (WISTAT), 132
unemployment, 119, 120, 191
unions, 82, 91, 92, 94
United States of America (USA), 97-114, 115-27, 171, 172, 173, 174, 177
urbanization, 159

veterinarians, women as, 42
violence against women, 158, 165, 239
Vision Terudo, 193
voluntary associations, importance of, 98

waged work, 76, 122, 158, 225
wages of women *see* pay of women
Walker, Meneal, 212
Ward, Lula, 201, 213
Washington, Gwen, 202
washrooms for women, 86, 88, 95
Weber, Lynn, 207
wedding rings, meaning of, 185
Weiss, Jane, 204
welfare policy, in the United States, 115-27
Westernization, 164; of women, 138

Westinghouse company, 92
white collar work, 36-52, 143
white feminists, 199-217
white privilege, acknowledging, 201
whiteness, interrogation of, 199
widowhood, fear of, 186
widows, 187, 191, 194; dispossessing of, 186
Widows' League (Uganda), 186
womanism, 109
women: as catalysts of social change, 97; as income earners, 168; as information transmitters, 56, 68
women in development (WID), 153, 193, 194, 205, 218-31
Women's Circle (Turkey), 158
women's groups, Black, 211
women's movement, 144, 153, 156, 234, 235, 237, 240, 241; economic agenda of, 245; in Turkey, 157-60; in US, 108, 232; White, 246
women's organizations, closed in Turkey, 155
Women's Studies, 161, 163, 200, 204, 209, 210, 220; rethinking of, 221
Women's Trust Fund, 193
women's work, 224; urban, 53-69
work: control of, 41, 42, 43; demarcation with leisure, 179; redefinition of, 212
work intensification: consequences of, 175-8; determinants of, 173-5
workforce, women's participation in, 133, 136, 138, 140, 142, 143, 144, 168, 174
working hours of women, 77, 168-81

ADG-8724

WITHDRAWN
From Bertrand Library